THE AGE OF REASON

BEING AN INVESTIGATION OF TRUE AND FABULOUS THEOLOGY

Thomas Paine

Edited by
Moncure Daniel Conway

DOVER PUBLICATIONS, INC.
Mineola, New York

Bibliographical Note

This Dover edition, first published in 2004, is an unabridged republication of the work originally published by G.P. Putnam's Sons, New York, 1896.

Library of Congress Cataloging-in-Publication Data

Paine, Thomas, 1737-1809.
  The age of reason : being an investigation of true and fabulous theology / Thomas Paine ; edited by Moncure Daniel Conway.
    p. cm.
  Originally published: New York : G.P. Putman's Sons, 1896.
  Includes bibliographical references and index.
  ISBN 0-486-43393-5 (pbk.)
    1. Rationalism—Early works to 1800. I. Conway, Moncure Daniel, 1832-1907. II. Title.

BL2740.A1 2004
211'.5—dc22

2003070117

Manufactured in the United States of America
Dover Publications, Inc., 31 East 2nd Street, Mineola, N.Y. 11501

CONTENTS.

PART I.

[Original title.]

THE

AGE OF REASON

BEING

AN INVESTIGATION OF TRUE AND FABULOUS THEOLOGY.

By THOMAS PAINE

Secretary of Foreign Affairs to Congress in the American War, and Author of
the Works entitled Common Sense, and Rights of Man, &c.

Paris:

PRINTED BY BARROIS.

1794.

[Second Year of the French Republic.]

TO MY FELLOW CITIZENS

OF THE

UNITED STATES OF AMERICA.

————

I PUT the following work under your protection. It contains my opinion upon Religion. You will do me the justice to remember, that I have always strenuously supported the Right of every man to his opinion, however different that opinion might be to mine. He who denies to another this right, makes a slave of himself to his present opinion, because he precludes himself the right of changing it.

The most formidable weapon against errors of every kind is Reason. I have never used any other, and I trust I never shall.

Your affectionate friend and fellow citizen,

THOMAS PAINE.[1]

LUXEMBOURG (PARIS), 8*th Pluviose*,
Second year of the French Republic, one and indivisible,
O. S. *January* 27, 1794.

[1] This dedication is not in the first editions printed in Paris (in English) and in London, and seems to have first appeared in America, 1794.—*Editor*.

THE AGE OF REASON.

EDITOR'S INTRODUCTION.

WITH SOME RESULTS OF RECENT RESEARCHES.

IN the opening year, 1793, when revolutionary France had beheaded its king, the wrath turned next upon the King of kings, by whose grace every tyrant claimed to reign. But eventualities had brought among them a great English and American heart—Thomas Paine. He had pleaded for Louis Capet—"Kill the king but spare the man." Now he pleaded,—" Disbelieve in the King of kings, but do not confuse with that idol the Father of Mankind !"

In Paine's Preface to the Second Part of "The Age of Reason" he describes himself as writing the First Part near the close of the year 1793. " I had not finished it more than six hours, in the state it has since appeared, before a guard came about three in the morning, with an order signed by the two Committees of Public Safety and Surety General, for putting me in arrestation." This was on the morning of December 28. But it is necessary to weigh the words just quoted—" in the state it has since appeared." For on August 5, 1794, François Lanthenas, in an appeal for Paine's liberation, wrote as follows : " I deliver to Merlin de Thionville a copy of the last work of T. Payne [The Age of Reason], formerly our colleague, and in custody since the decree excluding foreigners from the national representation. This book was written by the author in the beginning of the year '93 (old style). I undertook its translation before the revolution against priests, and it was published in French about the same time. Couthon, to whom I sent it, seemed offended with me for having translated this work."

Under the frown of Couthon, one of the most atrocious colleagues of Robespierre, this early publication seems to have been so effectually suppressed that no copy bearing that date, 1793, can be found in France or elsewhere. In Paine's letter to Samuel Adams, printed in the present volume, he says that he had it translated into French, to stay the progress of atheism, and that he endangered his life "by opposing atheism." The time indicated by Lanthenas as that in which he submitted the work to Couthon would appear to be the latter part of March, 1793, the fury against the priesthood having reached its climax in the decrees against them of March 19 and 26. If the moral deformity of Couthon, even greater than that of his body, be remembered, and the readiness with which death was inflicted for the most theoretical opinion not approved by the "Mountain," it will appear probable that the offence given Couthon by Paine's book involved danger to him and his translator. On May 31, when the Girondins were accused, the name of Lanthenas was included, and he barely escaped ; and on the same day Danton persuaded Paine not to appear in the Convention, as his life might be in danger. Whether this was because of the "Age of Reason," with its fling at the "Goddess Nature" or not, the statements of author and translator are harmonized by the fact that Paine prepared the manuscript, with considerable additions and changes, for publication in English, as he has stated in the Preface to Part II.

A comparison of the French and English versions, sentence by sentence, proved to me that the translation sent by Lanthenas to Merlin de Thionville in 1794 is the same as that he sent to Couthon in 1793. This discovery was the means of recovering several interesting sentences of the original work. I have given as footnotes translations of such clauses and phrases of the French work as appeared to be important. Those familiar with the translations of Lanthenas need not be reminded that he was too much of a literalist to depart from the manuscript before him, and indeed he did not even venture to alter it in an instance (presently considered) where it was obviously needed. Nor would Lanthenas have omitted any of the paragraphs lacking in his translation. This original work was divided into seventeen chapters, and these I have restored, translating their headings into English. The " Age of Reason " is thus for the first time given to the world with nearly its original completeness.

It should be remembered that Paine could not have read the proof of his " Age of Reason " (Part I.) which went through the press while he was in prison. To this must be ascribed the permanence of some sentences as abbreviated in the haste he has described. A notable instance is the dropping out of his estimate of Jesus the words rendered by Lanthenas " trop peu imité, trop oublié, trop meconnu." The addition of these words to Paine's tribute makes it the more notable that almost the only recognition of the human character and life of Jesus by any theological writer of that generation came from one long branded as an infidel.

To the inability of the prisoner to give his work any revision must be attributed the preservation in it of the singular error already alluded to, as one that Lanthenas, but for his extreme fidelity, would have corrected. This is Paine's repeated mention of six planets, and enumeration of them, twelve years after the discovery of Uranus. Paine was a devoted student of astronomy, and it cannot for a moment be supposed that he had not participated in the universal welcome of Herschel's discovery. The omission of any allusion to it convinces me that the astronomical episode was printed from a manuscript written before 1781, when Uranus was discovered. Unfamiliar with French in 1793, Paine might not have discovered the *erratum* in Lanthenas' translation, and, having no time for copying, he would naturally use as much as possible of the same manuscript in preparing his work for English readers. But he had no opportunity of revision, and there remains an *erratum* which, if my conjecture be correct, casts a significant light on the paragraphs in which he alludes to the preparation of the work. He states that soon after his publication of " Common Sense " (1776),

he " saw the exceeding probability that a revolution in the
system of government would be followed by a revolution in
the system of religion," and that "man would return to the
pure, unmixed, and unadulterated belief of one God and no
more." He tells Samuel Adams that it had long been his
intention to publish his thoughts upon religion, and he had
made a similar remark to John Adams in 1776. Like the
Quakers among whom he was reared Paine could then
readily use the phrase " word of God " for anything in the
Bible which approved itself to his "inner light," and as he
had drawn from the first Book of Samuel a divine condemnation of monarchy, John Adams, a Unitarian, asked him if he
believed in the inspiration of the Old Testament. Paine
replied that he did not, and at a later period meant to publish his views on the subject. There is little doubt that he
wrote from time to time on religious points, during the
American war, without publishing his thoughts, just as he
worked on the problem of steam navigation, in which he had
invented a practicable method (ten years before John Fitch
made his discovery) without publishing it. At any rate it
appears to me certain that the part of " The Age of Reason "
connected with Paine's favorite science, astronomy, was
written before 1781, when Uranus was discovered.

Paine's theism, however invested with biblical and Christian phraseology, was a birthright. It appears clear from
several allusions in " The Age of Reason " to the Quakers
that in his early life, or before the middle of the eighteenth
century, the people so called were substantially Deists. An
interesting confirmation of Paine's statements concerning
them appears as I write in an account sent by Count Leo
Tolstoi to the London *Times* of the Russian sect called
Dukhobortsy (*The Times*, October 23, 1895). This sect
sprang up in the last century, and the narrative says:

"The first seeds of the teaching called afterwards ' Duk-
hoborcheskaya' were sown by a foreigner, a Quaker, who
came to Russia. The fundamental idea of his Quaker teaching was that in the soul of man dwells God himself, and
that He himself guides man by His inner word. God lives

in nature physically and in man's soul spiritually. To Christ, as to an historical personage, the Dukhobortsy do not ascribe great importance. . . . Christ was God's son, but only in the sense in which we call ourselves 'sons of God.' The purpose of Christ's sufferings was no other than to show us an example of suffering for truth. The Quakers who, in 1818, visited the Dukhobortsy, could not agree with them upon these religious subjects; and when they heard from them their opinion about Jesus Christ (that he was a man), exclaimed 'Darkness!' . . . 'From the Old and New Testaments,' they say, 'we take only what is useful,' mostly the moral teaching. . . . The moral ideas of the Dukhobortsy are the following :—All men are, by nature, equal; external distinctions, whatsoever they may be, are worth nothing. This idea of men's equality the Dukhobortsy have directed further, against the State authority. . . . Amongst themselves they hold subordination, and much more, a monarchical Government, to be contrary to their ideas."

Here is an early Hicksite Quakerism carried to Russia long before the birth of Elias Hicks, who recovered it from Paine, to whom the American Quakers refused burial among them. Although Paine arraigned the union of Church and State, his ideal Republic was religious; it was based on a conception of equality based on the divine sonship of every man. This faith underlay equally his burden against claims to divine partiality by a "Chosen People," a Priesthood, a Monarch "by the grace of God," or an Aristocracy. Paine's "Reason" is only an expansion of the Quaker's "inner light"; and the greater impression, as compared with previous republican and deistic writings made by his "Rights of Man" and "Age of Reason" (really volumes of one work), is partly explained by the apostolic fervor which made him a spiritual successor of George Fox.

Paine's mind was by no means sceptical, it was eminently constructive. That he should have waited until his fifty-seventh year before publishing his religious convictions was due to a desire to work out some positive and practicable system to take the place of that which he believed was crumbling. The English engineer Hall, who assisted Paine in making the model of his iron bridge, wrote to his friends in England, in 1786 : " My employer has *Common Sense* enough to disbelieve most of the common systematic theories of Divinity, but does not seem to establish any for himself." But five years later Paine was able to lay the corner-stone of his temple : " With respect to religion itself, without regard to names, and as directing itself from the universal family of mankind to the Divine object of all adoration, *it is man bringing to his Maker the fruits of his heart ;* and though those fruits may differ from each other like the fruits of the earth, the grateful tribute of every one is accepted." ("Rights of Man." See my edition of Paine's Writings, ii., p. 326.) Here we have a reappearance of George Fox confuting the doctor in America who " denied the light and Spirit of God to be in every one ; and affirmed that it was not in the Indians. Whereupon I called an Indian to us, and asked him ' whether or not, when he lied, or did wrong to any one, there was not something in him that reproved him for it ?' He said, ' There was such a thing in him that did so reprove him ; and he was ashamed when he had done wrong, or spoken wrong.' So we shamed the doctor before the governor and the people." (Journal of George Fox, September 1672.)

Paine, who coined the phrase " Religion of Humanity " (The Crisis, vii., 1778), did but logically defend it in " The Age of Reason," by denying a special revelation to any particular tribe, or divine authority in any particular creed or church ; and the centenary of this much-abused publication has been celebrated by a great conservative champion of Church and State, Mr. Balfour, who, in his " Foundations of Belief," affirms that "inspiration" cannot be denied to the great Oriental teachers, unless grapes may be gathered from thorns.

The centenary of the complete publication of " The Age of Reason," (October 25, 1795), was also celebrated at the Church Congress, Norwich, on October 10, 1895, when Professor Bonney, F. R. S., Canon of Manchester, read a paper

in which he said : " I cannot deny that the increase of scientific knowledge has deprived parts of the earlier books of the
Bible of the historical value which was generally attributed
to them by our forefathers. The story of Creation in the
Book of Genesis, unless we play fast and loose either with
words or with science, cannot be brought into harmony with
what we have learnt from geology. Its ethnological statements are imperfect, if not sometimes inaccurate. The stories
of the Fall, of the Flood, and of the Tower of Babel, are incredible in their present form. Some historical element may
underlie many of the traditions in the first eleven chapters
in that book, but this we cannot hope to recover." Canon
Bonney proceeded to say of the New Testament also, that
" the Gospels are not, so far as we know, strictly con-
temporaneous records, so we must admit the possibility of
variations and even inaccuracies in details being introduced
by oral tradition." The Canon thinks the interval too short
for these importations to be serious, but that any question
of this kind is left open proves the Age of Reason fully
upon us. Reason alone can determine how many texts are
as spurious as the three heavenly witnesses (1 John v. 7),
and like it " serious " enough to have cost good men their
lives, and persecutors their charities. When men interpo-
late, it is because they believe their interpolation seriously
needed. It will be seen by a note in Part II. of the work,
that Paine calls attention to an interpolation introduced
into the first American edition without indication of its
being an editorial footnote. This footnote was : " The book
of Luke was carried by a majority of one only. Vide Mosheim's Ecc. History." Dr. Priestley, then in America, answered Paine's work, and in quoting less than a page from
the " Age of Reason " he made three alterations,—one of
which changed " church mythologists " into "Christian
mythologists,"—and also raised the editorial footnote into
the text, omitting the reference to Mosheim. Having done
this, Priestley writes : " As to the gospel of Luke being carried by a majority of one only, it is a legend, if not of Mr.
Paine's own invention, of no better authority whatever."

And so on with further castigation of the author for what he never wrote, and which he himself (Priestley) was the unconscious means of introducing into the text within the year of Paine's publication.

If this could be done, unintentionally by a conscientious and exact man, and one not unfriendly to Paine, if such a writer as Priestley could make four mistakes in citing half a page, it will appear not very wonderful when I state that in a modern popular edition of "The Age of Reason," including both parts, I have noted about five hundred deviations from the original. These were mainly the accumulated efforts of friendly editors to improve Paine's grammar or spelling; some were misprints, or developed out of such; and some resulted from the sale in London of a copy of Part Second surreptitiously made from the manuscript. These facts add significance to Paine's footnote (itself altered in some editions !), in which he says: " If this has happened within such a short space of time, notwithstanding the aid of printing, which prevents the alteration of copies individually; what may not have happened in a much greater length of time, when there was no printing, and when any man who could write, could make a written copy, and call it an original, by Matthew, Mark, Luke, or John.

Nothing appears to me more striking, as an illustration of the far-reaching effects of traditional prejudice, than the errors into which some of our ablest contemporary scholars have fallen by reason of their not having studied Paine. Professor Huxley, for instance, speaking of the freethinkers of the eighteenth century, admires the acuteness, common sense, wit, and the broad humanity of the best of them, but says "there is rarely much to be said for their work as an example of the adequate treatment of a grave and difficult investigation," and that they shared with their adversaries "to the full the fatal weakness of *a priori* philosophising."[1] Professor Huxley does not name Paine, evidently because he knows nothing about him. Yet Paine represents the turning-point of the

[1] Science and Christian Tradition, p. 18 (Lon. ed., 1894).

historical freethinking movement; he renounced the *a priori* method, refused to pronounce anything impossible outside pure mathematics, rested everything on evidence, and really founded the Huxleyan school. He plagiarized by anticipation many things from the rationalistic leaders of our time, from Strauss and Baur (being the first to expatiate on "Christian Mythology"), from Renan (being the first to attempt recovery of the human Jesus), and notably from Huxley, who has repeated Paine's arguments on the untrustworthiness of the biblical manuscripts and canon, on the inconsistencies of the narratives of Christ's resurrection, and various other points. None can be more loyal to the memory of Huxley than the present writer, and it is even because of my sense of his grand leadership that he is here mentioned as a typical instance of the extent to which the very elect of free-thought may be unconsciously victimized by the phantasm with which they are contending. He says that Butler overthrew freethinkers of the eighteenth century type, but Paine was of the nineteenth century type; and it was precisely because of his critical method that he excited more animosity than his deistical predecessors. He compelled the apologists to defend the biblical narratives in detail, and thus implicitly acknowledge the tribunal of reason and knowledge to which they were summoned. The ultimate answer by police was a confession of judgment. A hundred years ago England was suppressing Paine's works, and many an honest Englishman has gone to prison for printing and circulating his "Age of Reason." The same views are now freely expressed; they are heard in the seats of learning, and even in the Church Congress; but the suppression of Paine, begun by bigotry and ignorance, is continued in the long indifference of the representatives of our Age of Reason to their pioneer and founder. It is a grievous loss to them and to their cause. It is impossible to understand the religious history of England, and of America, without studying the phases of their evolution represented in the writings of Thomas Paine, in the controversies that grew out of them with such practical accompaniments as the

foundation of the Theophilanthropist Church in Paris and
New York, and of the great rationalist wing of Quakerism
in America.

Whatever may be the case with scholars in our time,
those of Paine's time took the " Age of Reason " very seriously indeed.   Beginning with the learned Dr. Richard
Watson, Bishop of Llandaff, a large number of learned men
replied to Paine's work, and it became a signal for the commencement of those concessions, on the part of theology,
which have continued to our time ; and indeed the so-called
" Broad Church " is to some extent an outcome of " The
Age of Reason."   It would too much enlarge this Introduction to cite here the replies made to Paine (thirty-six are
catalogued in the British Museum), but it may be remarked
that they were notably free, as a rule, from the personalities
that raged in the pulpits.   I must venture to quote one
passage from his very learned antagonist, the Rev. Gilbert
Wakefield, B.A., " late Fellow of Jesus College, Cambridge."
Wakefield, who had resided in London during all the Paine
panic, and was well acquainted with the slanders uttered
against the author of " Rights of Man," indirectly brands
them in answering Paine's argument that the original and
traditional unbelief of the Jews, among whom the alleged
miracles were wrought, is an important evidence against
them.   The learned divine writes:

" But the subject before us admits of further illustration
from the example of Mr. Paine himself.   In this country,
where his opposition to the corruptions of government has
raised him so many adversaries, and such a swarm of un-
principled hirelings have exerted themselves in blackening
his character and in misrepresenting all the transactions
and incidents of his life, will it not be a most difficult, nay
an impossible task, for posterity, after a lapse of 1700 years,
if such a wreck of modern literature as that of the ancient,
should intervene, to identify the real circumstances, moral
and civil, of the man?   And will a true historian, such as
the Evangelists, be credited at that future period against
such a predominant incredulity, without large and mighty

accessions of collateral attestation? And how trans-
cendantly extraordinary, I had almost said *miraculous*, will
it be estimated, by candid and reasonable minds, that a
writer whose object was a melioration of condition to the
common people, and their deliverance from oppression,
poverty, wretchedness, to the numberless blessings of upright and equal government, should be reviled, persecuted,
and burned in effigy, with every circumstance of insult and
execration, by these very objects of his benevolent inten-
tions, in every corner of the kingdom?"

After the execution of Louis XVI., for whose life Paine
pleaded so earnestly,—while in England he was denounced
as an accomplice in the deed,—he devoted himself to the
preparation of a Constitution, and also to gathering up his
religious compositions and adding to them. This manuscript I suppose to have been prepared in what was variously
known as White's Hotel or Philadelphia House, in Paris,
No. 7 Passage des Petits Pères. This compilation of early
and fresh manuscripts (if my theory be correct) was labelled,
" The Age of Reason," and given for translation to François
Lanthenas in March 1793. It is entered in Quérard *(La
France Littéraire)* under the year 1793, but with the title
"L'Age de la Raison" instead of that which it bore in 1794,
"Le Siècle de la Raison." The latter, printed "Au Bureau
de l'imprimérie, rue du Théâtre-Français, No. 4," is said
to be by "Thomas Paine, Citoyen et cultivateur de l'Amérique septentrionale, secrétaire du Congrès du département
des affaires étrangères pendant la guerre d'Amérique, et
auteur des ouvrages intitulés: LA SENS COMMUN et LES
DROITS DE L'HOMME."

When the Revolution was advancing to increasing terrors,
Paine, unwilling to participate in the decrees of a Convention whose sole legal function was to frame a Constitution,
retired to an old mansion and garden in the Faubourg St.
Denis, No. 63. Mr. J. G. Alger, whose researches in personal
details connected with the Revolution are original and useful, recently showed me, in the National Archives at Paris,
some papers connected with the trial of Georgeit, Paine's

landlord, by which it appears that the present No. 63 is not, as I had supposed, the house in which Paine resided. Mr. Alger accompanied me to the neighborhood, but we were not able to identify the house. The arrest of Georgeit is mentioned by Paine in his essay on "Forgetfulness" (Writings, iii., 319). When his trial came on one of the charges was that he had kept in his house "Paine and other Englishmen,"—Paine being then in prison,—but he (Georgeit) was acquitted of the paltry accusations brought against him by his Section, the "Faubourg du Nord." This Section took in the whole east side of the Faubourg St. Denis, whereas the present No. 63 is on the west side. After Georgeit (or Georget) had been arrested, Paine was left alone in the large mansion (said by Rickman to have been once the hotel of Madame de Pompadour), and it would appear, by his account, that it was after the execution (October 31, 1793) of his friends the Girondins, and political comrades, that he felt his end at hand, and set about his last literary bequest to the world,—"The Age of Reason,"—in the state in which it has since appeared, as he is careful to say. There was every probability, during the months in which he wrote (November and December 1793) that he would be executed. His religious testament was prepared with the blade of the guillotine suspended over him,—a fact which did not deter pious mythologists from portraying his death-bed remorse for having written the book.

In editing Part I. of "The Age of Reason," I follow closely the first edition, which was printed by Barrois in Paris from the manuscript, no doubt under the superintendence of Joel Barlow, to whom Paine, on his way to the Luxembourg, had confided it. Barlow was an American ex-clergyman, a speculator on whose career French archives cast an unfavorable light, and one cannot be certain that no liberties were taken with Paine's proofs.

I may repeat here what I have stated in the outset of my editorial work on Paine that my rule is to correct obvious misprints, and also any punctuation which seems to render

the sense less clear. And to that I will now add that in following Paine's quotations from the Bible I have adopted the
plan now generally used in place of his occasionally too
extended writing out of book, chapter, and verse.

Paine was imprisoned in the Luxembourg on December
28, 1793, and released on November 4, 1794. His liberation
was secured by his old friend, James Monroe (afterwards
President), who had succeeded his (Paine's) relentless enemy,
Gouverneur Morris, as American Minister in Paris. He was
found by Monroe more dead than alive from semi-starvation,
cold, and an abscess contracted in prison, and taken to the
Minister's own residence. It was not supposed that he could
survive, and he owed his life to the tender care of Mr. and
Mrs. Monroe. It was while thus a prisoner in his room, with
death still hovering over him, that Paine wrote Part Second
of "The Age of Reason."

The work was published in London by H. D. Symonds on
October 25, 1795, and claimed to be "from the Author's
manuscript." It is marked as "Entered at Stationers Hall,"
and prefaced by an apologetic note of "The Bookseller to
the Public," whose commonplaces about avoiding both
prejudice and partiality, and considering "both sides," need
not be quoted. While his volume was going through the
press in Paris, Paine heard of the publication in London,
which drew from him the following hurried note to a London
publisher, no doubt Daniel Isaacs Eaton :

"SIR,—I have seen advertised in the London papers the
second Edition [part] of the *Age of Reason*, printed, the
advertisement says, from the *Author's Manuscript*, and
entered at Stationers Hall. I have never sent any manuscript to any person. It is therefore a forgery to say it is
printed from the author's manuscript; and I suppose is done
to give the Publisher a pretence of Copy Right, which he
has no title to.

"I send you a printed copy, which is the only one I have
sent to London. I wish you to make a cheap edition of it.
I know not by what means any copy has got over to London.

If any person has made a manuscript copy I have no doubt
but it is full of errors. I wish you would talk to Mr. ——
upon this subject as I wish to know by what means this trick
has been played, and from whom the publisher has got
possession of any copy.

"T. PAINE.

"PARIS, December 4, 1795."

Eaton's cheap edition appeared January 1, 1796, with the
above letter on the reverse of the title. The blank in the
note was probably " Symonds " in the original, and possibly
that publisher was imposed upon. Eaton, already in trouble
for printing one of Paine's political pamphlets, fled to
America, and an edition of the "Age of Reason" was
issued under a new title; no publisher appears; it is said
to be "printed for, and sold by all the Booksellers in Great
Britain and Ireland." It is also said to be " By Thomas
Paine, author of several remarkable performances." I have
never found any copy of this anonymous edition except the
one in my possession. It is evidently the edition which was
suppressed by the prosecution of Williams for selling a copy
of it.

A comparison with Paine's revised edition reveals a good
many clerical and verbal errors in Symonds, though few that
affect the sense. The worst are in the preface, where, instead
of " 1793," the misleading date " 1790 " is given as the year
at whose close Paine completed Part First,—an error that
spread far and wide, and was fastened on by his calumnious
American "biographer," Cheetham, to prove his inconsistency. The editors have been fairly demoralized by, and
have altered in different ways, the following sentence of the
preface in Symonds: " The intolerant spirit of religious persecution had transferred itself into politics; the tribunals,
styled Revolutionary, supplied the place of the Inquisition;
and the Guillotine of the State outdid the Fire and Faggot
of the Church." The rogue who copied this little knew the
care with which Paine weighed words, and that he would
never call persecution " religious," nor connect the guillo-

tine with the " State," nor concede that with all it's horrors
it had outdone the history of fire and faggot. What Paine
wrote was : " The intolerant spirit of church persecution had
transferred itself into politics ; the tribunals, stiled Revolutionary, supplied the place of an Inquisition · and the Guillotine, of the Stake."

An original letter of Paine, in the possession of Joseph
Cowen, ex-M. P., which that gentleman permits me to bring
to light, besides being one of general interest makes clear
the circumstances of the original publication. Although the
name of the correspondent does not appear on the letter, it
was certainly written to Col. John Fellows of New York,
who copyrighted Part I. of the " Age of Reason." He published the pamphlets of Joel Barlow, to whom Paine confided
his manuscript on his way to prison. Fellows was afterwards
Paine's intimate friend in New York, and it was chiefly due
to him that some portions of the author's writings, left in
manuscript to Madame Bonneville while she was a freethinker, were rescued from her devout destructiveness after
her return to Catholicism. The letter which Mr. Cowen
sends me, is dated at Paris, January 20, 1797.

" SIR,—Your friend Mr. Caritat being on the point of his
departure for America, I make it the opportunity of writing
to you. I received two letters from you with some pamphlets a considerable time past, in which you inform me of
your entering a copyright of the first part of the Age of
Reason : when I return to America we will settle for that
matter.

" As Doctor Franklin has been my intimate friend for
thirty years past you will naturally see the reason of my continuing the connection with his grandson. I printed here
(Paris) about fifteen thousand of the second part of the Age
of Reason, which I sent to Mr. F[ranklin] Bache. I gave
him notice of it in September 1795 and the copy-right by
my own direction was entered by him. The books did not
arrive till April following, but he had advertised it long
before.

" I sent to him in August last a manuscript letter of about 70 pages, from me to Mr. Washington to be printed in a pamphlet. Mr. Barnes of Philadelphia carried the letter from me over to London to be forwarded to America. It went by the ship Hope, Cap: Harley, who since his return from America told me that he put it into the post office at New York for Bache. I have yet no certain account of its publication. I mention this that the letter may be enquired after, in case it has not been published or has not arrived to Mr. Bache. Barnes wrote to me, from London 29 August informing me that he was offered three hundred pounds sterling for the manuscript. The offer was refused because it was my intention it should not appear till it appeared in America, as that, and not England was the place for its operation.

" You ask me by your letter to Mr. Caritat for a list of my several works, in order to publish a collection of them. This is an undertaking I have always reserved for myself. It not only belongs to me of right, but nobody but myself can do it ; and as every author is accountable (at least in reputation) for his works, he only is the person to do it. If he neglects it in his life-time the case is altered. It is my intention to return to America in the course of the present year. I shall then [do] it by subscription, with historical notes. As this work will employ many persons in different parts of the Union, I will confer with you upon the subject, and such part of it as will suit you to undertake, will be at your choice. I have sustained so much loss, by disinterestedness and inattention to money matters, and by accidents, that I am obliged to look closer to my affairs than I have done. The printer (an Englishman) whom I employed here to print the second part of the Age of Reason made a manuscript copy of the work while he was printing it, which he sent to London and sold. It was by this means that an edition of it came out in London.

" We are waiting here for news from America of the state of the federal elections. You will have heard long before this reaches you that the French government has refused to

receive Mr. Pinckney as minister. While Mr. Monroe was
minister he had the opportunity of softening matters with
this government, for he was in good credit with them tho'
they were in high indignation at the infidelity of the Washington Administration. It is time that Mr. Washington
retire, for he has played off so much prudent hypocrisy between France and England that neither government believes
anything he says.

> "Your friend, etc.,
>
> "THOMAS PAINE."

It would appear that Symonds' stolen edition must have
got ahead of that sent by Paine to Franklin Bache, for some
of its errors continue in all modern American editions to the
present day, as well as in those of England. For in England
it was only the shilling edition—that revised by Paine—
which was suppressed. Symonds, who ministered to the
half-crown folk, and who was also publisher of replies to
Paine, was left undisturbed about his pirated edition, and
the new Society for the suppression of Vice and Immorality
fastened on one Thomas Williams, who sold pious tracts, but
was also convicted (June 24, 1797) of having sold one copy
of the "Age of Reason." Erskine, who had defended Paine
at his trial for the "Rights of Man," conducted the prosecution of Williams. He gained the victory from a packed
jury, but was not much elated by it, especially after a certain adventure on his way to Lincoln's Inn. He felt his
coat clutched and beheld at his feet a woman bathed in
tears. She led him into the small bookshop of Thomas
Williams, not yet called up for judgment, and there he beheld his victim stitching tracts in a wretched little room,
where there were three children, two suffering with small-
pox. He saw that it would be ruin and even a sort of murder to take away to prison the husband, who was not a
freethinker, and lamented his publication of the book, and
a meeting of the Society which had retained him was summoned. There was a full meeting, the Bishop of London
(Porteus) in the chair. Erskine reminded them that Wil-

liams was yet to be brought up for sentence, described the scene he had witnessed, and Williams' penitence, and, as the book was now suppressed, asked permission to move for a nominal sentence. Mercy, he urged, was a part of the Christianity they were defending. Not one of the Society took his side,—not even " philanthropic " Wilberforce—and Erskine threw up his brief. This action of Erskine led the Judge to give Williams only a year in prison instead of the three he said had been intended.

While Williams was in prison the orthodox colporteurs were circulating Erskine's speech on Christianity, but also an anonymous sermon " On the Existence and Attributes of the Deity," all of which was from Paine's " Age of Reason," except a brief " Address to the Deity " appended. This picturesque anomaly was repeated in the circulation of Paine's " Discourse to the Theophilanthropists " (their and the author's names removed) under the title of " Atheism Refuted." Both of these pamphlets are now before me, and beside them a London tract of one page just sent for my spiritual benefit. This is headed " A Word of Caution." It begins by mentioning the " pernicious doctrines of Paine," the first being " that there is NO GOD " (*sic*,) then proceeds to adduce evidences of divine existence taken from Paine's works. It should be added that this one dingy page is the only " survival " of the ancient Paine effigy in the tract form which I have been able to find in recent years, and to this no Society or Publisher's name is attached.

The imprisonment of Williams was the beginning of a thirty years' war for religious liberty in England, in the course of which occurred many notable events, such as Eaton receiving homage in his pillory at Charing Cross, and the whole Carlile family imprisoned,—its head imprisoned more than nine years for publishing the " Age of Reason." This last victory of persecution was suicidal. Gentlemen of wealth, not adherents of Paine, helped in setting Carlile up in business in Fleet Street, where freethinking publications have since been sold without interruption. But though Liberty triumphed in one sense, the " Age of Reason" remained to some extent suppressed among those whose attention it especially merited. Its original prosecution by a Society for the Suppression of Vice (a device to relieve the Crown) amounted to a libel upon a morally clean book, restricting its perusal in families; and the fact that the shilling book sold by and among humble people was alone prosecuted, diffused among the educated an equally false notion that the "Age of Reason" was vulgar and illiterate. The theologians, as we have seen, estimated more justly the ability of their antagonist, the *collaborateur* of Franklin, Rittenhouse, and Clymer, on whom the University of Pennsylvania had conferred the degree of Master of Arts,—but the gentry confused Paine with the class described by Burke as "the swinish multitude." Scepticism, or its free utterance, was temporarily driven out of polite circles by its complication with the outlawed vindicator of the "Rights of Man." But that long combat has now passed away. Time has reduced the "Age of Reason" from a flag of popular radicalism to a comparatively conservative treatise, so far as its negations are concerned. An old friend tells me that in his youth he heard a sermon in which the preacher declared that "Tom Paine" was so wicked that he could not be buried; his bones were thrown into a box which was bandied about the world till it came to a button-manufacturer; "and now Paine is travelling round the world in the form of buttons!" This variant of the Wandering Jew myth may now be regarded as unconscious homage to the author whose metaphorical bones may be recognized in buttons now fashionable, and some even found useful in holding clerical vestments together.

But the careful reader will find in Paine's "Age of Reason" something beyond negations, and in conclusion I will especially call attention to the new departure in Theism indicated in a passage corresponding to a famous aphorism of Kant, indicated by a note in Part II. The discovery already mentioned, that Part I. was written at least fourteen years before Part II., led me to compare the two; and it is plain that while the earlier work is an amplification of Newtonian

Deism, based on the phenomena of planetary motion, the work of 1795 bases belief in God on " the universal display of himself in the works of the creation *and by that repugnance we feel in ourselves to bad actions, and disposition to do good ones.*" This exaltation of the moral nature of man to be the foundation of theistic religion, though now familiar, was a hundred years ago a new affirmation ; it has led on a conception of deity subversive of last-century deism, it has steadily humanized religion, and its ultimate philosophical and ethical results have not yet been reached.

I.

THE AGE OF REASON.

CHAPTER I.

THE AUTHOR'S PROFESSION OF FAITH.

IT has been my intention, for several years past, to publish my thoughts upon religion; I am well aware of the difficulties that attend the subject, and from that consideration, had reserved it to a more advanced period of life. I intended it to be the last offering I should make to my fellow-citizens of all nations, and that at a time when the purity of the motive that induced me to it could not admit of a question, even by those who might disapprove the work.

The circumstance that has now taken place in France, of the total abolition of the whole national order of priesthood, and of everything appertaining to compulsive systems of religion, and compulsive articles of faith, has not only precipitated my intention, but rendered a work of this kind exceedingly necessary, lest, in the general wreck of superstition, of false systems of government, and false theology, we lose sight of morality, of humanity, and of the theology that is true.

As several of my colleagues, and others of my fellow-citizens of France, have given me the example of making their voluntary and individual profession of faith, I also will make mine; and I do this with all that sincerity and frankness with which the mind of man communicates with itself.

I believe in one God, and no more; and I hope for happiness beyond this life.

I believe the equality of man, and I believe that religious

duties consist in doing justice, loving mercy, and endeavouring to make our fellow-creatures happy.

But, lest it should be supposed that I believe many other things in addition to these, I shall, in the progress of this work, declare the things I do not believe, and my reasons for not believing them.

I do not believe in the creed professed by the Jewish church, by the Roman church, by the Greek church, by the Turkish church, by the Protestant church, nor by any church that I know of. My own mind is my own church.

All national institutions of churches, whether Jewish, Christian, or Turkish, appear to me no other than human inventions set up to terrify and enslave mankind, and monopolize power and profit.

I do not mean by this declaration to condemn those who believe otherwise ; they have the same right to their belief as I have to mine. But it is necessary to the happiness of man, that he be mentally faithful to himself. Infidelity does not consist in believing, or in disbelieving ; it consists in professing to believe what he does not believe.

It is impossible to calculate the moral mischief, if I may so express it, that mental lying has produced in society. When a man has so far corrupted and prostituted the chastity of his mind, as to subscribe his professional belief to things he does not believe, he has prepared himself for the commission of every other crime. He takes up the trade of a priest for the sake of gain, and, in order to qualify himself for that trade, he begins with a perjury. Can we conceive anything more destructive to morality than this?

Soon after I had published the pamphlet COMMON SENSE, in America, I saw the exceeding probability that a revolution in the system of government would be followed by a revolution in the system of religion. The adulterous connection of church and state, wherever it had taken place, whether Jewish, Christian, or Turkish, had so effectually prohibited, by pains and penalties, every discussion upon established creeds, and upon first principles of religion, that until the system of government should be changed, those subjects could not be brought fairly and openly before the world ; but that whenever this should be done, a revolution in the system of religion would follow. Human inventions and priest-craft would be detected; and man would return to the pure, unmixed, and unadulterated belief of one God, and no more.

CHAPTER II.

OF MISSIONS AND REVELATIONS.

EVERY national church or religion has established itself by pretending some special mission from God, communicated to certain individuals. The Jews have their Moses ; the Christians their Jesus Christ, their apostles and saints; and the Turks their Mahomet; as if the way to God was not open to every man alike.

Each of those churches shows certain books, which they call *revelation*, or the Word of God. The Jews say that their Word of God was given by God to Moses face to face ; the Christians say, that their Word of God came by divine inspiration ; and the Turks say, that their Word of God (the Koran) was brought by an angel from heaven. Each of those churches accuses the other of unbelief ; and, for my own part, I disbelieve them all.

As it is necessary to affix right ideas to words, I will, before I proceed further into the subject, offer some observations on the word *revelation*. Revelation when applied to religion, means something communicated *immediately* from God to man.

No one will deny or dispute the power of the Almighty to make such a communication if he pleases. But admitting, for the sake of a case, that something has been revealed to a certain person, and not revealed to any other person, it is revelation to that person only. When he tells it to a second person, a second to a third, a third to a fourth, and so on, it ceases to be a revelation to all those persons. It is revelation to the first person only, and *hearsay* to every other, and, consequently, they are not obliged to believe it.

It is a contradiction in terms and ideas to call anything a revelation that comes to us at second hand, either verbally or in writing. Revelation is necessarily limited to the first communication. After this, it is only an account of something which that person says was a revelation made to him; and though he may find himself obliged to believe it, it cannot be incumbent on me to believe it in the same manner, for it was not a revelation made to *me*, and I have only his word for it that it was made to *him*.

When Moses told the children of Israel that he received the two tables of the commandments from the hand of God, they were not obliged to believe him, because they had no other authority for it than his telling them so; and I have no other authority for it than some historian telling me so, the commandments carrying no internal evidence of divinity with them. They contain some good moral precepts such as any man qualified to be a lawgiver or a legislator could produce himself, without having recourse to supernatural intervention.*

When I am told that the Koran was written in Heaven, and brought to Mahomet by an angel, the account comes to near the same kind of hearsay evidence and second hand authority as the former. I did not see the angel myself, and therefore I have a right not to believe it.

When also I am told that a woman, called the Virgin Mary, said, or gave out, that she was with child without any cohabitation with a man, and that her betrothed husband, Joseph, said that an angel told him so, I have a right to believe them or not: such a circumstance required a much stronger evidence than their bare word for it: but we have not even this; for neither Joseph nor Mary wrote any such matter themselves. It is only reported by others that *they said so*. It is hearsay upon hearsay, and I do not chuse to rest my belief upon such evidence.

It is, however, not difficult to account for the credit that

---

* It is, however, necessary to except the declaration which says that God *visits the sins of the fathers upon the children.* This is contrary to every principle of moral justice.—*Author.*

was given to the story of Jesus Christ being the Son of God. He was born when the heathen mythology had still some fashion and repute in the world, and that mythology had prepared the people for the belief of such a story. Almost all the extraordinary men that lived under the heathen mythology were reputed to be the sons of some of their gods. It was not a new thing at that time to believe a man to have been celestially begotten ; the intercourse of gods with women was then a matter of familiar opinion. Their Jupiter, according to their accounts, had cohabited with hundreds; the story therefore had nothing in it either new, wonderful, or obscene ; it was conformable to the opinions that then prevailed among the people called Gentiles, or mythologists, and it was those people only that believed it. The Jews, who had kept strictly to the belief of one God, and no more, and who had always rejected the heathen mythology, never credited the story.

It is curious to observe how the theory of what is called the Christian Church, sprung out of the tail of the heathen mythology. A direct incorporation took place in the first instance, by making the reputed founder to be celestially begotten. The trinity of gods that then followed was no other than a reduction of the former plurality, which was about twenty or thirty thousand. The statue of Mary succeeded the statue of Diana of Ephesus. The deification of heroes changed into the canonization of saints. The Mythologists had gods for everything; the Christian Mythologists had saints for everything. The church became as crouded with the one, as the pantheon had been with the other ; and Rome was the place of both. The Christian theory is little else than the idolatry of the ancient mythologists, accommodated to the purposes of power and revenue; and it yet remains to reason and philosophy to abolish **the amphibious fraud.**

CHAPTER III.

CONCERNING THE CHARACTER OF JESUS CHRIST, AND HIS HISTORY.

NOTHING that is here said can apply, even with the most distant disrespect, to the *real* character of Jesus Christ. He was a virtuous and an amiable man. The morality that he preached and practised was of the most benevolent kind; and though similar systems of morality had been preached by Confucius, and by some of the Greek philosophers, many years before, by the Quakers since, and by many good men in all ages, it has not been exceeded by any.

Jesus Christ wrote no account of himself, of his birth, parentage, or anything else. Not a line of what is called the New Testament is of his writing. The history of him is altogether the work of other people; and as to the account given of his resurrection and ascension, it was the necessary counterpart to the story of his birth. His historians, having brought him into the world in a supernatural manner, were obliged to take him out again in the same manner, or the first part of the story must have fallen to the ground.

The wretched contrivance with which this latter part is told, exceeds everything that went before it. The first part, that of the miraculous conception, was not a thing that admitted of publicity; and therefore the tellers of this part of the story had this advantage, that though they might not be credited, they could not be detected. They could not be expected to prove it, because it was not one of those things that admitted of proof, and it was impossible that the person of whom it was told could prove it himself.

But the resurrection of a dead person from the grave, and his ascension through the air, is a thing very different, as to the evidence it admits of, to the invisible conception of a child in the womb. The resurrection and ascension, supposing them to have taken place, admitted of public and ocular demonstration, like that of the ascension of a balloon, or the sun at noon day, to all Jerusalem at least. A thing which everybody is required to believe, requires that the proof and evidence of it should be equal to all, and universal; and as the public visibility of this last related act was the only evidence that could give sanction to the former part, the whole of it falls to the ground, because that evidence never was given. Instead of this, a small number of persons, not more than eight or nine, are introduced as proxies for the whole world, to say they saw it, and all the rest of the world are called upon to believe it. But it appears that Thomas did not believe the resurrection; and, as they say, would not believe without having ocular and manual demonstration himself. *So neither will I;* and the reason is equally as good for me, and for every other person, as for Thomas.

It is in vain to attempt to palliate or disguise this matter. The story, so far as relates to the supernatural part, has every mark of fraud and imposition stamped upon the face of it. Who were the authors of it is as impossible for us now to know, as it is for us to be assured that the books in which the account is related were written by the persons whose names they bear. The best surviving evidence we now have respecting this affair is the Jews. They are regularly descended from the people who lived in the time this resurrection and ascension is said to have happened, and they say, *it is not true.* It has long appeared to me a strange inconsistency to cite the Jews as a proof of the truth of the story. It is just the same as if a man were to say, I will prove the truth of what I have told you, by producing the people who say it is false.

That such a person as Jesus Christ existed, and that he was crucified, which was the mode of execution at that day, are historical relations strictly within the limits of probability. He preached most excellent morality, and the equality of man; but he preached also against the corruptions and avarice of the Jewish priests, and this brought upon him the hatred and vengeance of the whole order of priesthood. The accusation which those priests brought against him was that of sedition and conspiracy against the Roman government, to which the Jews were then subject and tributary ; and it is not improbable that the Roman government might have some secret apprehension of the effects of his doctrine as well as the Jewish priests; neither is it improbable that Jesus Christ had in contemplation the delivery of the Jewish nation from the bondage of the Romans. Between the two, however, this virtuous reformer and revolutionist lost his life.[1]

CHAPTER IV.

OF THE BASES OF CHRISTIANITY.

IT is upon this plain narrative of facts, together with another case I am going to mention, that the Christian mythologists, calling themselves the Christian Church, have erected their fable, which for absurdity and extravagance is not exceeded by anything that is to be found in the mythology of the ancients.

The ancient mythologists tell us that the race of Giants made war against Jupiter, and that one of them threw a hundred rocks against him at one throw; that Jupiter defeated him with thunder, and confined him afterwards under Mount Etna; and that every time the Giant turns himself, Mount Etna belches fire. It is here easy to see that the circumstance of the mountain, that of its being a volcano, suggested the idea of the fable ; and that the fable is made to fit and wind itself up with that circumstance.

The Christian mythologists tell that their Satan made war against the Almighty, who defeated him, and confined him afterwards, not under a mountain, but in a pit. It is here easy to see that the first fable suggested the idea of the

---

[1] The French work has here: " Quoi qu'il en soit, ce verteux réformateur, ce révolutionnaire trop peu imité, trop oublié, trop méconnu, perdit la vie pour l'une ou pour l'autre de ces suppositions." However this may be, for one or the other of these suppositions this virtuous reformer, this revolutionist, too little imitated, too much forgotten, too much misunderstood, lost his life.—*Editor.*

second ; for the fable of Jupiter and the Giants was told many hundred years before that of Satan.

Thus far the ancient and the Christian mythologists differ very little from each other. But the latter have contrived to carry the matter much farther. They have contrived to connect the fabulous part of the story of Jesus Christ with the fable originating from Mount Etna; and, in order to make all the parts of the story tye together, they have taken to their aid the traditions of the Jews ; for the Christian mythology is made up partly from the ancient mythology, and partly from the Jewish traditions.

The Christian mythologists, after having confined Satan in a pit, were obliged to let him out again to bring on the sequel of the fable. He is then introduced into the garden of Eden in the shape of a snake, or a serpent, and in that shape he enters into familiar conversation with Eve, who is no ways surprised to hear a snake talk ; and the issue of this tête-à-tête is, that he persuades her to eat an apple, and the eating of that apple damns all mankind.

After giving Satan this triumph over the whole creation, one would have supposed that the church mythologists would have been kind enough to send him back again to the pit, or, if they had not done this, that they would have put a mountain upon him, (for they say that their faith can remove a mountain) or have put him under a mountain, as the former mythologists had done, to prevent his getting again among the women, and doing more mischief. But instead of this, they leave him at large, without even obliging him to give his parole. The secret of which is, that they could not do without him ; and after being at the trouble of making him, they bribed him to stay. They promised him ALL the Jews, ALL the Turks by anticipation, nine-tenths of the world beside, and Mahomet into the bargain. After this, who can doubt the bountifulness of the Christian Mythology ?

Having thus made an insurrection and a battle in heaven, in which none of the combatants could be either killed or wounded—put Satan into the pit—let him out again—given him a triumph over the whole creation—damned all mankind by the eating of an apple, these Christian mythologists bring the two ends of their fable together. They represent this virtuous and amiable man, Jesus Christ, to be at once both God and man, and also the Son of God, celestially begotten, on purpose to be sacrificed, because they say that Eve in her longing[1] had eaten an apple.

CHAPTER V.

EXAMINATION IN DETAIL OF THE PRECEDING BASES.

PUTTING aside everything that might excite laughter by its absurdity, or detestation by its prophaneness, and confining ourselves merely to an examination of the parts, it is impossible to conceive a story more derogatory to the Almighty, more inconsistent with his wisdom, more contradictory to his power, than this story is.

In order to make for it a foundation to rise upon, the inventors were under the necessity of giving to the being whom they call Satan a power equally as great, if not greater, than they attribute to the Almighty. They have not only given him the power of liberating himself from the pit, after what they call his fall, but they have made that power increase afterwards to infinity. Before this fall they represent him only as an angel of limited existence, as they represent the rest. After his fall, he becomes, by their account, omnipresent. He exists everywhere, and at the same time. He occupies the whole immensity of space.

Not content with this deification of Satan, they represent him as defeating by stratagem, in the shape of an animal of the creation, all the power and wisdom of the Almighty. They represent him as having compelled the Almighty to the *direct necessity* either of surrendering the whole of the creation to the government and sovereignty of this Satan, or of capitulating for its redemption by coming down upon earth, and exhibiting himself upon a cross in the shape of a man.

---

[1] The French work has : " cédant à une gourmandise effrénée " (yielding to an unrestrained appetite).—*Editor*.

Had the inventors of this story told it the contrary way, that is, had they represented the Almighty as compelling Satan to exhibit *himself* on a cross in the shape of a snake, as a punishment for his new transgression, the story would have been less absurd, less contradictory. But, instead of this they make the transgressor triumph, and the Almighty fall.

That many good men have believed this strange fable, and lived very good lives under that belief (for credulity is not a crime) is what I have no doubt of. In the first place, they were educated to believe it, and they would have believed anything else in the same manner. There are also many who have been so enthusiastically enraptured by what they conceived to be the infinite love of God to man, in making a sacrifice of himself, that the vehemence of the idea has forbidden and deterred them from examining into the absurdity and profaneness of the story. The more unnatural anything is, the more is it capable of becoming the object of dismal admiration.[1]

CHAPTER VI.

OF THE TRUE THEOLOGY.

BUT if objects for gratitude and admiration are our desire, do they not present themselves every hour to our eyes? Do we not see a fair creation prepared to receive us the instant we are born—a world furnished to our hands, that cost us nothing? Is it we that light up the sun; that pour down the rain; and fill the earth with abundance? Whether we sleep or wake, the vast machinery of the universe still goes on. Are these things, and the blessings they indicate in future, nothing to us? Can our gross feelings be excited by no other subjects than tragedy and suicide? Or is the gloomy pride of man become so intolerable, that nothing can flatter it but a sacrifice of the Creator?

---

[1] The French work has "aveugle et" (blind and) preceding "dismal."—
Editor.

I know that this bold investigation will alarm many, but it would be paying too great a compliment to their credulity to forbear it on that account. The times and the subject demand it to be done. The suspicion that the theory of what is called the Christian church is fabulous, is becoming very extensive in all countries; and it will be a consolation to men staggering under that suspicion, and doubting what to believe and what to disbelieve, to see the subject freely investigated. I therefore pass on to an examination of the books called the Old and the New Testament.

CHAPTER VII.

EXAMINATION OF THE OLD TESTAMENT.

THESE books, beginning with Genesis and ending with Revelations, (which, by the bye, is a book of riddles that requires a revelation to explain it) are, we are told, the word of God. It is, therefore, proper for us to know who told us so, that we may know what credit to give to the report. The answer to this question is, that nobody can tell, except that we tell one another so. The case, however, historically appears to be as follows:

When the church mythologists established their system, they collected all the writings they could find, and managed them as they pleased. It is a matter altogether of uncertainty to us whether such of the writings as now appear under the name of the Old and the New Testament, are in the same state in which those collectors say they found them; or whether they added, altered, abridged, or dressed them up.

Be this as it may, they decided by *vote* which of the books out of the collection they had made, should be the WORD OF GOD, and which should not. They rejected several; they voted others to be doubtful, such as the books called the Apocrypha; and those books which had a majority of votes, were voted to be the word of God. Had they voted otherwise, all the people since calling themselves Christians had believed otherwise ; for the belief of the one comes from the vote of the other. Who the people were that did all this, we know nothing of. They call themselves by the general name of the Church ; and this is all we know of the matter.

As we have no other external evidence or authority for believing these books to be the word of God, than what I have mentioned, which is no evidence or authority at all, I come, in the next place, to examine the internal evidence contained in the books themselves.

In the former part of this essay, I have spoken of revelation. I now proceed further with that subject, for the purpose of applying it to the books in question.

Revelation is a communication of something, which the person, to whom that thing is revealed, did not know before. For if I have done a thing, or seen it done, it needs no revelation to tell me I have done it, or seen it, nor to enable me to tell it, or to write it.

Revelation, therefore, cannot be applied to anything done upon earth of which man is himself the actor or the witness; and consequently all the historical and anecdotal part of the Bible, which is almost the whole of it, is not within the meaning and compass of the word revelation, and, therefore, is not the word of God.

When Samson ran off with the gate-posts of Gaza, if he ever did so, (and whether he did or not is nothing to us,) or when he visited his Delilah, or caught his foxes, or did anything else,[1] what has revelation to do with these things? If they were facts, he could tell them himself ; or his secretary, if he kept one, could write them, if they were worth either telling or writing ; and if they were fictions, revelation could not make them true ; and whether true or not, we are neither the better nor the wiser for knowing them.—When we contemplate the immensity of that Being, who directs and governs the incomprehensible WHOLE, of which the utmost ken of human sight can discover but a part, we ought to feel shame at calling such paltry stories the word of God.

As to the account of the creation, with which the book

---

[1] The French work has " frédaine " (prank).—*Editor.*

of Genesis opens, it has all the appearance of being a tradition which the Israelites had among them before they came
into Egypt; and after their departure from that country,
they put it at the head of their history, without telling, as it
is most probable that they did not know, how they came by
it. The manner in which the account opens, shews it to be
traditionary. It begins abruptly. It is nobody that speaks.
It is nobody that hears. It is addressed to nobody. It has
neither first, second, nor third person. It has every criterion of being a tradition. It has no voucher. Moses does
not take it upon himself by introducing it with the formality
that he uses on other occasions, such as that of saying, " *The*
Lord spake unto Moses, saying."

Why it has been called the Mosaic account of the creation, I am at a loss to conceive. Moses, I believe, was too
good a judge of such subjects to put his name to that account. He had been educated among the Egyptians, who
were a people as well skilled in science, and particularly in
astronomy, as any people of their day ; and the silence and
caution that Moses observes, in not authenticating the
account, is a good negative evidence that he neither told it
nor believed it.—The case is, that every nation of people
has been world-makers, and the Israelites had as much right
to set up the trade of world-making as any of the rest; and
as Moses was not an Israelite, he might not chuse to contradict the tradition. The account, however, is harmless;
and this is more than can be said for many other parts of the
Bible.

Whenever we read the obscene stories, the voluptuous
debaucheries, the cruel and torturous executions, the unre-
lenting vindictiveness, with which more than half the Bible[1]
is filled, it would be more consistent that we called it the
word of a demon, than the Word of God. It is a history of
wickedness, that has served to corrupt and brutalize mankind ; and, for my own part, I sincerely detest it, as I detest
everything that is cruel.

[1] It must be borne in mind that by the " Bible " Paine always means the Old
Testament alone.—*Editor.*

We scarcely meet with anything, a few phrases excepted, but what deserves either our abhorrence or our contempt, till we come to the miscellaneous parts of the Bible. In the anonymous publications, the Psalms, and the Book of Job, more particularly in the latter, we find a great deal of elevated sentiment reverentially expressed of the power and benignity of the Almighty ; but they stand on no higher rank than many other compositions on similar subjects, as well before that time as since.

The Proverbs which are said to be Solomon's, though most probably a collection, (because they discover a knowledge of life, which his situation excluded him from knowing) are an instructive table of ethics. They are inferior in keenness to the proverbs of the Spaniards, and not more wise and œconomical than those of the American Franklin.

All the remaining parts of the Bible, generally known by the name of the Prophets, are the works of the Jewish poets and itinerant preachers, who mixed poetry, anecdote, and devotion together—and those works still retain the air and stile of poetry, though in translation.*

There is not, throughout the whole book called the Bible, any word that describes to us what we call a poet, nor any

---

* As there are many readers who do not see that a composition is poetry, unless it be in rhyme, it is for their information that I add this note.

Poetry consists principally in two things—imagery and composition. The composition of poetry differs from that of prose in the manner of mixing long and short syllables together. Take a long syllable out of a line of poetry, and put a short one in the room of it, or put a long syllable where a short one should be, and that line will lose its poetical harmony. It will have an effect upon the line like that of misplacing a note in a song.

The imagery in those books called the Prophets appertains altogether to poetry. It is fictitious, and often extravagant, and not admissible in any other kind of writing than poetry.

To shew that these writings are composed in poetical numbers, I will take ten syllables, as they stand in the book, and make a line of the same number of syllables, (heroic measure) that shall rhyme with the last word. It will then be seen that the composition of those books is poetical measure. The instance I shall first produce is from Isaiah :—

" *Hear, O ye heavens, and give ear, O earth !*"
'T is God himself that calls attention forth.

Another instance I shall quote is from the mournful Jeremiah, to which I word that describes what we call poetry. The case is, that the word *prophet*, to which later times have affixed a new idea, was the Bible word for poet, and the word *prophesying* meant the art of making poetry. It also meant the art of playing poetry to a tune upon any instrument of music.

We read of prophesying with pipes, tabrets, and horns—of prophesying with harps, with psalteries, with cymbals, and with every other instrument of music then in fashion.[1] Were we now to speak of prophesying with a fiddle, or with a pipe and tabor, the expression would have no meaning, or would appear ridiculous, and to some people contemptuous, because we have changed the meaning of the word.

We are told of Saul being among the prophets, and also that he prophesied; but we are not told what they prophesied, nor what he prophesied. The case is, there was nothing to tell; for these prophets were a company of musicians and poets, and Saul joined in the concert, and this was called prophesying.

The account given of this affair in the book called Samuel, is, that Saul met a company of prophets; a whole company of them! coming down with a psaltery, a tabret, a pipe, and a harp, and that they prophesied, and that he prophesied with them. But it appears afterwards, that Saul prophesied badly, that is, he performed his part badly; for it is said that an "*evil spirit from God** came upon Saul, and he prophesied."[2]

shall add two other lines, for the purpose of carrying out the figure, and shewing the intention of the poet.

> " *O, that mine head were waters and mine eyes* "
> Were fountains flowing like the liquid skies ;
> Then would I give the mighty flood release
> And weep a deluge for the human race.—*Author.*

[This footnote is not included in the French work.]—*Editor.*

* As those men who call themselves divines and commentators are very fond of puzzling one another, I leave them to contest the meaning of the first part of the phrase, that of *an evil spirit of God.* I keep to my text. I keep to the meaning of the word prophesy.—*Author.*

[1] I Chron. xxv., I.—*Editor.*   [2] I Sam. xviii., 10.—*Editor.*

Now, were there no other passage in the book called the Bible, than this, to demonstrate to us that we have lost the original meaning of the word *prophesy*, and substituted another meaning in its place, this alone would be sufficient; for it is impossible to use and apply the word *prophesy*, in the place it is here used and applied, if we give to it the sense which later times have affixed to it. The manner in which it is here used strips it of all religious meaning, and shews that a man might then be a prophet, or he might *prophesy*, as he may now be a poet or a musician, without any regard to the morality or the immorality of his character. The word was originally a term of science, promiscuously applied to poetry and to music, and not restricted to any subject upon which poetry and music might be exercised.

Deborah and Barak are called prophets, not because they predicted anything, but because they composed the poem or song that bears their name, in celebration of an act already done. David is ranked among the prophets, for he was a musician, and was also reputed to be (though perhaps very erroneously) the author of the Psalms. But Abraham, Isaac, and Jacob are not called prophets; it does not appear from any accounts we have, that they could either sing, play music, or make poetry.

We are told of the greater and the lesser prophets. They might as well tell us of the greater and the lesser God; for there cannot be degrees in prophesying consistently with its modern sense. But there are degrees in poetry, and therefore the phrase is reconcilable to the case, when we understand by it the greater and the lesser poets.

It is altogether unnecessary, after this, to offer any observations upon what those men, stiled prophets, have written. The axe goes at once to the root, by shewing that the original meaning of the word has been mistaken, and consequently all the inferences that have been drawn from those books, the devotional respect that has been paid to them, and the laboured commentaries that have been written upon them, under that mistaken meaning, are not worth disputing about. —In many things, however, the writings of the Jewish poets deserve a better fate than that of being bound up, as they now are, with the trash that accompanies them, under the abused name of the Word of God.

If we permit ourselves to conceive right ideas of things, we must necessarily affix the idea, not only of unchangeableness, but of the utter impossibility of any change taking place, by any means or accident whatever, in that which we would honour with the name of the Word of God; and therefore the Word of God cannot exist in any written or human language.

The continually progressive change to which the meaning of words is subject, the want of an universal language which renders translation necessary, the errors to which translations are again subject, the mistakes of copyists and printers, together with the possibility of wilful alteration, are of themselves evidences that human language, whether in speech or in print, cannot be the vehicle of the Word of God.—The Word of God exists in something else.[1]

Did the book called the Bible excel in purity of ideas and expression all the books now extant in the world, I would not take it for my rule of faith, as being the Word of God; because the possibility would nevertheless exist of my being imposed upon. But when I see throughout the greatest part of this book scarcely anything but a history of the grossest vices, and a collection of the most paltry and contemptible tales, I cannot dishonour my Creator by calling it by his name.

CHAPTER VIII.

OF THE NEW TESTAMENT.

THUS much for the Bible; I now go on to the book called the New Testament. The *new* Testament! that is, the *new* Will, as if there could be two wills of the Creator.

Had it been the object or the intention of Jesus Christ to establish a new religion, he would undoubtedly have written

---

[1] This paragraph is not in the French work.—*Editor.*

the system himself, or *procured it to be written* in his life time. But there is no publication extant authenticated with his name. All the books called the New Testament were written after his death. He was a Jew by birth and by profession; and he was the son of God in like manner that every other person is; for the Creator is the Father of All.

The first four books, called Matthew, Mark, Luke, and John, do not give a history of the life of Jesus Christ, but only detached anecdotes of him. It appears from these books, that the whole time of his being a preacher was not more than eighteen months; and it was only during this short time that those men became acquainted with him. They make mention of him at the age of twelve years, sitting, they say, among the Jewish doctors, asking and answering them questions. As this was several years before their acquaintance with him began, it is most probable they had this anecdote from his parents. From this time there is no account of him for about sixteen years.[1] Where he lived, or how he employed himself during this interval, is not known. Most probably he was working at his father's trade, which was that of a carpenter.[2] It does not appear that he had any school education, and the probability is, that he could not write, for his parents were extremely poor, as appears from their not being able to pay for a bed when he was born.[3]

It is somewhat curious that the three persons whose names are the most universally recorded were of very obscure parentage. Moses was a foundling; Jesus Christ was born in a stable; and Mahomet was a mule driver. The first and the last of these men were founders of different systems of religion; but Jesus Christ founded no new sys-

[1] " A man named Jesus, and he about thirty years, chose us out."—*Gospel according to the Hebrews.—Editor.*

[2] τέκτων, a skilled worker in wood, stone, or iron ; a builder ; not necessarily a carpenter—*Editor.*

[3] One of the few errors traceable to Paine's not having a Bible at hand while writing Part I. There is no indication that the family was poor, but the reverse may in fact be inferred.—*Editor.*

tem. He called men to the practice of moral virtues, and the belief of one God. The great trait in his character is philanthropy.

The manner in which he was apprehended shews that he was not much known at that time ; and it shews also that the meetings he then held with his followers were in secret ; and that he had given over or suspended preaching publicly. Judas could no otherways betray him than by giving information where he was, and pointing him out to the officers that went to arrest him ; and the reason for employing and paying Judas to do this could arise only from the causes already mentioned, that of his not being much known, and living concealed.

The idea of his concealment, not only agrees very ill with his reputed divinity, but associates with it something of pusillanimity ; and his being betrayed, or in other words, his being apprehended, on the information of one of his followers, shews that he did not intend to be apprehended, and consequently that he did not intend to be crucified.

The Christian mythologists tell us that Christ died for the sins of the world, and that he came on *purpose to die.* Would it not then have been the same if he had died of a fever or of the small pox, of old age, or of anything else?

The declaratory sentence which, they say, was passed upon Adam, in case he ate of the apple, was not, that *thou shalt surely be crucified,* but, *thou shalt surely die.* The sentence was death, and not the *manner of dying.* Crucifixion, therefore, or any other particular manner of dying, made no part of the sentence that Adam was to suffer, and consequently, even upon their own tactic, it could make no part of the sentence that Christ was to suffer in the room of Adam. A fever would have done as well as a cross, if there was any occasion for either.

This sentence of death, which, they tell us, was thus passed upon Adam, must either have meant dying naturally, that is, ceasing to live, or have meant what these mythologists call damnation ; and consequently, the act of dying on the part of Jesus Christ, must, according to their system, apply as a prevention to one or other of these two *things* happening to Adam and to us.

That it does not prevent our dying is evident, because we all die; and if their accounts of longevity be true, men die faster since the crucifixion than before: and with respect to the second explanation, (including with it the *natural death* of Jesus Christ as a substitute for the *eternal death or damnation* of all mankind,) it is impertinently representing the Creator as coming off, or revoking the sentence, by a pun or a quibble upon the word *death.* That manufacturer of quibbles, St. Paul, if he wrote the books that bear his name, has helped this quibble on by making another quibble upon the word *Adam.* He makes there to be two Adams; the one who sins in fact, and suffers by proxy; the other who sins by proxy, and suffers in fact. A religion thus interlarded with quibble, subterfuge, and pun, has a tendency to instruct its professors in the practice of these arts. They acquire the habit without being aware of the cause.

If Jesus Christ was the being which those mythologists tell us he was, and that he came into this world to *suffer,* which is a word they sometimes use instead of *to die,* the only real suffering he could have endured would have been *to live.* His existence here was a state of exilement or transportation from heaven, and the way back to his original country was to die.—In fine, everything in this strange system is the reverse of what it pretends to be. It is the reverse of truth, and I become so tired of examining into its inconsistencies and absurdities, that I hasten to the conclusion of it, in order to proceed to something better.

How much, or what parts of the books called the New Testament, were written by the persons whose names they bear, is what we can know nothing of, neither are we certain in what language they were originally written. The matters they now contain may be classed under two heads: anecdote, and epistolary correspondence.

The four books already mentioned, Matthew, Mark, Luke, and John, are altogether anecdotal. They relate events after they had taken place. They tell what Jesus Christ

did and said, and what others did and said to him ; and in
several instances they relate the same event differently.
Revelation is necessarily out of the question with respect
to those books ; not only because of the disagreement of the
writers, but because revelation cannot be applied to the
relating of facts by the persons who saw them done, nor to
the relating or recording of any discourse or conversation
by those who heard it. The book called the Acts of the
Apostles (an anonymous work) belongs also to the anecdotal
part.

All the other parts of the New Testament, except the
book of enigmas, called the Revelations, are a collection of
letters under the name of epistles ; and the forgery of letters
has been such a common practice in the world, that the probability is at least equal, whether they are genuine or forged.
One thing, however, is much less equivocal, which is, that
out of the matters contained in those books, together with
the assistance of some old stories, the church has set up a
system of religion very contradictory to the character of the
person whose name it bears. It has set up a religion of
pomp and of revenue in pretended imitation of a person
whose life was humility and poverty.

The invention of a purgatory, and of the releasing of souls
therefrom, by prayers, bought of the church with money ;
the selling of pardons, dispensations, and indulgences, are
revenue laws, without bearing that name or carrying that
appearance. But the case nevertheless is, that those things
derive their origin from the proxysm of the crucifixion, and
the theory deduced therefrom, which was, that one person
could stand in the place of another, and could perform
meritorious services for him. The probability, therefore, is,
that the whole theory or doctrine of what is called the
redemption (which is said to have been accomplished by the
act of one person in the room of another) was originally
fabricated on purpose to bring forward and build all those
secondary and pecuniary redemptions upon ; and that the
passages in the books upon which the idea of theory of
redemption is built, have been manufactured and fabricated

for that purpose. Why are we to give this church credit, when she tells us that those books are genuine in every part, any more than we give her credit for everything else she has told us; or for the miracles she says she has performed? That she *could* fabricate writings is certain, because she could write; and the composition of the writings in question, is of that kind that anybody might do it; and that she *did* fabricate them is not more inconsistent with probability, than that she should tell us, as she has done, that she could and did work miracles.

Since, then, no external evidence can, at this long distance of time, be produced to prove whether the church fabricated the doctrine called redemption or not, (for such evidence, whether for or against, would be subject to the same suspicion of being fabricated,) the case can only be referred to the internal evidence which the thing carries of itself; and this affords a very strong presumption of its being a fabrication. For the internal evidence is, that the theory or doctrine of redemption has for its basis an idea of pecuniary justice, and not that of moral justice.

If I owe a person money, and cannot pay him, and he threatens to put me in prison, another person can take the debt upon himself, and pay it for me. But if I have committed a crime, every circumstance of the case is changed. Moral justice cannot take the innocent for the guilty even if the innocent would offer itself. To suppose justice to do this, is to destroy the principle of its existence, which is the thing itself. It is then no longer justice. It is indiscriminate revenge.

This single reflection will shew that the doctrine of redemption is founded on a mere pecuniary idea corresponding to that of a debt which another person might pay; and as this pecuniary idea corresponds again with the system of second redemptions, obtained through the means of money given to the church for pardons, the probability is that the same persons fabricated both the one and the other of those theories; and that, in truth, there is no such thing as redemption; that it is fabulous; and that man stands in the same relative condition with his Maker he ever did stand, since man existed ; and that it is his greatest consolation to think so.

Let him believe this, and he will live more consistently and morally, than by any other system. It is by his being taught to contemplate himself as an out-law, as an out-cast, as a beggar, as a mumper, as one thrown as it were on a dunghill, at an immense distance from his Creator, and who must make his approaches by creeping, and cringing to intermediate beings, that he conceives either a contemptuous disregard for everything under the name of religion, or becomes indifferent, or turns what he calls devout. In the latter case, he consumes his life in grief, or the affectation of it. His prayers are reproaches. His humility is ingratitude. He calls himself a worm, and the fertile earth a dunghill; and all the blessings of life by the thankless name of vanities. He despises the choicest gift of God to man, the GIFT OF REASON; and having endeavoured to force upon himself the belief of a system against which reason revolts, he ungratefully calls it *human reason*, as if man could give reason to himself.

Yet, with all this strange appearance of humility, and this contempt for human reason, he ventures into the boldest presumptions. He finds fault with everything. His selfishness is never satisfied ; his ingratitude is never at an end. He takes on himself to direct the Almighty what to do, even in the government of the universe. He prays dictatorially. When it is sunshine, he prays for rain, and when it is rain, he prays for sunshine. He follows the same idea in everything that he prays for ; for what is the amount of all his prayers, but an attempt to make the Almighty change his mind, and act otherwise than he does? It is as if he were to say—thou knowest not so well as I.

CHAPTER IX.

IN WHAT THE TRUE REVELATION CONSISTS.

BUT some perhaps will say—Are we to have no word of God—no revelation?[1] I answer yes. There is a Word of God; there is a revelation.

THE WORD OF GOD IS THE CREATION WE BEHOLD: And it is in *this word*, which no human invention can counterfeit or alter, that God speaketh universally to man.

Human language is local and changeable, and is therefore incapable of being used as the means of unchangeable and universal information. The idea that God sent Jesus Christ to publish, as they say, the glad tidings to all nations, from one end of the earth unto the other, is consistent only with the ignorance of those who know nothing of the extent of the world, and who believed, as those world-saviours believed, and continued to believe for several centuries, (and that in contradiction to the discoveries of philosophers and the experience of navigators,) that the earth was flat like a trencher; and that a man might walk to the end of it.

But how was Jesus Christ to make anything known to all nations? He could speak but one language, which was Hebrew; and there are in the world several hundred languages. Scarcely any two nations speak the same language, or understand each other; and as to translations, every man who knows anything of languages, knows that it is impossible to translate from one language into another, not only without losing a great part of the original, but frequently of mistaking the sense; and besides all this, the art of printing was wholly unknown at the time Christ lived.

It is always necessary that the means that are to accomplish any end be equal to the accomplishment of that end, or the end cannot be accomplished. It is in this that the difference between finite and infinite power and wisdom discovers

---

[1] French: "Je réponds hardiment que nous ne sommes point condamnés à ce malheur.". (I boldly answer that we are not condemned to this misfortune.)— *Editor.*

itself. Man frequently fails in accomplishing his end, from a natural inability of the power to the purpose; and frequently from the want of wisdom to apply power properly. But it is impossible for infinite power and wisdom to fail as man faileth. The means it useth are always equal to the end : but human language, more especially as there is not an universal language, is incapable of being used as an universal means of unchangeable and uniform information ; and therefore it is not the means that God useth in manifesting himself universally to man.

It is only in the CREATION that all our ideas and conceptions of a *word of God* can unite. The Creation speaketh an universal language, independently of human speech or human language, multiplied and various as they be. It is an ever existing original, which every man can read. It cannot be forged ; it cannot be counterfeited ; it cannot be lost ; it cannot be altered ; it cannot be suppressed. It does not depend upon the will of man whether it shall be published or not ; it publishes itself from one end of the earth to the other. It preaches to all nations and to all worlds ; and this *word of God* reveals to man all that is necessary for man to know of God.

Do we want to contemplate his power ? We see it in the immensity of the creation. Do we want to contemplate his wisdom ? We see it in the unchangeable order by which the incomprehensible Whole is governed. Do we want to contemplate his munificence ? We see it in the abundance with which he fills the earth. Do we want to contemplate his mercy ? We see it in his not withholding that abundance even from the unthankful. In fine, do we want to know what God is ? Search not the book called the scripture, which any human hand might make, but the scripture called the Creation.

CHAPTER X.

CONCERNING GOD, AND THE LIGHTS CAST ON HIS EXIST-
ENCE AND ATTRIBUTES BY THE BIBLE.

THE only idea man can affix to the name of God, is that
of a *first cause*, the cause of all things. And, incomprehen-
sibly difficult as it is for a man to conceive what a first
cause is, he arrives at the belief of it, from the tenfold
greater difficulty of disbelieving it. It is difficult beyond
description to conceive that space can have no end ; but it
is more difficult to conceive an end. It is difficult beyond
the power of man to conceive an eternal duration of what
we call time ; but it is more impossible to conceive a time
when there shall be no time.

In like manner of reasoning, everything we behold
carries in itself the internal evidence that it did not make
itself. Every man is an evidence to himself, that he did not
make himself ; neither could his father make himself, nor his
grandfather, nor any of his race ; neither could any tree,
plant, or animal make itself ; and it is the conviction arising
from this evidence, that carries us on, as it were, by necessity, to the belief of a first cause eternally existing, of a
nature totally different to any material existence we know
of, and by the power of which all things exist ; and this
first cause, man calls God.

It is only by the exercise of reason, that man can discover God. Take away that reason, and he would be incapable of understanding anything ; and in this case it
would be just as consistent to read even the book called the
Bible to a horse as to a man. How then is it that those
people pretend to reject reason ?

Almost the only parts in the book called the Bible, that
convey to us any idea of God, are some chapters in Job,
and the 19th Psalm ; I recollect no other. Those parts are
true *deistical* compositions ; for they treat of the *Deity*
through his works. They take the book of Creation
as the word of God ; they refer to no other book ;

and all the inferences they make are drawn from that volume.

I insert in this place the 19th Psalm, as paraphrased into English verse by Addison. I recollect not the prose, and where I write this I have not the opportunity of seeing it:

> The spacious firmament on high,
> With all the blue etherial sky,
> And spangled heavens, a shining frame,
> Their great original proclaim.
> The unwearied sun, from day to day,
> Does his Creator's power display,
> And publishes to every land
> The work of an Almighty hand.
> Soon as the evening shades prevail,
> The moon takes up the wondrous tale,
> And nightly to the list'ning earth
> Repeats the story of her birth ;
> Whilst all the stars that round her burn,
> And all the planets, in their turn,
> Confirm the tidings as they roll,
> And spread the truth from pole to pole.
> What though in solemn silence all
> Move round this dark terrestrial ball ;
> What though no real voice, nor sound,
> Amidst their radiant orbs be found,
> In reason's ear they all rejoice,
> And utter forth a glorious voice,
> Forever singing as they shine,
> THE HAND THAT MADE US IS DIVINE.[1]

What more does man want to know, than that the hand or power that made these things is divine, is omnipotent? Let him believe this, with the force it is impossible to repel if he permits his reason to act, and his rule of moral life will follow of course.

The allusions in Job have all of them the same tendency with this Psalm ; that of deducing or proving a truth that would be otherwise unknown, from truths already known.

I recollect not enough of the passages in Job to insert

---

[1] The French translator has substituted for this a version of the same psalm by Jean Baptiste Rousseau.—*Editor.*

them correctly ; but there is one that occurs to me that is applicable to the subject I am speaking upon. " Canst thou by searching find out God ; canst thou find out the Almighty to perfection ? "

I know not how the printers have pointed this passage, for I keep no Bible ; but it contains two distinct questions that admit of distinct answers.

First, Canst thou by *searching* find out God ? Yes. Because, in the first place, I know I did not make myself, and yet I have existence ; and by *searching* into the nature of other things, I find that no other thing could make itself ; and yet millions of other things exist ; therefore it is, that I know, by positive conclusion resulting from this search, that there is a power superior to all those things, and that power is God.

Secondly, Canst thou find out the Almighty to *perfection ?* No. Not only because the power and wisdom He has manifested in the structure of the Creation that I behold is to me incomprehensible ; but because even this manifestation, great as it is, is probably but a small display of that immensity of power and wisdom, by which millions of other worlds, to me invisible by their distance, were created and continue to exist.

It is evident that both of these questions were put to the reason of the person to whom they are supposed to have been addressed ; and it is only by admitting the first question to be answered affirmatively, that the second could follow. It would have been unnecessary, and even absurd, to have put a second question, more difficult than the first, if the first question had been answered negatively. The two questions have different objects ; the first refers to the existence of God, the second to his attributes. Reason can discover the one, but it falls infinitely short in discovering the whole of the other.

I recollect not a single passage in all the writings ascribed to the men called apostles, that conveys any idea of what God is. Those writings are chiefly controversial ; and the gloominess of the subject they dwell upon, that of a man

dying in agony on a cross, is better suited to the gloomy
genius of a monk in a cell, by whom it is not impossible they
were written, than to any man breathing the open air of the
Creation. The only passage that occurs to me, that has any
reference to the works of God, by which only his power and
wisdom can be known, is related to have been spoken by
Jesus Christ, as a remedy against distrustful care. "Behold
the lilies of the field, they toil not, neither do they spin."
This, however, is far inferior to the allusions in Job and in the
19th Psalm; but it is similar in idea, and the modesty of the
imagery is correspondent to the modesty of the man.

CHAPTER XI.

OF THE THEOLOGY OF THE CHRISTIANS; AND THE TRUE THEOLOGY.

As to the Christian system of faith, it appears to me as a
species of atheism; a sort of religious denial of God. It
professes to believe in a man rather than in God. It is a
compound made up chiefly of man-ism with but little
deism, and is as near to atheism as twilight is to darkness.
It introduces between man and his Maker an opaque body,
which it calls a redeemer, as the moon introduces her opaque
self between the earth and the sun, and it produces by this
means a religious or [1] an irreligious eclipse of light. It has
put the whole orbit of reason into shade.

The effect of this obscurity has been that of turning everything upside down, and representing it in reverse; and among
the revolutions it has thus magically produced, it has made
a revolution in Theology.

That which is now called natural philosophy, embracing
the whole circle of science, of which astronomy occupies
the chief place, is the study of the works of God, and of the
power and wisdom of God in his works, and is the true
theology.

[1] The French here has "plutôt" (rather).—*Editor*.

As to the theology that is now studied in its place, it is the study of human opinions and of human fancies *concerning* God.[1] It is not the study of God himself in the works that he has made, but in the works or writings that man has made ; and it is not among the least of the mischiefs that the Christian system has done to the world, that it has abandoned the original and beautiful system of theology,[2] like a beautiful innocent, to distress and reproach, to make room for the hag of superstition.

The Book of Job and the 19th Psalm, which even the church admits to be more ancient than the chronological order in which they stand in the book called the Bible, are theological orations conformable to the original system of theology. The internal evidence of those orations proves to a demonstration that the study and contemplation of the works of creation, and of the power and wisdom of God revealed and manifested in those works, made a great part of the religious devotion of the times in which they were written ; and it was this devotional study and contemplation that led to the discovery of the principles upon which what are now called Sciences are established ; and it is to the discovery of these principles that almost all the Arts that contribute to the convenience of human life owe their existence. Every principal art has some science for its parent, though the person who mechanically performs the work does not always, and but very seldom, perceive the connection.[3]

It is a fraud[4] of the Christian system to call the sciences *human inventions;* it is only the application of them that is human. Every science has for its basis a system of principles as fixed and unalterable as those by which the uni-

---

[1] French : " La suprême intelligence " instead of " God."—*Editor.*

[2] French : " La théologie naturelle."—*Editor.*

[3] In the French is added : " et que même, par l'ignorance que les gouvernemens modernes ont répandue, il soit très-rare aujourd'hui, que ces personnes s'en doutent " (and, such is the ignorance prevailing under modern governments, it is now even very rare for such persons to think about it).—*Editor.*

[4] French : " C'est un mensonge, une *fraude pieuse.*"—*Editor.*

verse is regulated and governed. Man cannot make principles, he can only discover them.

For example: Every person who looks at an almanack sees an account when an eclipse will take place, and he sees also that it never fails to take place according to the account there given. This shews that man is acquainted with the laws by which the heavenly bodies move. But it would be something worse than ignorance, were any church on earth to say that those laws are an human invention.

It would also be ignorance, or something worse, to say that the scientific principles, by the aid of which man is enabled to calculate and foreknow when an eclipse will take place, are an human invention. Man cannot invent any thing that is eternal and immutable; and the scientific principles he employs for this purpose must, and are, of necessity, as eternal and immutable as the laws by which the heavenly bodies move, or they could not be used as they are to ascertain the time when, and the manner how, an eclipse will take place.

The scientific principles that man employs to obtain the foreknowledge of an eclipse, or of any thing else relating to the motion of the heavenly bodies, are contained chiefly in that part of science that is called trigonometry, or the properties of a triangle, which, when applied to the study of the heavenly bodies, is called astronomy; when applied to direct the course of a ship on the ocean, it is called navigation; when applied to the construction of figures drawn by a rule and compass, it is called geometry; when applied to the construction of plans of edifices, it is called architecture; when applied to the measurement of any portion of the surface of the earth, it is called land-surveying. In fine, it is the soul of science. It is an eternal truth: it contains the *mathematical demonstration* of which man speaks, and the extent of its uses are unknown.

It may be said, that man can make or draw a triangle, and therefore a triangle is an human invention.

But the triangle, when drawn, is no other than the image of the principle: it is a delineation to the eye, and from thence to the mind, of a principle that would otherwise be imperceptible. The triangle does not make the principle, any more than a candle taken into a room that was dark, makes the chairs and tables that before were invisible. All the properties of a triangle exist independently of the figure, and existed before any triangle was drawn or thought of by man. Man had no more to do in the formation of those properties or principles, than he had to do in making the laws by which the heavenly bodies move ; and therefore the one must have the same divine origin as the other.

In the same manner as, it may be said, that man can make a triangle, so also, may it be said, he can make the mechanical instrument called a lever. But the principle by which the lever acts, is a thing distinct from the instrument, and would exist if the instrument did not ; it attaches itself to the instrument after it is made; the instrument, therefore, can act no otherwise than it does act ; neither can all the efforts of human invention make it act otherwise. That which, in all such cases, man calls the *effect*, is no other than the principle itself rendered perceptible to the senses.

Since, then, man cannot make principles, from whence did he gain a knowledge of them, so as to be able to apply them, not only to things on earth, but to ascertain the motion of bodies so immensely distant from him as all the heavenly bodies are ? From whence, I ask, *could* he gain that knowledge, but from the study of the true theology ?

It is the structure of the universe that has taught this knowledge to man. That structure is an ever-existing exhibition of every principle upon which every part of mathematical science is founded. The offspring of this science is mechanics ; for mechanics is no other than the principles of science applied practically. The man who proportions the several parts of a mill uses the same scientific principles as if he had the power of constructing an universe, but as he cannot give to matter that invisible agency by which all the component parts of the immense machine of the universe have influence upon each other, and act in motional unison together, without any apparent contact, and to which man has given the name of attraction, gravitation, and repulsion, he supplies the place of that agency by the humble imitation of teeth and cogs. All the parts of man's microcosm must visibly touch. But could he gain a knowledge of that agency, so as to be able to apply it in practice, we might then say that another *canonical book* of the word of God had been discovered.

If man could alter the properties of the lever, so also could he alter the properties of the triangle: for a lever (taking that sort of lever which is called a steel-yard, for the sake of explanation) forms, when in motion, a triangle. The line it descends from, (one point of that line being in the fulcrum,) the line it descends to, and the chord of the arc, which the end of the lever describes in the air, are the three sides of a triangle. The other arm of the lever describes also a triangle; and the corresponding sides of those two triangles, calculated scientifically, or measured geometrically,—and also the sines, tangents, and secants generated from the angles, and geometrically measured,—have the same proportions to each other as the different weights have that will balance each other on the lever, leaving the weight of the lever out of the case.

It may also be said, that man can make a wheel and axis; that he can put wheels of different magnitudes together, and produce a mill. Still the case comes back to the same point, which is, that he did not make the principle that gives the wheels those powers. This principle is as unalterable as in the former cases, or rather it is the same principle under a different appearance to the eye.

The power that two wheels of different magnitudes have upon each other is in the same proportion as if the semi-diameter of the two wheels were joined together and made into that kind of lever I have described, suspended at the part where the semi-diameters join; for the two wheels, scientifically considered, are no other than the two circles generated by the motion of the compound lever.

It is from the study of the true theology that all our knowledge of science is derived; and it is from that knowledge that all the arts have originated.

The Almighty lecturer, by displaying the principles of science in the structure of the universe, has invited man to study and to imitation. It is as if he had said to the inhabitants of this globe that we call ours, " I have made an earth for man to dwell upon, and I have rendered the starry heavens visible, to teach him science and the arts. He can now provide for his own comfort, AND LEARN FROM MY MUNIFICENCE TO ALL, TO BE KIND TO EACH OTHER."

Of what use is it, unless it be to teach man something, that his eye is endowed with the power of beholding, to an incomprehensible distance, an immensity of worlds revolving in the ocean of space? Or of what use is it that this immensity of worlds is visible to man? What has man to do with the Pleiades, with Orion, with Sirius, with the star he calls the north star, with the moving orbs he has named Saturn, Jupiter, Mars, Venus, and Mercury, if no uses are to follow from their being visible? A less power of vision would have been sufficient for man, if the immensity he now possesses were given only to waste itself, as it were, on an immense desert of space glittering with shows.

It is only by contemplating what he calls the starry heavens, as the book and school of science, that he discovers any use in their being visible to him, or any advantage resulting from his immensity of vision. But when he contemplates the subject in this light, he sees an additional motive for saying, that *nothing was made in vain;* for in vain would be this power of vision if it taught man nothing.

CHAPTER XII.

THE EFFECTS OF CHRISTIANISM ON EDUCATION. PROPOSED REFORMS.

As the Christian system of faith has made a revolution in theology, so also has it made a revolution in the state of learning. That which is now called learning, was not learning originally. Learning does not consist, as the schools now make it consist, in the knowledge of languages, but in the knowledge of things to which language gives names.

The Greeks were a learned people, but learning with them did not consist in speaking Greek, any more than in a Roman's speaking Latin, or a Frenchman's speaking French, or an Englishman's speaking English. From what we know of the Greeks, it does not appear that they knew or studied any language but their own, and this was one cause of their becoming so learned ; it afforded them more time to apply themselves to better studies. The schools of the Greeks were schools of science and philosophy, and not of languages ; and it is in the knowledge of the things that science and philosophy teach that learning consists.

Almost all the scientific learning that now exists, came to us from the Greeks, or the people who spoke the Greek language. It therefore became necessary to the people of other nations, who spoke a different language, that some among them should learn the Greek language, in order that the learning the Greeks had might be made known in those nations, by translating the Greek books of science and philosophy into the mother tongue of each nation.

The study, therefore, of the Greek language (and in the same manner for the Latin) was no other than the drudgery business of a linguist ; and the language thus obtained, was no other than the means, or as it were the tools, employed to obtain the learning the Greeks had. It made no part of the learning itself ; and was so distinct from it as to make it exceedingly probable that the persons who had studied Greek sufficiently to translate those works, such for instance as Euclid's Elements, did not understand any of the learning the works contained.

As there is now nothing new to be learned from the dead languages, all the useful books being already translated, the languages are become useless, and the time expended in teaching and in learning them is wasted. So far as the study of languages may contribute to the progress and communication of knowledge (for it has nothing to do with the *creation* of knowledge) it is only in the living languages that new knowledge is to be found; and certain it is, that, in general, a youth will learn more of a living language in one year, than of a dead language in seven; and it is but seldom that the teacher knows much of it himself. The difficulty of learning the dead languages does not arise from any superior abstruseness in the languages themselves, but in their *being dead*, and the pronunciation entirely lost. It would be the same thing with any other language when it becomes dead. The best Greek linguist that now exists does not understand Greek so well as a Grecian plowman did, or a Grecian milkmaid; and the same for the Latin, compared with a plowman or a milkmaid of the Romans; and with respect to pronunciation and idiom, not so well as the cows that she milked. It would therefore be advantageous to the state of learning to abolish the study of the dead languages, and to make learning consist, as it originally did, in scientific knowledge.

The apology that is sometimes made for continuing to teach the dead languages is, that they are taught at a time when a child is not capable of exerting any other mental faculty than that of memory. But this is altogether erroneous. The human mind has a natural disposition to scientific knowledge, and to the things connected with it. The first and favourite amusement of a child, even before it begins to play, is that of imitating the works of man. It builds houses with cards or sticks; it navigates the little ocean of a bowl of water with a paper boat; or dams the stream of a gutter, and contrives something which it calls a mill; and it interests itself in the fate of its works with a care that resembles affection. It afterwards goes to school, where its genius is killed by the barren study of a dead language, and the philosopher is lost in the linguist.

But the apology that is now made for continuing to teach the dead languages, could not be the cause at first of cutting down learning to the narrow and humble sphere of linguistry; the cause therefore must be sought for elsewhere. In all researches of this kind, the best evidence that can be produced, is the internal evidence the thing carries with itself, and the evidence of circumstances that unites with it ; both of which, in this case, are not difficult to be discovered.

Putting then aside, as matter of distinct consideration, the outrage offered to the moral justice of God, by supposing him to make the innocent suffer for the guilty, and also the loose morality and low contrivance of supposing him to change himself into the shape of a man, in order to make an excuse to himself for not executing his supposed sentence upon Adam ; putting, I say, those things aside as matter of distinct consideration, it is certain that what is called the christian system of faith, including in it the whimsical account of the creation—the strange story of Eve, the snake, and the apple—the amphibious idea of a man-god—the corporeal idea of the death of a god—the mythological idea of a family of gods, and the christian system of arithmetic, [1] that three are one, and one is three, are all irreconcilable, not only to the divine gift of reason, that God has given to man, but to the knowledge that man gains of the power and wisdom of God by the aid of the sciences, and by studying the structure of the universe that God has made.

The setters up, therefore, and the advocates of the Christian system of faith, [2] could not but foresee that the continually progressive knowledge that man would gain by the aid of science, of the power and wisdom of God, manifested in the structure of the universe, and in all the works of creation, would militate against, and call into question, the truth of their system of faith ; and therefore it became necessary to their purpose to cut learning down to a size less dangerous to their project, and this they effected by restricting the idea of learning to the dead [3] study of dead languages.

They not only rejected the study of science out of the christian schools, but they persecuted it ; and it is only within about the last two centuries that the study has been

---

[1] French : " ce *nonsense* arithmetique." The words " christian system " do not occur in the clause.—*Editor.*

[2] Instead of " christian system of faith," the French has " ce tissu d' absurdités."—*Editor.*

[3] French : " aride."—*Editor.*

revived. So late as 1610, Galileo, a Florentine, discovered and introduced the use of telescopes, and by applying them to observe the motions and appearances of the heavenly bodies, afforded additional means for ascertaining the true structure of the universe. Instead of being esteemed for these discoveries, he was sentenced to renounce them, or the opinions resulting from them, as a damnable heresy. And prior to that time Virgilius was condemned to be burned for asserting the antipodes, or in other words, that the earth was a globe, and habitable in every part where there was land ; yet the truth of this is now too well known even to be told.[1]

If the belief of errors not morally bad did no mischief, it would make no part of the moral duty of man to oppose and remove them. There was no moral ill in believing the earth was flat like a trencher, any more than there was moral virtue in believing it was round like a globe ; neither was there any moral ill in believing that the Creator made no other world than this, any more than there was moral virtue in believing that he made millions, and that

[1] I cannot discover the source of this statement concerning the ancient author whose Irish name Feirghill was Latinized into Virgilius. The British Museum possesses a copy of the work (*Decalogium*) which was the pretext of the charge of heresy made by Boniface, Archbishop of Mayence, against Virgilius, Abbot-bishop of Salzburg. These were leaders of the rival " British " and " Roman " parties, and the British champion made a countercharge against Boniface of " irreligious practices." Boniface had to express a " regret," but none the less pursued his rival. The Pope, Zachary II., decided that if his alleged " doctrine, against God and his soul, that beneath the earth there is another world, other men, or sun and moon," should be acknowledged by Virgilius, he should be excommunicated by a Council and condemned with canonical sanctions. Whatever may have been the fate involved by condemnation with " canonicis sanctionibus," in the middle of the eighth century, it did not fall on Virgilius. His accuser, Boniface, was martyred, 755, and it is probable that Virgilius harmonized his Antipodes with orthodoxy. The *gravamen* of the heresy seems to have been the suggestion that there were men not of the progeny of Adam. Virgilius was made Bishop of Salzburg in 768. He bore until his death, 789, the curious title, " Geometer and Solitary," or "lone wayfarer" (*Solivagus*). A suspicion of heresy clung to his memory until 1233, when he was raised by Gregory IX. to sainthood beside his accuser, St. Boniface.—*Editor.*

the infinity of space is filled with worlds. But when a system of religion is made to grow out of a supposed system of creation that is not true, and to unite itself therewith in a manner almost inseparable therefrom, the case assumes an entirely different ground. It is then that errors, not morally bad, become fraught with the same mischiefs as if they were. It is then that the truth, though otherwise indifferent itself, becomes an essential, by becoming the criterion that either confirms by corresponding evidence, or denies by contradictory evidence, the reality of the religion itself. In this view of the case it is the moral duty of man to obtain every possible evidence that the structure of the heavens, or any other part of creation affords, with respect to systems of religion. But this, the supporters or partizans of the christian system, as if dreading the result, incessantly opposed, and not only rejected the sciences, but persecuted the professors. Had Newton or Descartes lived three or four hundred years ago, and pursued their studies as they did, it is most probable they would not have lived to finish them ; and had Franklin drawn lightning from the clouds at the same time, it would have been at the hazard of expiring for it in flames.

Later times have laid all the blame upon the Goths and Vandals, but, however unwilling the partizans of the Christian system may be to believe or to acknowledge it, it is nevertheless true, that the age of ignorance commenced with the Christian system. There was more knowledge in the world before that period, than for many centuries afterwards ; and as to religious knowledge, the Christian system, as already said, was only another species of mythology ; and the mythology to which it succeeded, was a corruption of an ancient system of theism.*

---

* It is impossible for us now to know at what time the heathen mythology began ; but it is certain, from the internal evidence that it carries, that it did not begin in the same state or condition in which it ended. All the gods of that mythology, except Saturn, were of modern invention. The supposed reign of Saturn was prior to that which is called the heathen mythology, and was so far a species of theism that it admitted the belief of only one God. Saturn is sup-.

It is owing to this long interregnum of science, *and to no other cause*, that we have now to look back through a vast chasm of many hundred years to the respectable characters we call the Ancients. Had the progression of knowledge gone on proportionably with the stock that before existed, that chasm would have been filled up with characters rising superior in knowledge to each other; and those Ancients we now so much admire would have appeared respectably in the background of the scene. But the christian system laid all waste; and if we take our stand about the beginning of the sixteenth century, we look back through that long chasm, to the times of the Ancients, as over a vast sandy desert, in which not a shrub appears to intercept the vision to the fertile hills beyond.

It is an inconsistency scarcely possible to be credited, that any thing should exist, under the name of a religion, that held it to be *irreligious* to study and contemplate the structure of the universe that God had made. But the fact is too well established to be denied. The event that served more than any other to break the first link in this long chain of despotic ignorance, is that known by the name of the Reformation by Luther. From that time, though it does not appear to have made any part of the intention of

posed to have abdicated the government in favour of his three sons and one daughter, Jupiter, Pluto, Neptune, and Juno ; after this, thousands of other gods and demi-gods were imaginarily created, and the calendar of gods increased as fast as the calendar of saints and the calendar of courts have increased since.

All the corruptions that have taken place, in theology and in religion have been produced by admitting of what man calls *revealed religion*. The mythologists pretended to more revealed religion than the christians do. They had their oracles and their priests, who were supposed to receive and deliver the word of God verbally on almost all occasions.

Since then all corruptions down from Moloch to modern predestinarianism, and the human sacrifices of the heathens to the christian sacrifice of the Creator, have been produced by admitting of what is called *revealed religion*, the most effectual means to prevent all such evils and impositions is, not to admit of any other revelation than that which is manifested in the book of Creation, and to contemplate the Creation as the only true and real word of God that ever did or ever will exist ; and every thing else called the word of God is fable and imposition.—*Author.*

Luther,[1] or of those who are called Reformers, the Sciences began to revive, and Liberality,[2] their natural associate, began to appear. This was the only public good the Reformation did; for, with respect to religious good, it might as well not have taken place. The mythology still continued the same; and a multiplicity of National Popes grew out of the downfal of the Pope of Christendom.

CHAPTER XIII.

COMPARISON OF CHRISTIANISM WITH THE RELIGIOUS IDEAS INSPIRED BY NATURE.

HAVING thus shewn, from the internal evidence of things, the cause that produced a change in the state of learning, and the motive for substituting the study of the dead languages, in the place of the Sciences, I proceed, in addition to the several observations already made in the former part of this work, to compare, or rather to confront, the evidence that the structure of the universe affords, with the christian system of religion. But as I cannot begin this part better than by referring to the ideas that occurred to me at an early part of life, and which I doubt not have occurred in some degree to almost every other person at one time or other, I shall state what those ideas were, and add thereto such other matter as shall arise out of the subject, giving to the whole, by way of preface, a short introduction.

My father being of the quaker profession, it was my good fortune to have an exceedingly good moral education, and a tolerable stock of useful learning. Though I went to the grammar school,* I did not learn Latin, not only because I had no inclination to learn languages, but because of the objection the quakers have against the books in which the language is taught. But this did not prevent me from

---

[1] French : " ce moine " (this monk) instead of " Luther."—*Editor.*

[2] French : " la civilisation " instead of " liberality."—*Editor.*

* The same school, Thetford in Norfolk, that the present Counsellor Mingay went to, and under the same master—*Author.* [This note is not in the French work.—*Editor.*]

being acquainted with the subjects of all the Latin books used in the school.

The natural bent of my mind was to science. I had some turn, and I believe some talent for poetry ; but this I rather repressed than encouraged, as leading too much into the field of imagination. As soon as I was able, I pur- chased a pair of globes, and attended the philosophical lectures of Martin and Ferguson, and became afterwards acquainted with Dr. Bevis, of the society called the Royal Society, then living in the Temple, and an excellent astron- omer.

I had no disposition for what was called politics. It pre- sented to my mind no other idea than is contained in the word Jockeyship. When, therefore, I turned my thoughts towards matters of government, I had to form a system for myself, that accorded with the moral and philosophic prin- ciples in which I had been educated. I saw, or at least I thought I saw, a vast scene opening itself to the world in the affairs of America ; and it appeared to me, that unless the Americans changed the plan they were then pursuing, with respect to the government of England, and declared themselves independent, they would not only involve them- selves in a multiplicity of new difficulties, but shut out the prospect that was then offering itself to mankind through their means. It was from these motives that I published the work known by the name of *Common Sense,* which is the first work I ever did publish, and so far as I can judge of myself, I believe I should never have been known in the world as an author on any subject whatever, had it not been for the affairs of America. I wrote *Common Sense* the latter end of the year 1775, and published it the first of January, 1776.[1] Independence was declared the fourth of July following.

---

[1] The pamphlet *Common Sense* was first advertised, as "just published," on January 10, 1776. His plea for the Officers of Excise, written before leaving England, was printed, but not published until 1793. Despite his reiterated assertion that *Common Sense* was the first work he ever published the notion that he was "Junius" still finds some believers. An indirect comment on our

Any person, who has made observations on the state and progress of the human mind, by observing his own, cannot but have observed, that there are two distinct classes of what are called Thoughts; those that we produce in ourselves by reflection and the act of thinking, and those that bolt into the mind of their own accord. I have always made it a rule to treat those voluntary visitors with civility, taking care to examine, as well as I was able, if they were worth entertaining; and it is from them I have acquired almost all the knowledge that I have. As to the learning that any person gains from school education, it serves only, like a small capital, to put him in the way of beginning learning for himself afterwards. Every person of learning is finally his own teacher; the reason of which is, that principles, being of a distinct quality to circumstances, cannot be impressed upon the memory; their place of mental residence is the understanding, and they are never so lasting as when they begin by conception. Thus much for the introductory part.[1]

From the time I was capable of conceiving an idea, and acting upon it by reflection, I either doubted the truth of the christian system, or thought it to be a strange affair; I scarcely knew which it was: but I well remember, when about seven or eight years of age, hearing a sermon read by a relation of mine, who was a great devotee of the church,[2] upon the subject of what is called *Redemption by the death of the Son of God.* After the sermon was ended, I went into the garden, and as I was going down the garden steps

---

Paine-Junians may be found in Part 2 of this work where Paine says a man capable of writing Homer " would not have thrown away his own fame by giving it to another." It is probable that Paine ascribed the Letters of Junius to Thomas Hollis. His friend F. Lanthenas, in his translation of the Age of Reason (1794) advertises his translation of the Letters of Junius from the English " (Thomas Hollis)." This he could hardly have done without consultation with Paine. Unfortunately this translation of Junius cannot be found either in the Bibliothèque Nationale or the British Museum, and it cannot be said whether it contains any attempt at an identification of Junius—*Editor.*

[1] This sentence is not in the French work.—*Editor.*

[2] No doubt Paine's aunt, Miss Cooke, who managed to have him confirmed in the parish church at Thetford.—*Editor.*

(for I perfectly recollect the spot) I revolted at the recollection of what I had heard, and thought to myself that it was making God Almighty act like a passionate man, that killed his son, when he could not revenge himself any other way; and as I was sure a man would be hanged that did such a thing, I could not see for what purpose they preached such sermons. This was not one of those kind of thoughts that had any thing in it of childish levity; it was to me a serious reflection, arising from the idea I had that God was too good to do such an action, and also too almighty to be under any necessity of doing it. I believe in the same manner to this moment; and I moreover believe, that any system of religion that has any thing in it that shocks the mind of a child, cannot be a true system.

It seems as if parents of the christian profession were ashamed to tell their children any thing about the principles of their religion. They sometimes instruct them in morals, and talk to them of the goodness of what they call Providence; for the Christian mythology has five deities: there is God the Father, God the Son, God the Holy Ghost, the God Providence, and the Goddess Nature. But the christian story of God the Father putting his son to death, or employing people to do it, (for that is the plain language of the story,) cannot be told by a parent to a child; and to tell him that it was done to make mankind happier and better, is making the story still worse; as if mankind could be improved by the example of murder; and to tell him that all this is a mystery, is only making an excuse for the incredibility of it.

How different is this to the pure and simple profession of Deism! The true deist has but one Deity; and his religion consists in contemplating the power, wisdom, and benignity of the Deity in his works, and in endeavouring to imitate him in every thing moral, scientifical, and mechanical.

The religion that approaches the nearest of all others to true Deism, in the moral and benign part thereof, is that professed by the quakers: but they have contracted themselves too much by leaving the works of God out of their system. Though I reverence their philanthropy, I can not help smiling at the conceit, that if the taste of a quaker could have been consulted at the creation, what a silent and drab-colored creation it would have been! Not a flower would have blossomed its gaieties, nor a bird been permitted to sing.

Quitting these reflections, I proceed to other matters. After I had made myself master of the use of the globes, and of the orrery,* and conceived an idea of the infinity of space, and of the eternal divisibility of matter, and obtained, at least, a general knowledge of what was called natural philosophy, I began to compare, or, as I have before said, to confront, the internal evidence those things afford with the christian system of faith.

Though it is not a direct article of the christian system that this world that we inhabit is the whole of the habitable creation, yet it is so worked up therewith, from what is called the Mosaic account of the creation, the story of Eve and the apple, and the counterpart of that story, the death of the Son of God, that to believe otherwise, that is, to believe that God created a plurality of worlds, at least as numerous as what we call stars, renders the christian system of faith at once little and ridiculous; and scatters it in the mind like feathers in the air. The two beliefs can not be held together in the same mind ; and he who thinks that he believes both, has thought but little of either.

Though the belief of a plurality of worlds was familiar to the ancients, it is only within the last three centuries that the extent and dimensions of this globe that we inhabit have been ascertained. Several vessels, following the tract of the

---

* As this book may fall into the hands of persons who do not know what an orrery is, it is for their information I add this note, as the name gives no idea of the uses of the thing. The orrery has its name from the person who invented it. It is a machinery of clock-work, representing the universe in miniature : and in which the revolution of the earth round itself and round the sun, the revolution of the moon round the earth, the revolution of the planets round the sun, their relative distances from the sun, as the center of the whole system, their relative distances from each other, and their different magnitudes, are represented as they really exist in what we call the heavens.—*Author*.

ocean, have sailed entirely round the world, as a man may march in a circle, and come round by the contrary side of the circle to the spot he set out from. The circular dimensions of our world, in the widest part, as a man would measure the widest round of an apple, or a ball, is only twenty-five thousand and twenty English miles, reckoning sixty-nine miles and an half to an equatorial degree, and may be sailed round in the space of about three years.*

A world of this extent may, at first thought, appear to us to be great; but if we compare it with the immensity of space in which it is suspended, like a bubble or a balloon in the air, it is infinitely less in proportion than the smallest grain of sand is to the size of the world, or the finest particle of dew to the whole ocean, and is therefore but small; and, as will be hereafter shewn, is only one of a system of worlds, of which the universal creation is composed.

It is not difficult to gain some faint idea of the immensity of space in which this and all the other worlds are suspended, if we follow a progression of ideas. When we think of the size or dimensions of a room, our ideas limit themselves to the walls, and there they stop. But when our eye, or our imagination darts into space, that is, when it looks upward into what we call the open air, we cannot conceive any walls or boundaries it can have; and if for the sake of resting our ideas we suppose a boundary, the question immediately renews itself, and asks, what is beyond that boundary? and in the same manner, what beyond the next boundary? and so on till the fatigued imagination returns and says, *there is no end.* Certainly, then, the Creator was not pent for room when he made this world no larger than it is; and we have to seek the reason in something else.

If we take a survey of our own world, or rather of this, of which the Creator has given us the use as our portion in the immense system of creation, we find every part of it, the earth, the waters, and the air that surround it, filled,

---

* Allowing a ship to sail, on an average, three miles in an hour, she would sail entirely round the world in less than one year, if she could sail in a direct circle, but she is obliged to follow the course of the ocean.—*Author.*

and as it were crouded with life, down from the largest animals that we know of to the smallest insects the naked eye can behold, and from thence to others still smaller, and totally invisible without the assistance of the microscope. Every tree, every plant, every leaf, serves not only as an habitation, but as a world to some numerous race, till animal existence becomes so exceedingly refined, that the effluvia of a blade of grass would be food for thousands.

Since then no part of our earth is left unoccupied, why is it to be supposed that the immensity of space is a naked void, lying in eternal waste? There is room for millions of worlds as large or larger than ours, and each of them millions of miles apart from each other.

Having now arrived at this point, if we carry our ideas only one thought further, we shall see, perhaps, the true reason, at least a very good reason for our happiness, why the Creator, instead of making one immense world, extending over an immense quantity of space, has preferred dividing that quantity of matter into several distinct and separate worlds, which we call planets, of which our earth is one. But before I explain my ideas upon this subject, it is necessary (not for the sake of those that already know, but for those who do not) to shew what the system of the universe is.

CHAPTER XIV.

SYSTEM OF THE UNIVERSE.

THAT part of the universe that is called the solar system (meaning the system of worlds to which our earth belongs, and of which Sol, or in English language, the Sun, is the center) consists, besides the Sun, of six distinct orbs, or planets, or worlds, besides the secondary bodies, called the satellites, or moons, of which our earth has one that attends her in her annual revolution round the Sun, in like manner as the other satellites or moons, attend the planets or worlds to which they severally belong, as may be seen by the assistance of the telescope.

The Sun is the center round which those six worlds or planets revolve at different distances therefrom, and in circles concentric to each other. Each world keeps constantly in nearly the same tract round the Sun, and continues at the same time turning round itself, in nearly an upright position, as a top turns round itself when it is spinning on the ground, and leans a little sideways.

It is this leaning of the earth ($23\frac{1}{2}$ degrees) that occasions summer and winter, and the different length of days and nights. If the earth turned round itself in a position perpendicular to the plane or level of the circle it moves in round the Sun, as a top turns round when it stands erect on the ground, the days and nights would be always of the same length, twelve hours day and twelve hours night, and the season would be uniformly the same throughout the year.

Every time that a planet (our earth for example) turns round itself, it makes what we call day and night; and every time it goes entirely round the Sun, it makes what we call a year, consequently our world turns three hundred and sixty-five times round itself, in going once round the Sun. *

The names that the ancients gave to those six worlds, and which are still called by the same names, are Mercury, Venus, this world that we call ours, Mars, Jupiter, and Saturn.[1] They appear larger to the eye than the stars, being many million miles nearer to our earth than any of the stars

[1] With reference to the omission of any mention of Uranus, see the Introduction. In the New York edition, 1794, edited by Col. John Fellows, occurs this footnote : "Mr. Paine had made no mention of the planet Herschel, which was first discovered, by the person whose name it bears, in 1781. It is at a greater distance from the Sun than either of the other planets and consequently occupies a greater length of time in performing its revolutions."—*Editor.*

* Those who supposed that the Sun went round the earth every 24 hours made the same mistake in idea that a cook would do in fact, that should make the fire go round the meat, instead of the meat turning round itself towards the fire.—*Author.*

are. The planet Venus is that which is called the evening star, and sometimes the morning star, as she happens to set after, or rise before the Sun, which in either case is never more than three hours.

The Sun as before said being the center, the planet or world nearest the Sun is Mercury; his distance from the Sun is thirty-four million miles, and he moves round in a circle always at that distance from the Sun, as a top may be supposed to spin round in the tract in which a horse goes in a mill. The second world is Venus; she is fifty-seven million miles distant from the Sun, and consequently moves round in a circle much greater than that of Mercury. The third world is this that we inhabit, and which is eighty-eight million miles distant from the Sun, and consequently moves round in a circle greater than that of Venus. The fourth world is Mars; he is distant from the sun one hundred and thirty-four million miles, and consequently moves round in a circle greater than that of our earth. The fifth is Jupiter; he is distant from the Sun five hundred and fifty-seven million miles, and consequently moves round in a circle greater than that of Mars. The sixth world is Saturn; he is distant from the Sun seven hundred and sixty-three million miles, and consequently moves round in a circle that surrounds the circles or orbits of all the other worlds or planets.

The space, therefore, in the air, or in the immensity of space, that our solar system takes up for the several worlds to perform their revolutions in round the Sun, is of the extent in a strait line of the whole diameter of the orbit or circle in which Saturn moves round the Sun, which being double his distance from the Sun, is fifteen hundred and twenty-six million miles; and its circular extent is nearly five thousand million; and its globical content is almost three thousand five hundred million times three thousand five hundred million square miles. *

* If it should be asked, how can man know these things? I have one plain answer to give, which is, that man knows how to calculate an eclipse, and also how to calculate to a minute of time when the planet Venus, in making her

But this, immense as it is, is only one system of worlds. Beyond this, at a vast distance into space, far beyond all power of calculation, are the stars called the fixed stars. They are called fixed, because they have no revolutionary motion, as the six worlds or planets have that I have been describing. Those fixed stars continue always at the same distance from each other, and always in the same place, as the Sun does in the center of our system. The probability, therefore, is, that each of those fixed stars is also a Sun, round which another system of worlds or planets, though too remote for us to discover, performs its revolutions, as our system of worlds does round our central Sun.[1]

By this easy progression of ideas, the immensity of space will appear to us to be filled with systems of worlds; and that no part of space lies at waste, any more than any part of our globe of earth and water is left unoccupied.

Having thus endeavoured to convey, in a familiar and easy manner, some idea of the structure of the universe, I return to explain what I before alluded to, namely, the great benefits arising to man in consequence of the Creator having made a *plurality* of worlds, such as our system is, consisting of a central Sun and six worlds,[2] besides satellites, in preference to that of creating one world only of a vast extent.

revolutions round the Sun, will come in a strait line between our earth and the Sun, and will appear to us about the size of a large pea passing across the face of the Sun. This happens but twice in about a hundred years, at the distance of about eight years from each other, and has happened twice in our time, both of which were foreknown by calculation. It can also be known when they will happen again for a thousand years to come, or to any other portion of time. As therefore, man could not be able to do these things if he did not understand the solar system, and the manner in which the revolutions of the several planets or worlds are performed, the fact of calculating an eclipse, or a transit of Venus, is a proof in point that the knowledge exists ; and as to a few thousand, or even a few million miles, more or less, it makes scarcely any sensible difference in such immense distances.—*Author.*

[1] This speculation has been confirmed by nineteenth-century astronomy. " The stars, speaking broadly, are suns "(Clarke's *System of the Stars*, ch. iii). See Herschel's *Outlines of Astronomy*, Part III. ch. xv.—*Editor.*

[2] The French work has " plusieurs planètes " (many planets) instead of " six worlds."—*Editor.*

CHAPTER XV.

ADVANTAGES OF THE EXISTENCE OF MANY WORLDS IN EACH SOLAR SYSTEM.

IT is an idea I have never lost sight of, that all our knowledge of science is derived from the revolutions (exhibited to our eye and from thence to our understanding) which those several planets or worlds of which our system is composed make in their circuit round the Sun.

Had then the quantity of matter which these six worlds contain been blended into one solitary globe, the consequence to us would have been, that either no revolutionary motion would have existed, or not a sufficiency of it to give us the ideas and the knowledge of science we now have; and it is from the sciences that all the mechanical arts that contribute so much to our earthly felicity and comfort are derived.

As therefore the Creator made nothing in vain, so also must it be believed that he organized the structure of the universe in the most advantageous manner for the benefit of man; and as we see, and from experience feel, the benefits we derive from the structure of the universe, formed as it is, which benefits we should not have had the opportunity of enjoying if the structure, so far as relates to our system, had been a solitary globe, we can discover at least one reason why a *plurality* of worlds has been made, and that reason calls forth the devotional gratitude of man, as well as his admiration.

But it is not to us, the inhabitants of this globe, only, that the benefits arising from a plurality of worlds are limited. The inhabitants of each of the worlds of which our system is composed, enjoy the same opportunities of knowledge as we do. They behold the revolutionary motions of our earth, as we behold theirs. All the planets revolve in sight of each other; and, therefore, the same universal school of science presents itself to all.

Neither does the knowledge stop here. The system of worlds next to us exhibits, in its revolutions, the same principles and school of science, to the inhabitants of their system, as our system does to us, and in like manner throughout the immensity of space.

Our ideas, not only of the almightiness of the Creator, but of his wisdom and his beneficence, become enlarged in proportion as we contemplate the extent and the structure of the universe. The solitary [1] idea of a solitary world, rolling or at rest in the immense ocean of space, gives place to the cheerful idea of a society of worlds, so happily contrived as to administer, even by their motion, instruction to man.[2] We see our own earth filled with abundance ; but we forget to consider how much of that abundance is owing to the scientific knowledge the vast machinery of the universe has unfolded.

CHAPTER XVI.

APPLICATION OF THE PRECEDING TO THE SYSTEM OF THE CHRISTIANS.

BUT, in the midst of those reflections, what are we to think of the christian system of faith that forms itself upon the idea of only one world, and that of no greater extent, as is before shewn, than twenty-five thousand miles. An extent which a man, walking at the rate of three miles an hour for twelve hours in the day, could he keep on in a circular direction, would walk entirely round in less than two years. Alas! what is this to the mighty ocean of space, and the almighty power of the Creator!

From whence then could arise the solitary and strange conceit that the Almighty, who had millions of worlds equally dependent on his protection, should quit the care of all the rest, and come to die in our world, because, they say, one man and one woman had eaten an apple! And, on the

---

[1] The French work has " triste."—*Editor*.

[2] The French work has : " leur mouvement même est le premier éveil, la première instruction de la raison dans l'homme." (Their motion itself is the first awakening, the first instruction of the reason in man).—*Editor*.

other hand, are we to suppose that every world in the bound-
less creation had an Eve, an apple, a serpent, and a redeemer? In this case, the person who is irreverently called
the Son of God, and sometimes God himself, would have
nothing else to do than to travel from world to world,
in an endless succession of death, with scarcely a momentary
interval of life.[1]

It has been by rejecting the evidence, that the word, or
works of God in the creation, affords to our senses, and the
action of our reason upon that evidence, that so many wild
and whimsical systems of faith, and of religion, have been
fabricated and set up. There may be many systems of religion that so far from being morally bad are in many
respects morally good: but there can be but ONE that is true;
and that one necessarily must, as it ever will, be in all things
consistent with the ever existing word of God that we behold in his works. But such is the strange construction of the
christian system of faith, that every evidence the heavens affords to man, either directly contradicts it or renders it absurd.

It is possible to believe, and I always feel pleasure in
encouraging myself to believe it, that there have been men
in the world who persuaded themselves that what is called
a *pious fraud*, might, at least under particular circumstances,
be productive of some good. But the fraud being once
established, could not afterwards be explained; for it is with
a pious fraud as with a bad action, it begets a calamitous
necessity of going on.

The persons who first preached the christian system of
faith, and in some measure combined with it the morality
preached by Jesus Christ, might persuade themselves that
it was better than the heathen mythology that then prevailed. From the first preachers the fraud went on to the
second, and to the third, till the idea of its being a pious
fraud became lost in the belief of its being true; and that
belief became again encouraged by the interest of those
who made a livelihood by preaching it.

---

[1] Such constant rebirth of the Son was the doctrine of Master Eckhardt, (4th
cent.).—*Editor.*

But though such a belief might, by such means, be rendered almost general among the laity, it is next to impossible to account for the continual persecution carried on by
the church, for several hundred years, against the sciences,
and against the professors of science, if the church had not
some record or tradition that it was originally no other than
a pious fraud, or did not foresee that it could not be maintained against the evidence that the structure of the universe
afforded.

CHAPTER XVII.

OF THE MEANS EMPLOYED IN ALL TIME, AND ALMOST UNIVERSALLY, TO DECEIVE THE PEOPLES.

HAVING thus shewn the irreconcileable inconsistencies
between the real word of God existing in the universe, and
that which is called *the word of God,* as shewn to us in a
printed book that any man might make, I proceed to speak
of the three principal means that have been employed in all
ages, and perhaps in all countries, to impose upon mankind.

Those three means are Mystery, Miracle, and Prophecy.
The first two are incompatible with true religion, and the
third ought always to be suspected.

With respect to Mystery, every thing we behold is, in
one sense, a mystery to us. Our own existence is a mystery: the whole vegetable world is a mystery. We cannot
account how it is that an acorn, when put into the ground,
is made to develop itself and become an oak. We know
not how it is that the seed we sow unfolds and multiplies
itself, and returns to us such an abundant interest for so
small a capital.

The fact however, as distinct from the operating cause,
is not a mystery, because we see it; and we know also the
means we are to use, which is no other than putting the seed
in the ground. We know, therefore, as much as is necessary
for us to know; and that part of the operation that we
do not know, and which if we did, we could not perform,

the Creator takes upon himself and performs it for us. We are, therefore, better off than if we had been let into the secret, and left to do it for ourselves.

But though every created thing is, in this sense, a mystery, the word mystery cannot be applied to *moral truth,* any more than obscurity can be applied to light. The God in whom we believe is a God of moral truth, and not a God of mystery or obscurity. Mystery is the antagonist of truth. It is a fog of human invention that obscures truth, and represents it in distortion. Truth never invelops *itself* in mystery; and the mystery in which it is at any time enveloped, is the work of its antagonist, and never of itself.

Religion, therefore, being the belief of a God, and the practice of moral truth, cannot have connection with mystery. The belief of a God, so far from having any thing of mystery in it, is of all beliefs the most easy, because it arises to us, as is before observed, out of necessity. And the practice of moral truth, or, in other words, a practical imitation of the moral goodness of God, is no other than our acting towards each other as he acts benignly towards all. We cannot *serve* God in the manner we serve those who cannot do without such service; and, therefore, the only idea we can have of serving God, is that of contributing to the happiness of the living creation that God has made. This cannot be done by retiring ourselves from the society of the world, and spending a recluse life in selfish devotion.

The very nature and design of religion, if I may so express it, prove even to demonstration that it must be free from every thing of mystery, and unincumbered with every thing that is mysterious. Religion, considered as a duty, is incumbent upon every living soul alike, and, therefore, must be on a level to the understanding and comprehension of all. Man does not learn religion as he learns the secrets and mysteries of a trade. He learns the theory of religion by reflection. It arises out of the action of his own mind upon the things which he sees, or upon what he may happen to hear or to read, and the practice joins itself thereto.

When men, whether from policy or pious fraud, set up

systems of religion incompatible with the word or works of God in the creation, and not only above but repugnant to human comprehension, they were under the necessity of inventing or adopting a word that should serve as a bar to all questions, inquiries and speculations. The word *mystery* answered this purpose, and thus it has happened that religion, which is in itself without mystery, has been corrupted into a fog of mysteries.

As *mystery* answered all general purposes, *miracle* followed as an occasional auxiliary. The former served to bewilder the mind, the latter to puzzle the senses. The one was the lingo, the other the legerdemain.

But before going further into this subject, it will be proper to inquire what is to be understood by a miracle.

In the same sense that every thing may be said to be a mystery, so also may it be said that every thing is a miracle, and that no one thing is a greater miracle than another. The elephant, though larger, is not a greater miracle than a mite : nor a mountain a greater miracle than an atom. To an almighty power it is no more difficult to make the one than the other, and no more difficult to make a million of worlds than to make one. Every thing, therefore, is a miracle, in one sense ; whilst, in the other sense, there is no such thing as a miracle. It is a miracle when compared to our power, and to our comprehension. It is not a miracle compared to the power that performs it. But as nothing in this description conveys the idea that is affixed to the word miracle, it is necessary to carry the inquiry further.

Mankind have conceived to themselves certain laws, by which what they call nature is supposed to act ; and that a miracle is something contrary to the operation and effect of those laws. But unless we know the whole extent of those laws, and of what are commonly called the powers of nature, we are not able to judge whether any thing that may appear to us wonderful or miraculous, be within, or be beyond, or be contrary to, her natural power of acting.

The ascension of a man several miles high into the air, would have everything in it that constitutes the idea of a

miracle, if it were not known that a species of air can be
generated several times lighter than the common atmos-
pheric air, and yet possess elasticity enough to prevent the
balloon, in which that light air is inclosed, from being com-
pressed into as many times less bulk, by the common air
that surrounds it. In like manner, extracting flashes or
sparks of fire from the human body, as visibly as from a
steel struck with a flint, and causing iron or steel to move
without any visible agent, would also give the idea of a
miracle, if we were not acquainted with electricity and
magnetism ; so also would many other experiments in natural philosophy, to those who are not acquainted with the
subject. The restoring persons to life who are to appearance dead, as is practised upon drowned persons, would also
be a miracle, if it were not known that animation is capable
of being suspended without being extinct.

Besides these, there are performances by slight of hand,
and by persons acting in concert, that have a miraculous
appearance, which, when known, are thought nothing of.
And, besides these, there are mechanical and optical decep-
tions. There is now an exhibition in Paris of ghosts or
spectres, which, though it is not imposed upon the specta-
tors as a fact, has an astonishing appearance. As, therefore,
we know not the extent to which either nature or art can
go, there is no criterion to determine what a miracle is ;
and mankind, in giving credit to appearances, under the
idea of their being miracles, are subject to be continually
imposed upon.

Since then appearances are so capable of deceiving, and
things not real have a strong resemblance to things that are,
nothing can be more inconsistent than to suppose that the
Almighty would make use of means, such as are called miracles, that would subject the person who performed them to
the suspicion of being an impostor, and the person who
related them to be suspected of lying, and the doctrine
intended to be supported thereby to be suspected as a fabulous invention.

Of all the modes of evidence that ever were invented to

obtain belief to any system or opinion to which the name of religion has been given, that of miracle, however successful the imposition may have been, is the most inconsistent. For, in the first place, whenever recourse is had to show, for the purpose of procuring that belief (for a miracle, under any idea of the word, is a show) it implies a lameness or weakness in the doctrine that is preached. And, in the second place, it is degrading the Almighty into the character of a show-man, playing tricks to amuse and make the people stare and wonder. It is also the most equivocal sort of evidence that can be set up ; for the belief is not to depend upon the thing called a miracle, but upon the credit of the reporter, who says that he saw it ; and, therefore, the thing, were it true, would have no better chance of being believed than if it were a lie.

Suppose I were to say, that when I sat down to write this book, a hand presented itself in the air, took up the pen and wrote every word that is herein written ; would any body believe me? Certainly they would not. Would they believe me a whit the more if the thing had been a fact? Certainly they would not. Since then a real miracle, were it to happen, would be subject to the same fate as the falsehood, the inconsistency becomes the greater of supposing the Almighty would make use of means that would not answer the purpose for which they were intended, even if they were real.

If we are to suppose a miracle to be something so entirely out of the course of what is called nature, that she must go out of that course to accomplish it, and we see an account given of such a miracle by the person who said he saw it, it raises a question in the mind very easily decided, which is,—Is it more probable that nature should go out of her course, or that a man should tell a lie? We have never seen, in our time, nature go out of her course ; but we have good reason to believe that millions of lies have been told in the same time ; it is, therefore, at least millions to one, that the reporter of a miracle tells a lie.

The story of the whale swallowing Jonah, though a whale

is large enough to do it, borders greatly on the marvellous;
but it would have approached nearer to the idea of a miracle,
if Jonah had swallowed the whale. In this, which may serve
for all cases of miracles, the matter would decide itself as before stated, namely, Is it more probable that a man should
have swallowed a whale, or told a lie?

But suppose that Jonah had really swallowed the whale,
and gone with it in his belly to Nineveh, and to convince
the people that it was true have cast it up in their sight,
of the full length and size of a whale, would they not have
believed him to have been the devil instead of a prophet?
or if the whale had carried Jonah to Nineveh, and cast him
up in the same public manner, would they not have believed
the whale to have been the devil, and Jonah one of his
imps?

The most extraordinary of all the things called miracles,
related in the New Testament, is that of the devil flying
away with Jesus Christ, and carrying him to the top of a
high mountain; and to the top of the highest pinnacle of
the temple, and showing him and promising to him *all the
kingdoms of the world.* How happened it that he did not
discover America? or is it only with *kingdoms* that his sooty
highness has any interest.

I have too much respect for the moral character of Christ
to believe that he told this whale of a miracle himself:
neither is it easy to account for what purpose it could have
been fabricated, unless it were to impose upon the connois-
seurs of miracles, as is sometimes practised upon the con-
noisseurs of Queen Anne's farthings, and collectors of relics
and antiquities; or to render the belief of miracles ridiculous,
by outdoing miracle, as Don Quixote outdid chivalry; or
to embarrass the belief of miracles, by making it doubtful by
what power, whether of God or of the devil, any thing called a
miracle was performed. It requires, however, a great deal
of faith in the devil to believe this miracle.

In every point of view in which those things called miracles
can be placed and considered, the reality of them is improbable, and their existence unnecessary. They would not, as

before observed, answer any useful purpose, even if they were true; for it is more difficult to obtain belief to a miracle, than to a principle evidently moral, without any miracle. Moral principle speaks universally for itself. Miracle could be but a thing of the moment, and seen but by a few; after this it requires a transfer of faith from God to man to believe a miracle upon man's report. Instead, therefore, of admitting the recitals of miracles as evidence of any system of religion being true, they ought to be considered as symptoms of its being fabulous. It is necessary to the full and upright character of truth that it rejects the crutch; and it is consistent with the character of fable to seek the aid that truth rejects. Thus much for Mystery and Miracle.

As Mystery and Miracle took charge of the past and the present, Prophecy took charge of the future, and rounded the tenses of *faith*.¹ It was not sufficient to know what had been done, but what would be done. The supposed prophet was the supposed historian of times to come; and if he happened, in shooting with a long bow of a thousand years, to strike within a thousand miles of a mark, the ingenuity of posterity could make it point-blank; and if he happened to be directly wrong, it was only to suppose, as in the case of Jonah and Nineveh, that God had repented himself and changed his mind. What a fool do fabulous systems make of man!

It has been shewn, in a former part of this work, that the original meaning of the words *prophet* and *prophesying* has been changed, and that a prophet, in the sense of the word as now used, is a creature of modern invention; and it is owing to this change in the meaning of the words, that the flights and metaphors of the Jewish poets, and phrases and expressions now rendered obscure by our not being acquainted with the local circumstances to which they applied at the time they were used, have been erected into prophecies, and made to bend to explanations at the will and whimsical conceits of sectaries, expounders, and commentators. Every thing unintelligible was prophetical, and

¹ In the French work : " du verbe *croire.*"—*Editor.*

every thing insignificant was typical.   A blunder would have
served for a prophecy ; and a dish-clout for a type.

If by a prophet we are to suppose a man to whom the
Almighty communicated some event that would take place
in future, either there were such men, or there were not.
If there were, it is consistent to believe that the event so
communicated would be told in terms that could be understood, and not related in such a loose and obscure manner
as to be out of the comprehension of those that heard it,
and so equivocal as to fit almost any circumstance that
might happen afterwards.   It is conceiving very irreverently
of the Almighty, to suppose he would deal in this jesting
manner with mankind ; yet all the things called prophecies
in the book called the Bible come under this description.

But it is with Prophecy as it is with Miracle.   It could
not answer the purpose even if it were real.   Those to whom
a prophecy should be told could not tell whether the man
prophesied or lied, or whether it had been revealed to him,
or whether he conceited it ; and if the thing that he prophesied, or pretended to prophesy, should happen, or some thing
like it, among the multitude of things that are daily happening, nobody could again know whether he foreknew it,
or guessed at it, or whether it was accidental.   A prophet,
therefore, is a character useless and unnecessary ; and the
safe side of the case is to guard against being imposed upon,
by not giving credit to such relations.

Upon the whole, Mystery, Miracle, and Prophecy, are
appendages that belong to fabulous and not to true religion.
They are the means by which so many *Lo heres!* and *Lo
theres!* have been spread about the world, and religion been
made into a trade.   The success of one impostor gave en-
couragement to another, and the quieting salvo of doing
some good by keeping up a *pious fraud* protected them from
remorse

RECAPITULATION.

HAVING now extended the subject to a greater length than I first intended, I shall bring it to a close by abstracting a summary from the whole.

First, That the idea or belief of a word of God existing in print, or in writing, or in speech, is inconsistent in itself for the reasons already assigned. These reasons, among many others, are the want of an universal language; the mutability of language; the errors to which translations are subject; the possibility of totally suppressing such a word; the probability of altering it, or of fabricating the whole, and imposing it upon the world.

Secondly, That the Creation we behold is the real and ever existing word of God, in which we cannot be deceived. It proclaimeth his power, it demonstrates his wisdom, it manifests his goodness and beneficence.

Thirdly, That the moral duty of man consists in imitating the moral goodness and beneficence of God manifested in the creation towards all his creatures. That seeing as we daily do the goodness of God to all men, it is an example calling upon all men to practise the same towards each other; and, consequently, that every thing of persecution and revenge between man and man, and every thing of cruelty to animals, is a violation of moral duty.

I trouble not myself about the manner of future existence. I content myself with believing, even to positive conviction, that the power that gave me existence is able to continue it, in any form and manner he pleases, either with or without this body; and it appears more probable to me that I shall continue to exist hereafter than that I should have had existence, as I now have, before that existence began.

It is certain that, in one point, all nations of the earth and all religions agree. All believe in a God, The things in which they disagree are the redundancies annexed to that belief; and therefore, if ever an universal religion should prevail, it will not be believing any thing new, but in getting rid of redundancies, and believing as man believed at first.[1] Adam, if ever there was such a man, was created a Deist; but in the mean time, let every man follow, as he has a right to do, the religion and worship he prefers.

[1] "In the childhood of the world," according to the first (French) version; and the strict translation of the final sentence is: "Deism was the religion of Adam, supposing him not an imaginary being; but none the less must it be left to all men to follow, as is their right, the religion and worship they prefer."— *Editor.*

II.

THE AGE OF REASON.

PART II.

PREFACE.

I HAVE mentioned in the former part of *The Age of Reason* that it had long been my intention to publish my thoughts upon Religion; but that I had originally reserved it to a later period in life, intending it to be the last work I should undertake. The circumstances, however, which existed in France in the latter end of the year 1793, determined me to delay it no longer. The just and humane principles of the Revolution which Philosophy had first diffused, had been departed from. The Idea, always dangerous to Society as it is derogatory to the Almighty,—that priests could forgive sins,—though it seemed to exist no longer, had blunted the feelings of humanity, and callously prepared men for the commission of all crimes. The intolerant spirit of church persecution had transferred itself into politics; the tribunals, stiled Revolutionary, supplied the place of an Inquisition; and the Guillotine of the Stake. I saw many of my most intimate friends destroyed; others daily carried to prison; and I had reason to believe, and had also intimations given me, that the same danger was approaching myself.

Under these disadvantages, I began the former part of the Age of Reason; I had, besides, neither Bible nor Testament [1] to refer to, though I was writing against both; nor could I procure any; notwithstanding which I have pro-

[1] It must be borne in mind that throughout this work Paine generally means by "Bible" only the Old Testament, and speaks of the New as the "Testament."—*Editor*.

duced a work that no Bible Believer, though writing at his ease, and with a Library of Church Books about him, can refute.   Towards the latter end of December of that year, a motion was made and carried, to exclude foreigners from the Convention.   There were but two, Anacharsis Cloots and myself; and I saw I was particularly pointed at by Bourdon de l'Oise, in his speech on that motion.

Conceiving, after this, that I had but a few days of liberty, I sat down and brought the work to a close as speedily as possible; and I had not finished it more than six hours, in the state it has since appeared,[1] before a guard came there, about three in the morning, with an order signed by the two Committees of Public Safety and Surety General, for putting me in arrestation as a foreigner, and conveying me to the prison of the Luxembourg.   I contrived, in my way there, to call on Joel Barlow, and I put the Manuscript of the work into his hands, as more safe than in my possession in prison; and not knowing what might be the fate in France either of the writer or the work, I addressed it to the protection of the citizens of the United States.

It is justice that I say, that the guard who executed this order, and the interpreter to the Committee of General Surety, who accompanied them to examine my papers, treated me not only with civility, but with respect.   The keeper of the Luxembourg, Benoit, a man of good heart, shewed to me every friendship in his power, as did also all his family, while he continued in that station.   He was removed from it, put into arrestation, and carried before the tribunal upon a malignant accusation, but acquitted.

After I had been in Luxembourg about three weeks, the Americans then in Paris went in a body to the Convention, to reclaim me as their countryman and friend; but were answered by the President, Vadier, who was also President of the Committee of Surety General, and had signed the order for my arrestation, that I was born in England.[2]   I

---

[1] This is an allusion to the essay which Paine wrote at an earlier part of 1793. See Introduction.—*Editor*.

[2] These excited Americans do not seem to have understood or reported the

heard no more, after this, from any person out of the walls of the prison, till the fall of Robespierre, on the 9th of Thermidor—July 27, 1794.

About two months before this event, I was seized with a fever that in its progress had every symptom of becoming mortal, and from the effects of which I am not recovered. It was then that I remembered with renewed satisfaction, and congratulated myself most sincerely, on having written the former part of *The Age of Reason.* I had then but little expectation of surviving, and those about me had less. I know therefore by experience the conscientious trial of my own principles.

I was then with three chamber comrades: Joseph Vanheule of Bruges, Charles Bastíni, and Michael Robyns of Louvain. The unceasing and anxious attention of these three friends to me, by night and day, I remember with gratitude and mention with pleasure. It happened that a physician (Dr. Graham) and a surgeon, (Mr. Bond,) part of the suite of General O'Hara,[1] were then in the Luxembourg: I ask not myself whether it be convenient to them, as men under the English Government, that I express to them my thanks; but I should reproach myself if I did not; and also to the physician of the Luxembourg, Dr. Markoski.

I have some reason to believe, because I cannot discover any other, that this illness preserved me in existence. Among the papers of Robespierre that were examined and reported upon to the Convention by a Committee of Deputies, is a note in the hand writing of Robespierre, in the following words:

" Démander que Thomas Paine soit décrété d'accusation, pour l'intérêt de l'Amérique autant que de la France."

Demand that Thomas Paine be decreed of accusation, for the interest of America, as well as of France.

most important item in Vadier's reply, namely that their application was " unoffi. cial," i. e. not made through or sanctioned by Gouverneur Morris, American Minister.   For the detailed history of all this see vol. iii.—*Editor*.

[1] The officer who at Yorktown, Virginia, carried out the sword of Cornwallis for surrender, and satirically offered it to Rochambeau instead of Washington. Paine loaned him £300 when he (O'Hara) left the prison, the money he had concealed in the lock of his cell-door.—*Editor*.

From what cause it was that the intention was not put in execution, I know not, and cannot inform myself; and therefore I ascribe it to impossibility, on account of that illness.

The Convention, to repair as much as lay in their power the injustice I had sustained, invited me publickly and unanimously to return into the Convention, and which I accepted, to shew I could bear an injury without permitting it to injure my principles or my disposition. It is not because right principles have been violated, that they are to be abandoned.

I have seen, since I have been at liberty, several publications written, some in America, and some in England, as answers to the former part of "The Age of Reason." If the authors of these can amuse themselves by so doing, I shall not interrupt them. They may write against the work, and against me, as much as they please; they do me more service than they intend, and I can have no objection that they write on. They will find, however, by this Second Part, without its being written as an answer to them, that they must return to their work, and spin their cobweb over again. The first is brushed away by accident.

They will now find that I have furnished myself with a Bible and Testament; and I can say also that I have found them to be much worse books than I had conceived. If I have erred in any thing, in the former part of the Age of Reason, it has been by speaking better of some parts than they deserved.

I observe, that all my opponents resort, more or less, to what they call Scripture Evidence and Bible authority, to help them out. They are so little masters of the subject, as to confound a dispute about authenticity with a dispute about doctrines; I will, however, put them right, that if they should be disposed to write any more, they may know how to begin.

THOMAS PAINE.

October, 1795.

CHAPTER I.

THE OLD TESTAMENT.

IT has often been said that any thing may be proved from the Bible; but before any thing can be admitted as proved by Bible, the Bible itself must be proved to be true; for if the Bible be not true, or the truth of it be doubtful, it ceases to have authority, and cannot be admitted as proof of any thing.

It has been the practice of all Christian commentators on the Bible, and of all Christian priests and preachers, to impose the Bible on the world as a mass of truth, and as the word of God; they have disputed and wrangled, and have anathematized each other about the supposeable meaning of particular parts and passages therein; one has said and insisted that such a passage meant such a thing, another that it meant directly the contrary, and a third, that it meant neither one nor the other, but something different from both; and this they have called *understanding* the Bible.

It has happened, that all the answers that I have seen to the former part of *The Age of Reason* have been written by priests: and these pious men, like their predecessors, contend and wrangle, and *understand* the Bible; each understands it differently, but each understands it best; and they have agreed in nothing but in telling their readers that Thomas Paine understands it not.

Now instead of wasting their time, and heating themselves in fractious disputations about doctrinal points drawn from the Bible, these men *ought to know*, and if they do not it is civility to inform them, that the first thing to be *understood* is, whether there is sufficient authority for believing the Bible to be the word of God, or whether there is not?

There are matters in that book, said to be done by the *express command* of God, that are as shocking to humanity, and to every idea we have of moral justice, as any thing done by Robespierre, by Carrier, by Joseph le Bon, in France, by the English government in the East Indies, or by any other assassin in modern times. When we read in the books ascribed to Moses, Joshua, etc., that they (the Israelites) came by stealth upon whole nations of people, who, as the history itself shews, had given them no offence ; *that they put all those nations to the sword ; that they spared neither age nor infancy ; that they utterly destroyed men, women and childreu ; that they left not a soul to breathe ;* expressions that are repeated over and over again in those books, and that too with exulting ferocity ; are we sure these things are facts ? are we sure that the Creator of man commissioned those things to be done ? Are we sure that the books that tell us so were written by his authority ?

It is not the antiquity of a tale that is any evidence of its truth ; on the contrary, it is a symptom of its being fabulous ; for the more ancient any history pretends to be, the more it has the resemblance of a fable. The origin of every nation is buried in fabulous tradition, and that of the Jews is as much to be suspected as any other.

To charge the commission of things upon the Almighty, which in their own nature, and by every rule of moral justice, are crimes, as all assassination is, and more especially the assassination of infants, is matter of serious concern. The Bible tells us, that those assassinations were done by the *express command of God.* To believe therefore the Bible to be true, we must *unbelieve* all our belief in the moral justice of God ; for wherein could crying or smiling infants offend? And to read the Bible without horror, we must undo every thing that is tender, sympathising, and benevolent in the heart of man. Speaking for myself, if I had no other evidence that the Bible is fabulous, than the sacrifice I must make to believe it to be true, that alone would be sufficient to determine my choice.

But in addition to all the moral evidence against the

Bible, I will, in the progress of this work, produce such other evidence as even a priest cannot deny ; and shew, from that evidence, that the Bible is not entitled to credit, as being the word of God.

But, before I proceed to this examination, I will shew wherein the Bible differs from all other ancient writings with respect to the nature of the evidence necessary to establish its authenticity ; and this is the more proper to be done, because the advocates of the Bible, in their answers to the former part of *The Age of Reason*, undertake to say, and they put some stress thereon, that the authenticity of the Bible is as well established as that of any other ancient book : as if our belief of the one could become any rule for our belief of the other.

I know, however, but of one ancient book that authoritatively challenges universal consent and belief, and that is *Euclid's Elements of Geometry ;* * and the reason is, because it is a book of self-evident demonstration, entirely independent of its author, and of every thing relating to time, place, and circumstance. The matters contained in that book would have the same authority they now have, had they been written by any other person, or had the work been anonymous, or had the author never been known ; for the identical certainty of who was the author makes no part of our belief of the matters contained in the book. But it is quite otherwise with respect to the books ascribed to Moses, to Joshua, to Samuel, etc. : those are books of *testimony*, and they testify of things naturally incredible ; and therefore the whole of our belief, as to the authenticity of those books, rests, in the first place, upon the *certainty* that they were written by Moses, Joshua, and Samuel ; secondly, upon the credit we give to their testimony. We may believe the first, that is, may believe the certainty of the authorship, and yet not the testimony ; in the same manner that we may believe that a certain person gave evidence

* Euclid, according to chronological history, lived three hundred years before Christ, and about one hundred before Archimedes ; he was of the city of Alexandria, in Egypt.—*Author.*

upon a case, and yet not believe the evidence that he gave.
But if it should be found that the books ascribed to Moses,
Joshua, and Samuel, were not written by Moses, Joshua,
and Samuel, every part of the authority and authenticity of those books is gone at once ; for there can be no
such thing as forged or invented testimony ; neither can
there be anonymous testimony, more especially as to things
naturally incredible ; such as that of talking with God face
to face, or that of the sun and moon standing still at the
command of a man.

The greatest part of the other ancient books are works
of genius ; of which kind are those ascribed to Homer, to
Plato, to Aristotle, to Demosthenes, to Cicero, etc.   Here
again the author is not an essential in the credit we give to
any of those works ; for as works of genius they would have
the same merit they have now, were they anonymous.
Nobody believes the Trojan story, as related by Homer, to
be true ; for it is the poet only that is admired, and the
merit of the poet will remain, though the story be fabulous.
But if we disbelieve the matters related by the Bible authors
(Moses for instance) as we disbelieve the things related by
Homer, there remains nothing of Moses in our estimation,
but an imposter.   As to the ancient historians, from Herod-
otus to Tacitus, we credit them as far as they relate things
probable and credible, and no further : for if we do, we must
believe the two miracles which Tacitus relates were performed by Vespasian, that of curing a lame man, and a
blind man, in just the same manner as the same things are
told of Jesus Christ by his historians.   We must also believe
the miracles cited by Josephus, that of the sea of Pamphilia
opening to let Alexander and his army pass, as is related of
the Red Sea in Exodus.   These miracles are quite as well
authenticated as the Bible miracles, and yet we do not
believe them ; consequently the degree of evidence necessary to establish our belief of things naturally incredible,
whether in the Bible or elsewhere, is far greater than that
which obtains our belief to natural and probable things ;
and therefore the advocates for the Bible have no claim

to our belief of the Bible because that we believe things stated in other ancient writings; since that we believe the things stated in those writings no further than they are probable and credible, or because they are self-evident, like Euclid; or admire them because they are elegant, like Homer; or approve them because they are sedate, like Plato; or judicious, like Aristotle.

Having premised these things, I proceed to examine the authenticity of the Bible; and I begin with what are called the five books of Moses, *Genesis, Exodus, Leviticus, Numbers,* and *Deuteronomy.* My intention is to shew that those books are spurious, and that Moses is not the author of them; and still further, that they were not written in the time of Moses nor till several hundred years afterwards; that they are no other than an attempted history of the life of Moses, and of the times in which he is said to have lived, and also of the times prior thereto, written by some very ignorant and stupid pretenders to authorship, several hundred years after the death of Moses; as men now write histories of things that happened, or are supposed to have happened, several hundred or several thousand years ago.

The evidence that I shall produce in this case is from the books themselves; and I will confine myself to this evidence only. Were I to refer for proofs to any of the ancient authors, whom the advocates of the Bible call prophane authors, they would controvert that authority, as I controvert theirs: I will therefore meet them on their own ground, and oppose them with their own weapon, the Bible.

In the first place, there is no affirmative evidence that Moses is the author of those books; and that he is the author, is altogether an unfounded opinion, got abroad nobody knows how. The style and manner in which those books are written give no room to believe, or even to suppose, they were written by Moses; for it is altogether the style and manner of another person speaking of Moses. In Exodus, Leviticus and Numbers, (for every thing in Genesis is prior to the times of Moses and not the least allusion is made to him therein,) the whole, I say, of these books is in the third person; it is always, *the Lord said unto Moses, or Moses said unto the Lord; or Moses said unto the people, or the people said unto Moses;* and this is the style and manner that historians use in speaking of the person whose lives and actions they are writing. It may be said, that a man may speak of himself in the third person, and, therefore, it may be supposed that Moses did; but supposition proves nothing; and if the advocates for the belief that Moses wrote those books himself have nothing better to advance than supposition, they may as well be silent.

But granting the grammatical right, that Moses might speak of himself in the third person, because any man might speak of himself in that manner, it cannot be admitted as a fact in those books, that it is Moses who speaks, without rendering Moses truly ridiculous and absurd:—for example, Numbers xii. 3: " *Now the man Moses was very* MEEK, *above all the men which were on the face of the earth.* If Moses said this of himself, instead of being the meekest of men, he was one of the most vain and arrogant coxcombs; and the advocates for those books may now take which side they please, for both sides are against them: if Moses was not the author, the books are without authority; and if he was the author, the author is without credit, because to boast of *meekness* is the reverse of meekness, and is *a lie in sentiment.*

In Deuteronomy, the style and manner of writing marks more evidently than in the former books that Moses is not the writer. The manner here used is dramatical; the writer opens the subject by a short introductory discourse, and then introduces Moses as in the act of speaking, and when he has made Moses finish his harrangue, he (the writer) resumes his own part, and speaks till he brings Moses forward again, and at last closes the scene with an account of the death, funeral, and character of Moses.

This interchange of speakers occurs four times in this book: from the first verse of the first chapter, to the end of the fifth verse, it is the writer who speaks; he then introduces Moses as in the act of making his harrangue, and this continues to the end of the 40th verse of the fourth chapter; here the writer drops Moses, and speaks histori-cally of what was done in consequence of what Moses, when living, is supposed to have said, and which the writer has dramatically rehearsed.

The writer opens the subject again in the first verse of the fifth chapter, though it is only by saying that Moses called the people of Israel together; he then introduces Moses as before, and continues him as in the act of speak-ing, to the end of the 26th chapter. He does the same thing at the beginning of the 27th chapter; and continues Moses as in the act of speaking, to the end of the 28th chapter. At the 29th chapter the writer speaks again through the whole of the first verse, and the first line of the second verse, where he introduces Moses for the last time, and continues him as in the act of speaking, to the end of the 33d chapter.

The writer having now finished the rehearsal on the part of Moses, comes forward, and speaks through the whole of the last chapter: he begins by telling the reader, that Moses went up to the top of Pisgah, that he saw from thence the land which (the writer says) had been promised to Abraham, Isaac, and Jacob; that *he*, Moses, died there in the land of Moab, that he buried him in a valley in the land of Moab, but that no man knoweth of his sepulchre unto this day, that is unto the time in which the writer lived who wrote the book of Deuteronomy. The writer then tells us, that Moses was one hundred and ten years of age when he died—that his eye was not dim, nor his natural force abated ; and he concludes by saying, that there arose not a prophet *since* in Israel like unto Moses, whom, says this anonymous writer, the Lord knew face to face.

Having thus shewn, as far as grammatical evidence im-plies, that Moses was not the writer of those books, I will, after making a few observations on the inconsistencies of the writer of the book of Deuteronomy, proceed to shew, from the historical and chronological evidence contained in those books, that Moses *was not*, because *he could not be*, the writer of them; and consequently, that there is no authority for believing that the inhuman and horrid butcheries of men, women, and children, told of in those books, were done, as those books say they were, at the command of God. It is a duty incumbent on every true deist, that he vindicates the moral justice of God against the calumnies of the Bible.

The writer of the book of Deuteronomy, whoever he was, for it is an anonymous work, is obscure, and also contradictory with himself in the account he has given of Moses.

After telling that Moses went to the top of Pisgah (and it does not appear from any account that he ever came down again) he tells us, that Moses died *there* in the land of Moab, and that *he* buried him in a valley in the land of Moab; but as there is no antecedent to the pronoun *he*, there is no knowing who *he* was, that did bury him. If the writer meant that he (God) buried him, how should *he* (the writer) know it? or why should we (the readers) believe him? since we know not who the writer was that tells us so, for certainly Moses could not himself tell where he was buried.

The writer also tells us, that no man knoweth where the sepulchre of Moses is unto this day, meaning the time in which this writer lived; how then should he know that Moses was buried in a valley in the land of Moab? for as the writer lived long after the time of Moses, as is evident from his using the expression of *unto this day*, meaning a great length of time after the death of Moses, he certainly was not at his funeral; and on the other hand, it is impossible that Moses himself could say that *no man knoweth where the sepulchre is unto this day*. To make Moses the speaker, would be an improvement on the play of a child that hides himself and cries *nobody can find me*; nobody can find Moses.

This writer has no where told us how he came by the speeches which he has put into the mouth of Moses to speak, and therefore we have a right to conclude that he either composed them himself, or wrote them from oral tradition. One or other of these is the more probable, since he has given, in the fifth chapter, a table of commandments, in which that called the fourth commandment is different from the fourth commandment in the twentieth chapter of Exodus. In that of Exodus, the reason given for keeping the seventh day is, because (says the commandment) God made the heavens and the earth in six days, and rested on the seventh; but in that of Deuteronomy, the reason given is, that it was the day on which the children of Israel came out of Egypt, and *therefore,* says this commandment, *the Lord thy God commanded thee to keep the sabbath-day.* *This* makes no mention of the creation, nor *that* of the coming out of Egypt. There are also many things given as laws of Moses in this book, that are not to be found in any of the other books; among which is that inhuman and brutal law, xxi. 18, 19, 20, 21, which authorizes parents, the father and the mother, to bring their own children to have them stoned to death for what it pleased them to call stubbornness.—But priests have always been fond of preaching up Deuteronomy, for Deuteronomy preaches up tythes; and it is from this book, xxv. 4, they have taken the phrase, and applied it to tything, that *thou shalt not muzzle the ox when he treadeth out the corn :* and that this might not escape observation, they have noted it in the table of contents at the head of the chapter, though it is only a single verse of less than two lines. O priests! priests! ye are willing to be compared to an ox, for the sake of tythes.[1]—Though it is impossible for us to know *identically* who the writer of Deuteronomy was, it is not difficult to discover him *professionally,* that he was some Jewish priest, who lived, as I shall shew in the course of this work, at least three hundred and fifty years after the time of Moses.

I come now to speak of the historical and chronological evidence. The chronology that I shall use is the Bible chronology; for I mean not to go out of the Bible for

[1] An elegant pocket edition of Paine's Theological Works (London : R. Carlile, 1822) has in its title a picture of Paine, as a Moses in evening dress, unfolding the two tables of his "Age of Reason" to a farmer from whom the Bishop of Llandaff (who replied to this work) has taken a sheaf and a lamb which he is carrying to a church at the summit of a well-stocked hill.—*Editor.*

evidence of any thing, but to make the Bible itself prove historically and chronologically that Moses is not the author of the books ascribed to him.   It is therefore proper that I inform the readers (such an one at least as may not have the opportunity of knowing it) that in the larger Bibles, and also in some smaller ones, there is a series of chronology printed in the margin of every page for the purpose of shewing how long the historical matters stated in each page happened, or are supposed to have happened, before Christ, and consequently the distance of time between one historical circumstance and another.

I begin with the book of Genesis.—In Genesis xiv., the writer gives an account of Lot being taken prisoner in a battle between the four kings against five, and carried off; and that when the account of Lot being taken came to Abraham, that he armed all his household and marched to rescue Lot from the captors; and that he pursued them unto Dan. (ver. 14.)

To shew in what manner this expression of *pursuing them unto Dan* applies to the case in question, I will refer to two circumstances, the one in America, the other in France.   The city now called New York, in America, was originally New Amsterdam; and the town in France, lately called Havre Marat, was before called Havre-de-Grace.   New Amsterdam was changed to New York in the year 1664; Havre-de-Grace to Havre Marat in the year 1793.   Should, therefore, any writing be found, though without date, in which the name of New-York should be mentioned, it would be certain evidence that such a writing could not have been written before, and must have been written after New Amsterdam was changed to New York, and consequently not till after the year 1664, or at least during the course of that year.   And in like manner, any dateless writing, with the name of Havre Marat, would be certain evidence that such a writing must have been written after Havre-de-Grace became Havre Marat, and consequently not till after the year 1793, or at least during the course of that year.

I now come to the application of those cases, and to shew

that there was no such place as *Dan* till many years after the death of Moses; and .consequently, that Moses could not be the writer of the book of Genesis, where this account of pursuing them unto *Dan* is given.

The place that is called Dan in the Bible was originally a town of the Gentiles, called Laish; and when the tribe of Dan seized upon this town, they changed its name to Dan, in commemoration of Dan, who was the father of that tribe, and the great grandson of Abraham.

To establish this in proof, it is necessary to refer from Genesis to chapter xviii. of the book called the Book of Judges. It is there said (ver. 27) that *they* (the Danites) *came unto Laish to a people that were quiet and secure, and they smote them with the edge of the sword* [the Bible is filled with murder] *and burned the city with fire; and they built a city*, (ver. 28,) and dwelt therein, *and* [ver. 29,] *they called the name of the city Dan, after the name of Dan, their father; howbeit the name of the city was Laish at the first.*

This account of the Danites taking possession of Laish and changing it to Dan, is placed in the book of Judges immediately after the death of Samson. The death of Samson is said to have happened B. C. 1120 and that of Moses B. C. 1451; and, therefore, according to the historical arrangement, the place was not called Dan till 331 years after the death of Moses.

There is a striking confusion between the historical and the chronological arrangement in the book of Judges. The last five chapters, as they stand in the book, 17, 18, 19, 20, 21, are put chronologically before all the preceding chapters; they are made to be 28 years before the 16th chapter, 266 before the 15th, 245 before the 13th, 195 before the 9th, 90 before the 4th, and 15 years before the 1st chapter. This shews the uncertain and fabulous state of the Bible. According to the chronological arrangement, the taking of Laish, and giving it the name of Dan, is made to be twenty years after the death of Joshua, who was the successor of Moses; and by the historical order, as it stands in the book, it is made to be 306 years after the death of Joshua, and 331

after that of Moses; but they both exclude Moses from
being the writer of Genesis, because, according to either of
the statements, no such a place as Dan existed in the time of
Moses; and therefore the writer of Genesis must have been
some person who lived after the town of Laish had the name
of Dan; and who that person was nobody knows, and consequently the book of Genesis is anonymous, and without
authority.

I come now to state another point of historical and chronological evidence, and to shew therefrom, as in the preceding
case, that Moses is not the author of the book of Genesis.

In Genesis xxxvi. there is given a genealogy of the sons
and descendants of Esau, who are called Edomites, and also
a list by name of the kings of Edom; in enumerating of
which, it is said, verse 31, "*And these are the kings that
reigned in Edom, before there reigned any king over the children of Israel.*"

Now, were any dateless writing to be found, in which,
speaking of any past events, the writer should say, these
things happened before there was any Congress in America,
or before there was any Convention in France, it would be
evidence that such writing could not have been written
before, and could only be written after there was a Congress
in America, or a Convention in France, as the case might
be; and, consequently, that it could not be written by any
person who died before there was a Congress in the one
country, or a Convention in the other.

Nothing is more frequent, as well in history as in conversation, than to refer to a fact in the room of a date: it is
most natural so to do, because a fact fixes itself in the memory better than a date; secondly, because the fact includes
the date, and serves to give two ideas at once; and this
manner of speaking by circumstances implies as positively
that the fact alluded to is past, as if it was so expressed.
When a person in speaking upon any matter, says, it was
before I was married, or before my son was born, or before
I went to America, or before I went to France, it is absolutely
understood, and intended to be understood, that he has been

married, that he has had a son, that he has been in America, or been in France. Language does not admit of using this mode of expression in any other sense; and whenever such an expression is found anywhere, it can only be understood in the sense in which only it could have been used.

The passage, therefore, that I have quoted—that "these are the kings that reigned in Edom, before there reigned *any* king over the children of Israel," could only have been written after the first king began to reign over them ; and consequently that the book of Genesis, so far from having been written by Moses, could not have been written till the time of Saul at least. This is the positive sense of the passage ; but the expression, *any* king, implies more kings than one, at least it implies two, and this will carry it to the time of David ; and, if taken in a general sense, it carries itself through all times of the Jewish monarchy.

Had we met with this verse in any part of the Bible that professed to have been written after kings began to reign in Israel, it would have been impossible not to have seen the application of it. It happens then that this is the case ; the two books of Chronicles, which give a history of all the kings of Israel, are *professedly*, as well as in fact, written after the Jewish monarchy began ; and this verse that I have quoted, and all the remaining verses of Genesis xxxvi. are, word for word, in 1 Chronicles i., beginning at the 43d verse.

It was with consistency that the writer of the Chronicles could say as he has said, 1 Chron. i. 43, *These are the kings that reigned in Edom, before there reigned any king over the children of Israel*, because he was going to give, and has given, a list of the kings that had reigned in Israel ; but as it is impossible that the same expression could have been used before that period, it is as certain as any thing can be proved from historical language, that this part of Genesis is taken from Chronicles, and that Genesis is not so old as Chronicles, and probably not so old as the book of Homer, or as Æsop's Fables ; admitting Homer to have been, as the tables of chronology state, contemporary with David or Solomon, and Æsop to have lived about the end of the Jewish monarchy.

Take away from Genesis the belief that Moses was the author, on which only the strange belief that it is the word of God has stood, and there remains nothing of Genesis but an anonymous book of stories, fables, and traditionary or invented absurdities, or of downright lies. The story of Eve and the serpent, and of Noah and his ark, drops to a level with the Arabian Tales, without the merit of being entertaining, and the account of men living to eight and nine hundred years becomes as fabulous as the immortality of the giants of the Mythology.

Besides, the character of Moses, as stated in the Bible, is the most horrid that can be imagined. If those accounts be true, he was the wretch that first began and carried on wars on the score or on the pretence of religion ; and under that mask, or that infatuation, committed the most unexampled atrocities that are to be found in the history of any nation.   Of which I will state only one instance :

When the Jewish army returned from one of their plundering and murdering excursions, the account goes on as follows (Numbers xxxi. 13) : " And Moses, and Eleazar the priest, and all the princes of the congregation, went forth to meet them without the camp ; and Moses was wroth with the officers of the host, with the captains over thousands, and captains over hundreds, which came from the battle ; and Moses said unto them, *Have ye saved all the women alive ?* behold, these caused the children of Israel, through the counsel of Balaam, to commit trespass against the Lord in the matter of Peor, and there was a plague among the congregation of the Lord.   Now therefore, *kill every male among the little ones, and kill every woman that hath known a man by lying with him ; but all the women-children that have not known a man by lying with him, keep alive for yourselves.*"

Among the detestable villains that in any period of the world have disgraced the name of man, it is impossible to find a greater than Moses, if this account be true.   Here is an order to butcher the boys, to massacre the mothers, and debauch the daughters.

Let any mother put herself in the situation of those

mothers, one child murdered, another destined to violation, and herself in the hands of an executioner : let any daughter put herself in the situation of those daughters, destined as a prey to the murderers of a mother and a brother, and what will be their feelings? It is in vain that we attempt to impose upon nature, for nature will have her course, and the religion that tortures all her social ties is a false religion.

After this detestable order, follows an account of the plunder taken, and the manner of dividing it; and here it is that the profaneness of priestly hypocrisy increases the catalogue of crimes. Verse 37, "*And the Lord's tribute* of the sheep was six hundred and threescore and fifteen ; and the beeves were thirty and six thousand, of which the *Lord's tribute* was threescore and twelve ; and the asses were thirty thousand, of which the *Lord's tribute* was threescore and one; and the persons were sixteen thousand, of which the *Lord's tribute* was thirty and two." In short, the matters contained in this chapter, as well as in many other parts of the Bible, are too horrid for humanity to read, or for decency to hear; for it appears, from the 35th verse of this chapter, that the number of women-children consigned to debauchery by the order of Moses was thirty-two thousand.

People in general know not what wickedness there is in this pretended word of God. Brought up in habits of superstition, they take it for granted that the Bible is true, and that it is good ; they permit themselves not to doubt of it, and they carry the ideas they form of the benevolence of the Almighty to the book which they have been taught to believe was written by his authority. Good heavens! it is quite another thing, it is a book of lies, wickedness, and blasphemy; for what can be greater blasphemy, than to ascribe the wickedness of man to the orders of the Almighty!

But to return to my subject, that of shewing that Moses is not the author of the books ascribed to him, and that the Bible is spurious. The two instances I have already given would be sufficient, without any additional evidence, to invalidate the authenticity of any book that pretended to be four or five hundred years more ancient than the matters it speaks of, or refers to, as facts; for in the case of *pursuing them unto Dan,* and of *the kings that reigned over the children of Israel,* not even the flimsy pretence of prophecy can be pleaded. The expressions are in the preter tense, and it would be downright idiotism to say that a man could prophecy in the preter tense.

But there are many other passages scattered throughout those books that unite in the same point of evidence. It is said in Exodus, (another of the books ascribed to Moses,) xvi. 35 : "And the children of Israel did eat manna *until they came to a land inhabited;* they did eat manna *until they came unto the borders of the land of Canaan.*"

Whether the children of Israel ate manna or not, or what manna was, or whether it was anything more than a kind of fungus or small mushroom, or other vegetable substance common to that part of the country, makes no part of my argument; all that I mean to shew is, that it is not Moses that could write this account, because the account extends itself beyond the life time of Moses. Moses, according to the Bible, (but it is such a book of lies and contradictions there is no knowing which part to believe, or whether any) died in the wilderness, and never came upon the borders of the land of Canaan ; and, consequently, it could not be he that said what the children of Israel did, or what they ate when they came there. This account of eating manna, which they tell us was written by Moses, extends itself to the time of Joshua, the successor of Moses, as appears by the account given in the book of Joshua, after the children of Israel had passed the river Jordan, and came into the borders of the land of Canaan. Joshua, v. 12 : "*And the manna ceased on the morrow, after they had eaten of the old corn of the land ; neither had the children of Israel manna any more, but they did eat of the fruit of the land of Canaan that year.*"

But a more remarkable instance than this occurs in Deuteronomy ; which, while it shews that Moses could not be the writer of that book, shews also the fabulous notions that prevailed at that time about giants. In Deuteronomy iii. 11, among the conquests said to be made by Moses, is an account of the taking of Og, king of Bashan : "For only Og, king of Bashan, remained of the race of giants; behold, his bedstead was a bedstead of iron ; is it not in Rabbath of the children of Ammon? nine cubits was the length thereof, and four cubits the breadth of it, after the cubit of a man." A cubit is 1 foot $9\frac{888}{1000}$ inches; the length therefore of the bed was 16 feet 4 inches, and the breadth 7 feet 4 inches; thus much for this giant's bed. Now for the historical part, which, though the evidence is not so direct and positive as in the former cases, is nevertheless very presumable and corroborating evidence, and is better than the *best* evidence on the contrary side.

The writer, by way of proving the existence of this giant, refers to his bed, as an *ancient relick*, and says, is it not in Rabbath (or Rabbah) of the children of Ammon? meaning that it is; for such is frequently the bible method of affirming a thing. But it could not be Moses that said this, because Moses could know nothing about Rabbah, nor of what was in it. Rabbah was not a city belonging to this giant king, nor was it one of the cities that Moses took. The knowledge therefore that this bed was at Rabbah, and of the particulars of its dimensions, must be referred to the time when Rabbah was taken, and this was not till four hundred years after the death of Moses; for which, see 2 Sam. xii. 26: "And Joab [David's general] fought against *Rabbah of the children of Ammon*, and took the royal city," etc.

As I am not undertaking to point out all the contradictions in time, place, and circumstance that abound in the books ascribed to Moses, and which prove to demonstration that those books could not be written by Moses, nor in the time of Moses, I proceed to the book of Joshua, and to shew that Joshua is not the author of that book, and that it is anonymous and without authority. The evidence I shall produce is contained in the book itself: I will not go out of the Bible for proof against the supposed authenticity of the Bible. False testimony is always good against itself.

Joshua, according to Joshua i., was the immediate successor of Moses; he was, moreover, a military man, which Moses was not; and he continued as chief of the people of Israel twenty-five years; that is, from the time that Moses died, which, according to the Bible chronology, was B.C. 1451, until B.C. 1426, when, according to the same chronology, Joshua died. If, therefore, we find in this book, said to have been written by Joshua, references to *facts done* after the death of Joshua, it is evidence that Joshua could not be the author; and also that the book could not have been written till after the time of the latest fact which it records. As to the character of the book, it is horrid; it is a military history of rapine and murder, as savage and brutal as those recorded of his predecessor in villainy and hypocrisy, Moses; and the blasphemy consists, as in the former books, in ascribing those deeds to the orders of the Almighty.

In the first place, the book of Joshua, as is the case in the preceding books, is written in the third person; it is the historian of Joshua that speaks, for it would have been absurd and vainglorious that Joshua should say of himself, as is said of him in the last verse of the sixth chapter, that "*his fame was noised throughout all the country.*"—I now come more immediately to the proof.

In Joshua xxiv. 31, it is said "And Israel served the Lord all the days of Joshua, and *all the days of the elders that over-lived Joshua.*" Now, in the name of common sense, can it be Joshua that relates what people had done after he was dead? This account must not only have been written by some historian that lived after Joshua, but that lived also after the elders that out-lived Joshua.

There are several passages of a general meaning with respect to time, scattered throughout the book of Joshua, that carries the time in which the book was written to a distance from the time of Joshua, but without marking by exclusion any particular time, as in the passage above quoted. In that passage, the time that intervened between the death of Joshua and the death of the elders is excluded descriptively and absolutely, and the evidence substantiates that the book could not have been written till after the death of the last.

But though the passages to which I allude, and which I am going to quote, do not designate any particular time by exclusion, they imply a time far more distant from the days of Joshua than is contained between the death of Joshua and the death of the elders. Such is the passage, x. 14, where, after giving an account that the sun stood still upon Gibeon, and the moon in the valley of Ajalon, at the command of Joshua, (a tale only fit to amuse children*) the passage says: "And there was no day like that, before it, nor *after it*, that the Lord hearkened to the voice of a man."

The time implied by the expression *after it*, that is, after that day, being put in comparison with all the time that passed *before it*, must, in order to give any expressive signification to the passage, mean a *great length of time :*—for example, it would have been ridiculous to have said so the next day, or the next week, or the next month, or the next year; to give therefore meaning to the passage, comparative with the wonder it relates, and the prior time it alludes to,

---

* This tale of the sun standing still upon Mount Gibeon, and the moon in the valley of Ajalon, is one of those fables that detects itself. Such a circumstance could not have happened without being known all over the world. One half would have wondered why the sun did not rise, and the other why it did not set; and the tradition of it would be universal; whereas there is not a nation in the world that knows any thing about it. But why must the moon stand still? What occasion could there be for moonlight in the daytime, and that too whilst the sun shined? As a poetical figure, the whole is well enough; it is akin to that in the song of Deborah and Barak, *The stars in their courses fought against Sisera;* but it is inferior to the figurative declaration of Mahomet to the persons who came to expostulate with him on his goings on, *Wert thou*, said he, *to come to me with the sun in thy right hand and the moon in thy left, it should not alter my career.* For Joshua to have exceeded Mahomet, he should have put the sun and moon, one in each pocket, and carried them as Guy Faux carried his dark lanthorn, and taken them out to shine as he might happen to want them. The sublime and the ridiculous are often so nearly related that it is difficult to class them separately. One step above the sublime makes the ridiculous, and one step above the ridiculous makes the sublime again; the account, however, abstracted from the poetical fancy, shews the ignorance of Joshua, for he should have commanded the earth to have stood still.—*Author.*

it must mean centuries of years; less however than one would be trifling, and less than two would be barely admissible.

A distant, but general time is also expressed in chapter viii.; where, after giving an account of the taking the city of Ai, it is said, ver. 28th, "And Joshua burned Ai, and made it an heap for ever, a desolation *unto this day;*" and again, ver. 29, where speaking of the king of Ai, whom Joshua had hanged, and buried at the entering of the gate, it is said, "And he raised thereon a great heap of stones, which remaineth *unto this day*," that is, unto the day or time in which the writer of the book of Joshua lived. And again, in chapter x. where, after speaking of the five kings whom Joshua had hanged on five trees, and then thrown in a cave, it is said, "And he laid great stones on the cave's mouth, which remain unto this very day."

In enumerating the several exploits of Joshua, and of the tribes, and of the places which they conquered or attempted, it is said, xv. 63, "As for the Jebusites, the inhabitants of Jerusalem, the children of Judah could not drive them out; but the Jebusites dwell with the children of Judah AT JERU-SALEM *unto this day.*" The question upon this passage is, At what time did the Jebusites and the children of Judah dwell together at Jerusalem? As this matter occurs again in Judges i. I shall reserve my observations till I come to that part.

Having thus shewn from the book of Joshua itself, without any auxiliary evidence whatever, that Joshua is not the author of that book, and that it is anonymous, and consequently without authority, I proceed, as before-mentioned, to the book of Judges.

The book of Judges is anonymous on the face of it; and, therefore, even the pretence is wanting to call it the word of God; it has not so much as a nominal voucher; it is altogether fatherless.

This book begins with the same expression as the book of Joshua. That of Joshua begins, chap i. 1, *Now after the death of Moses*, etc., and this of the Judges begins, *Now after*

the death of Joshua, etc. This, and the similarity of stile between the two books, indicate that they are the work of the
same author ; but who he was, is altogether unknown ; the
only point that the book proves is that the author lived long
after the time of Joshua ; for though it begins as if it followed immediately after his death, the second chapter is an
epitome or abstract of the whole book, which, according to
the Bible chronology, extends its history through a space
of 306 years ; that is, from the death of Joshua, B.C. 1426
to the death of Samson, B.C. 1120, and only 25 years before
Saul went *to seek his father's asses, and was made king.* But
there is good reason to believe, that it was not written till
the time of David, at least, and that the book of Joshua was
not written before the same time.

In Judges i., the writer, after announcing the death of
Joshua, proceeds to tell what happened between the children
of Judah and the native inhabitants of the land of Canaan.
In this statement the writer, having abruptly mentioned
Jerusalem in the 7th verse, says immediately after, in the
8th verse, by way of explanation, " Now the children of
Judah *had* fought against Jerusalem, and *taken* it ;" consequently this book could not have been written before Jerusalem had been taken. The reader will recollect the quotation I have just before made from Joshua xv. 63, where it
said that *the Jebusites dwell with the children of Judah at
Jerusalem at this day ;* meaning the time when the book of
Joshua was written.

The evidence I have already produced to prove that the
books I have hitherto treated of were not written by the
persons to whom they are ascribed, nor till many years after
their death, if such persons ever lived, is already so abundant, that I can afford to admit this passage with less weight
than I am entitled to draw from it. For the case is, that
so far as the Bible can be credited as an history, the city of
Jerusalem was not taken till the time of David ; and consequently, that the book of Joshua, and of Judges, were not
written till after the commencement of the reign of David,
which was 370 years after the death of Joshua.

The name of the city that was afterward called Jerusalem was originally Jebus, or Jebusi, and was the capital of the Jebusites. The account of David's taking this city is given in 2 Samuel, v. 4, etc.; also in 1 Chron. xiv. 4, etc. There is no mention in any part of the Bible that it was ever taken before, nor any account that favours such an opinion. It is not said, either in Samuel or in Chronicles, that they "utterly destroyed men, women and children, that they left not a soul to breathe," as is said of their other conquests; and the silence here observed implies that it was taken by capitulation; and that the Jebusites, the native inhabitants, continued to live in the place after it was taken. The account therefore, given in Joshua, that "the Jebusites dwell with the children of Judah" at Jerusalem at this day, corresponds to no other time than after taking the city by David.

Having now shown that every book in the Bible, from Genesis to Judges, is without authenticity, I come to the book of Ruth, an idle, bungling story, foolishly told, nobody knows by whom, about a strolling country-girl creeping slily to bed to her cousin Boaz.[1] Pretty stuff indeed to be called the word of God. It is, however, one of the best books in the Bible, for it is free from murder and rapine.

I come next to the two books of Samuel, and to shew that those books were not written by Samuel, nor till a great length of time after the death of Samuel; and that they are, like all the former books, anonymous, and without authority.

To be convinced that these books have been written much later than the time of Samuel, and consequently not by him, it is only necessary to read the account which the writer gives of Saul going to seek his father's asses, and of his interview with Samuel, of whom Saul went to enquire about those lost asses, as foolish people now-a-days go to a conjuror to enquire after lost things.

The writer, in relating this story of Saul, Samuel, and the asses, does not tell it as a thing that had just then happened, but as *an ancient story in the time this writer lived ;* for he tells

---

[1] The text of Ruth does not imply the unpleasant sense Paine's words are likely to convey.—*Editor.*

it in the language or terms used at the time that *Samuel* lived, which obliges the writer to explain the story in the terms or language used in the time the *writer* lived.

Samuel, in the account given of him in the first of those books, chap. ix. is called *the seer;* and it is by this term that Saul enquires after him, ver. 11, "And as they [Saul and his servant] went up the hill to the city, they found young maidens going out to draw water; and they said unto them, *Is the seer here?*" Saul then went according to the direction of these maidens, and met Samuel without knowing him, and said unto him, ver. 18, "Tell me, I pray thee, where the *seer's house is?* and Samuel answered Saul, and said, *I am the seer.*"

As the writer of the book of Samuel relates these questions and answers, in the language or manner of speaking used in the time they are said to have been spoken, and as that manner of speaking was out of use when this author wrote, he found it necessary, in order to make the story understood, to explain the terms in which these questions and answers are spoken; and he does this in the 9th verse, where he says, "*Before-time* in Israel, when a man went to enquire of God, thus he spake, Come let us go to the seer; for he that is now called a prophet, was *before-time* called a seer." This proves, as I have before said, that this story of Saul, Samuel, and the asses, was an ancient story at the time the book of Samuel was written, and consequently that Samuel did not write it, and that the book is without authenticity.

But if we go further into those books the evidence is still more positive that Samuel is not the writer of them; for they relate things that did not happen till several years after the death of Samuel. Samuel died before Saul; for 1 Samuel, xxviii. tells, that Saul and the witch of Endor conjured Samuel up after he was dead; yet the history of matters contained in those books is extended through the remaining part of Saul's life, and to the latter end of the life of David, who succeeded Saul. The account of the death and burial of Samuel (a thing which he could not write himself) is related in 1 Samuel xxv.; and the chronology affixed to this chapter makes this to be B.C. 1060; yet the history of this *first* book is brought down to B.C. 1056, that is, to the death of Saul, which was not till four years after the death of Samuel.

The second book of Samuel begins with an account of things that did not happen till four years after Samuel was dead; for it begins with the reign of David, who succeeded Saul, and it goes on to the end of David's reign, which was forty-three years after the death of Samuel; and, therefore, the books are in themselves positive evidence that they were not written by Samuel.

I have now gone through all the books in the first part of the Bible, to which the names of persons are affixed, as being the authors of those books, and which the church, stiling itself the Christian church, have imposed upon the world as the writings of Moses, Joshua and Samuel; and I have detected and proved the falsehood of this imposition.—And now ye priests, of every description, who have preached and written against the former part of the *Age of Reason,* what have ye to say? Will ye with all this mass of evidence against you, and staring you in the face, still have the assurance to march into your pulpits, and continue to impose these books on your congregations, as the works of *inspired penmen,* and the word of God? when it is as evident as demonstration can make truth appear, that the persons who ye say are the authors, are *not* the authors, and that ye know not who the authors are. What shadow of pretence have ye now to produce for continuing the blasphemous fraud? What have ye still to offer against the pure and moral religion of deism, in support of your system of falsehood, idolatry, and pretended revelation? Had the cruel and murdering orders, with which the Bible is filled, and the numberless torturing executions of men, women, and children, in consequence of those orders, been ascribed to some friend, whose memory you revered, you would have glowed with satisfaction at detecting the falsehood of the charge, and gloried in defending his injured fame. It is because ye are sunk in the cruelty of superstition, or feel no

interest in the honour of your Creator, that ye listen to the
horrid tales of the Bible, or hear them with callous indifference. The evidence I have produced, and shall still produce
in the course of this work, to prove that the Bible is without
authority, will, whilst it wounds the stubbornness of a priest,
relieve and tranquillize the minds of millions: it will free
them from all those hard thoughts of the Almighty which
priestcraft and the Bible had infused into their minds, and
which stood in everlasting opposition to all their ideas of
his moral justice and benevolence.

I come now to the two books of Kings, and the two
books of Chronicles.—Those books are altogether historical,
and are chiefly confined to the lives and actions of the
Jewish kings, who in general were a parcel of rascals: but
these are matters with which we have no more concern than
we have with the Roman emperors, or Homer's account of
the Trojan war. Besides which, as those books are anonymous, and as we know nothing of the writer, or of his character, it is impossible for us to know what degree of credit
to give to the matters related therein. Like all other ancient
histories, they appear to be a jumble of fable and of fact,
and of probable and of improbable things, but which distance
of time and place, and change of circumstances in the world,
have rendered obsolete and uninteresting.

The chief use I shall make of those books will be that of
comparing them with each other, and with other parts of the
Bible, to shew the confusion, contradiction, and cruelty in
this pretended word of God.

The first book of Kings begins with the reign of Solomon,
which, according to the Bible chronology, was B.C. 1015;
and the second book ends B.C. 588, being a little after the
reign of Zedekiah, whom Nebuchadnezzar, after taking
Jerusalem and conquering the Jews, carried captive to Babylon. The two books include a space of 427 years.

The two books of Chronicles are an history of the same
times, and in general of the same persons, by another
author; for it would be absurd to suppose that the same
author wrote the history twice over. The first book of

Chronicles (after giving the genealogy from Adam to Saul, which takes up the first nine chapters) begins with the reign of David; and the last book ends, as in the last book of Kings, soon after the reign of Zedekiah, about B.C. 588. The last two verses of the last chapter bring the history 52 years more forward, that is, to 536. But these verses do not belong to the book, as I shall shew when I come to speak of the book of Ezra.

The two books of Kings, besides the history of Saul, David, and Solomon, who reigned over *all* Israel, contain an abstract of the lives of seventeen kings and one queen, who are stiled kings of Judah; and of nineteen, who are stiled kings of Israel; for the Jewish nation, immediately on the death of Solomon, split into two parties, who chose separate kings, and who carried on most rancorous wars against each other.

These two books are little more than a history of assassinations, treachery, and wars. The cruelties that the Jews had accustomed themselves to practise on the Canaanites, whose country they had savagely invaded, under a pretended gift from God, they afterwards practised as furiously on each other. Scarcely half their kings died a natural death, and in some instances whole families were destroyed to secure possession to the successor, who, after a few years, and sometimes only a few months, or less, shared the same fate. In 2 Kings x., an account is given of two baskets full of children's heads, seventy in number, being exposed at the entrance of the city; they were the children of Ahab, and were murdered by the orders of Jehu, whom Elisha, the pretended man of God, had anointed to be king over Israel, on purpose to commit this bloody deed, and assassinate his predecessor. And in the account of the reign of Menahem, one of the kings of Israel who had murdered Shallum, who had reigned but one month, it is said, 2 Kings xv. 16, that Menahem smote the city of Tiphsah, because they opened not the city to him, *and all the women therein that were with child he ripped up.*

Could we permit ourselves to suppose that the Almighty

would distinguish any nation of people by the name of *his chosen people*, we must suppose that people to have been an example to all the rest of the world of the purest piety and humanity, and not such a nation of ruffians and cut-throats as the ancient Jews were,—a people who, corrupted by and copying after such monsters and imposters as Moses and Aaron, Joshua, Samuel, and David, had distinguished themselves above all others on the face of the known earth for barbarity and wickedness. If we will not stubbornly shut our eyes and steel our hearts it is impossible not to see, in spite of all that long-established superstition imposes upon the mind, that the flattering appellation of *his chosen people* is no other than a LIE which the priests and leaders of the Jews had invented to cover the baseness of their own characters ; and which Christian priests sometimes as corrupt, and often as cruel, have professed to believe.

The two books of Chronicles are a repetition of the same crimes; but the history is broken in several places, by the author leaving out the reign of some of their kings ; and in this, as well as in that of Kings, there is such a frequent transition from kings of Judah to kings of Israel, and from kings of Israel to kings of Judah, that the narrative is obscure in the reading. In the same book the history sometimes contradicts itself : for example, in 2 Kings, i. 17, we are told, but in rather ambiguous terms, that after the death of Ahaziah, king of Israel, Jehoram, or Joram, (who was of the house of Ahab, reigned in his stead in the *second year of* Jehoram, or Joram, son of Jehoshaphat, king of Judah ; and in viii. 16, of the same book, it is said, " And in the *fifth year* of Joram, the son of Ahab, king of Israel, Jehoshaphat being then king of Judah, Jehoram, the son of Jehoshaphat king of Judah, began to reign." That is, one chapter says Joram of Judah began to reign in the *second year* of Joram of Israel ; and the other chapter says, that Joram of Israel began to reign in the *fifth year* of Joram of Judah.

Several of the most extraordinary matters related in one history, as having happened during the reign of such or such of their kings, are not to be found in the other, in relating the reign of the same king: for example, the two first rival kings, after the death of Solomon, were Rehoboam and Jeroboam ; and in 1 Kings xii. and xiii. an account is given of Jeroboam making an offering of burnt incense, and that a man, who is there called a man of God, cried out against the altar (xiii. 2): "O altar, altar! thus saith the Lord: Behold, a child shall be born unto the house of David, Josiah by name, and upon thee shall he offer the priests of the high places that burn incense upon thee, and men's bones shall be burned upon thee." Verse 4: "And it came to pass, when king Jeroboam heard the saying of the man of God, which had cried against the altar in Bethel, that he put forth his hand from the altar, saying, *Lay hold on him;* and his hand which he put out against him *dried up, so that he could not pull it again to him.*"

One would think that such an extraordinary case as this, (which is spoken of as a judgement,) happening to the chief of one of the parties, and that at the first moment of the separation of the Israelites into two nations, would, if it had been true, have been recorded in both histories. But though men, in later times, have believed *all that the prophets have said unto them,* it does not appear that those prophets, or historians, believed each other: they knew each other too well.

A long account also is given in Kings about Elijah. It runs through several chapters, and concludes with telling, 2 Kings ii. 11, "And it came to pass, as they (Elijah and Elisha) still went on, and talked, that, behold, there appeared *a chariot of fire and horses of fire,* and parted them both asunder, and Elijah *went up by a whirlwind into heaven.*" Hum! this the author of Chronicles, miraculous as the story is, makes no mention of, though he mentions Elijah by name ; neither does he say anything of the story related in the second chapter of the same book of Kings, of a parcel of children calling Elisha *bald head;* and that this *man of God* (ver. 24) "turned back, and looked upon them, *and cursed them in the name of the Lord;* and there came forth two she-bears out of the wood, and tare forty and two children of them." He also passes over in silence the story told, 2 Kings xiii., that when they were burying a man in the sepulchre where Elisha had been buried, it happened that the dead man, as they were letting him down, (ver. 21) "touched the bones of Elisha, and he (the dead man) *revived, and stood up on his feet.*" The story does not tell us whether they buried the man, notwithstanding he revived and stood upon his feet, or drew him up again. Upon all these stories the writer of the Chronicles is as silent as any writer of the present day, who did not chuse to be accused of *lying*, or at least of romancing, would be about stories of the same kind.

But, however these two historians may differ from each other with respect to the tales related by either, they are silent alike with respect to those men stiled prophets whose writings fill up the latter part of the Bible. Isaiah, who lived in the time of Hezekiah, is mentioned in Kings, and again in Chronicles, when these histories are speaking of that reign; but except in one or two instances at most, and those very slightly, none of the rest are so much as spoken of, or even their existence hinted at; though, according to the Bible chronology, they lived within the time those histories were written; and some of them long before. If those prophets, as they are called, were men of such importance in their day, as the compilers of the Bible, and priests and commentators have since represented them to be, how can it be accounted for that not one of those histories should say anything about them?

The history in the books of Kings and of Chronicles is brought forward, as I have already said, to the year B.C. 588; it will, therefore, be proper to examine which of these prophets lived before that period.

Here follows a table of all the prophets, with the times in which they lived before Christ, according to the chronology affixed to the first chapter of each of the books of the prophets; and also of the number of years they lived before the books of Kings and Chronicles were written:

TABLE of the Prophets, with the time in which they lived
before Christ, and also before the books of Kings and
Chronicles were written:

NAMES.	Years before Christ.	Years before Kings and Chronicles.	Observations.
Isaiah	760	172	mentioned.
Jeremiah	629	41	{ mentioned only in the last [two] chapters of Chronicles.
Ezekiel	595	7	not mentioned.
Daniel	607	19	not mentioned.
Hosea	785	97	not mentioned.
Joel	800	212	not mentioned.
Amos	789	199	not mentioned.
Obadiah	789	199	not mentioned.
Jonah	862	274	see the note.*
Micah	750	162	not mentioned.
Nahum	713	125	not mentioned.
Habakkuk	620	38	not mentioned.
Zephaniah	630	42	not mentioned.
Haggai } Zechariah } after the year 588 Malachi }			

This table is either not very honourable for the Bible
historians, or not very honourable for the Bible prophets;
and I leave to priests and commentators, who are very
learned in little things, to settle the point of *etiquette* between the two; and to assign a reason, why the authors
of Kings and of Chronicles have treated those prophets,
whom, in the former part of the *Age of Reason*, I have
considered as poets, with as much degrading silence as
any historian of the present day would treat Peter Pindar.

I have one more observation to make on the book of
Chronicles; after which I shall pass on to review the
remaining books of the Bible.

In my observations on the book of Genesis, I have quoted
a passage from xxxvi. 31, which evidently refers to a time,
after that kings began to reign over the children of Israel;
and I have shewn that as this verse is verbatim the same as

---

* In 2 Kings xiv. 25, the name of Jonah is mentioned on account of the
restoration of a tract of land by Jeroboam; but nothing further is said of him,
nor is any allusion made to the book of Jonah, nor to his expedition to Nineveh,
nor to his encounter with the whale.—*Author.*

in 1 Chronicles i. 43, where it stands consistently with the order of history, which in Genesis it does not, that the verse in Genesis, and a great part of the 36th chapter, have been taken from Chronicles ; and that the book of Genesis, though it is placed first in the Bible, and ascribed to Moses, has been manufactured by some unknown person, after the book of Chronicles was written, which was not until at least eight hundred and sixty years after the time of Moses.

The evidence I proceed by to substantiate this, is regular, and has in it but two stages. First, as I have already stated, that the passage in Genesis refers itself for *time* to Chronicles; secondly, that the book of Chronicles, to which this passage refers itself, was not *begun* to be written until at least eight hundred and sixty years after the time of Moses. To prove this, we have only to look into 1 Chronicles iii. 15, where the writer, in giving the genealogy of the descendants of David, mentions *Zedekiah;* and it was in the time of *Zedekiah* that Nebuchadnezzar conquered Jerusalem, B.C. 588, and consequently more than 860 years after Moses. Those who have superstitiously boasted of the antiquity of the Bible, and particularly of the books ascribed to Moses, have done it without examination, and without any other authority than that of one credulous man telling it to another : for, so far as historical and chronological evidence applies, the very first book in the Bible is not so ancient as the book of Homer, by more than three hundred years, and is about the same age with Æsop's Fables.

I am not contending for the morality of Homer; on the contrary, I think it a book of false glory, and tending to inspire immoral and mischievous notions of honour ; and with respect to Æsop, though the moral is in general just, the fable is often cruel ; and the cruelty of the fable does more injury to the heart, especially in a child, than the moral does good to the judgment.

Having now dismissed Kings and Chronicles, I come to the next in course, the book of Ezra.

As one proof, among others I shall produce to shew the disorder in which this pretended word of God, the Bible, has been put together, and the uncertainty of who the authors were, we have only to look at the first three verses in Ezra, and the last two in 2 Chronicles ; for by what kind of cutting and shuffling has it been that the first three verses in Ezra should be the last two verses in 2 Chronicles, or that the last two in 2 Chronicles should be the first three in Ezra? Either the authors did not know their own works or the compilers did not know the authors.

Last Two Verses of 2 Chronicles.

Ver. 22. Now in the first year of Cyrus, King of Persia, that the word of the Lord, spoken by the mouth of Jeremiah, might be accomplished, the Lord stirred up the spirit of Cyrus, king of Persia, that he made a proclamation throughout all his kingdom, and put it also in writing, saying,

23. Thus saith Cyrus, king of Persia, all the kingdoms of the earth hath the Lord God of heaven given me ; and he hath charged me to build him an house in Jerusalem which is in Judah. Who is there among you of all his people? the Lord his God be with him, and let him go up.*⁎*

First Three Verses of Ezra.

Ver. 1. Now in the first year of Cyrus, king of Persia, that the word of the Lord, by the mouth of Jeremiah, might be fulfilled, the Lord stirred up the spirit of Cyrus, king of Persia, that he made a proclamation throughout all his kingdom, and put it also in writing, saying,

2. Thus saith Cyrus, king of Persia, The Lord God of heaven hath given me all the kingdoms of the earth ; and he hath charged me to build him an house at Jerusalem, which is in Judah.

3. Who is there among you of all his people? his God be with him, and let him go up *to Jerusalem, which is in Judah, and build the house of the Lord God of Israel (he is the God) which is in Jerusalem.*

*⁎*The last verse in Chronicles is broken abruptly, and ends in the middle of the phrase with the word *up*, without signifying to what place. This abrupt break, and the appearance of the same verses in different books, shew as I have already said, the disorder and ignorance in which the Bible has been put together, and that the compilers of it had no

authority for what they were doing, nor we any authority for believing what they have done.*

The only thing that has any appearance of certainty in the book of Ezra is the time in which it was written, which was immediately after the return of the Jews from the Babylonian captivity, about B.C. 536. Ezra (who, according to the Jewish commentators, is the same person as is called Esdras in the Apocrypha) was one of the persons who returned, and who, it is probable, wrote the account of that affair. Nehemiah, whose book follows next to Ezra, was

---

*I observed, as I passed along, several broken and senseless passages in the Bible, without thinking them of consequence enough to be introduced in the body of the work ; such as that, 1 Samuel xiii. 1, where it is said, "Saul reigned one year ; and when he had reigned two years over Israel, Saul chose him three thousand men," &c. The first part of the verse, that Saul reigned *one year* has no sense, since it does not tell us what Saul did, nor say any thing of what happened at the end of that one year ; and it is, besides, mere absurdity to say he reigned *one year*, when the very next phrase says he had reigned two ; for if he had reigned two, it was impossible not to have reigned one.

Another instance occurs in Joshua v. where the writer tells us a story of an angel (for such the table of contents at the head of the chapter calls him) appearing unto Joshua ; and the story ends abruptly, and without any conclusion. The story is as follows :—Ver. 13. "And it came to pass, when Joshua was by Jericho, that he lifted up his eyes and looked, and behold there stood a man over against him with his sword drawn in his hand ; and Joshua went unto him and said unto him, Art thou for us, or for our adversaries ?" Verse 14, "And he said, Nay ; but as captain of the host of the Lord am I now come. And Joshua fell on his face to the earth, and did worship and said unto him, What saith my Lord unto his servant ?" Verse 15, "And the captain of the Lord's host said unto Joshua, Loose thy shoe from off thy foot ; for the place whereon thou standeth is holy. And Joshua did so."—And what then ? nothing : for here the story ends, and the chapter too.

Either this story is broken off in the middle, or it is a story told by some Jewish humourist in ridicule of Joshua's pretended mission from God, and the compilers of the Bible, not perceiving the design of the story, have told it as a serious matter. As a story of humour and ridicule it has a great deal of point ; for it pompously introduces an angel in the figure of a man, with a drawn sword in his hand, before whom Joshua falls on his face to the earth, and worships (which is contrary to their second commandment ;) and then, this most important embassy from heaven ends in telling Joshua to *pull off his shoe.* It might as well have told him to pull up his breeches.

It is certain, however, that the Jews did not credit every thing their leaders told them, as appears from the cavalier manner in which they speak of Moses, when he was gone into the mount. As for *this* Moses, say they. *we wot not what is become of him.* Exod. xxxii. 1.—*Author.*

another of the returned persons; and who, it is also probable, wrote the account of the same affair, in the book that bears his name. But those accounts are nothing to us, nor to any other person, unless it be to the Jews, as a part of the history of their nation; and there is just as much of the word of God in those books as there is in any of the histories of France, or Rapin's history of England, or the history of any other country.

But even in matters of historical record, neither of those writers are to be depended upon. In Ezra ii., the writer gives a list of the tribes and families, and of the precise number of souls of each, that returned from Babylon to Jerusalem; and this enrolment of the persons so returned appears to have been one of the principal objects for writing the book; but in this there is an error that destroys the intention of the undertaking.

The writer begins his enrolment in the following manner (ii. 3): "The children of Parosh, two thousand one hundred seventy and four." Ver. 4, "The children of Shephatiah, three hundred seventy and two." And in this manner he proceeds through all the families; and in the 64th verse, he makes a total, and says, the whole congregation together was *forty and two thousand three hundred and threescore.*

But whoever will take the trouble of casting up the several particulars, will find that the total is but 29,818; so that the error is 12,542.* What certainty then can there be in the Bible for any thing?

* Particulars of the Families from Ezra ii.

Verse			Bro't forw. 11577		Bro't forw. 15783		Bro't forw. 19444
	3	2172	Ver. 13 666	Ver. 23 128	Ver. 33 725
	4	372	14 2056	24 42	34 345
	5	775	15 454	25 743	35 3630
	6	2812	16 98	26 621	36 973
	7	1254	17 323	27 122	37 1052
	8	945	18 112	28 223	38 1247
	9	760	19 223	29 52	39 1017
	10	642	20 95	30 156	40 74
	11	623	21 123	31 1254	41 128
	12	1222	22 56	32 320	42 139
					58 392
					60 652
		11,577	15,783	19,444	Total, 29,818

—*Author.*

Nehemiah, in like manner, gives a list of the returned families, and of the number of each family. He begins as in Ezra, by saying (vii. 8): "The children of Parosh, two thousand three hundred and seventy-two;" and so on through all the families. (The list differs in several of the particulars from that of Ezra.) In ver. 66, Nehemiah makes a total, and says, as Ezra had said, "The whole congregation together was forty and two thousand three hundred and threescore." But the particulars of this list make a total but of 31,089, so that the error here is 11,271. These writers may do well enough for Bible-makers, but not for any thing where truth and exactness is necessary.

The next book in course is the book of Esther. If Madam Esther thought it any honour to offer herself as a kept mistress to Ahasuerus, or as a rival to Queen Vashti, who had refused to come to a drunken king in the midst of a drunken company, to be made a shew of, (for the account says, they had been drinking seven days, and were merry,) let Esther and Mordecai look to that, it is no business of ours, at least it is none of mine; besides which, the story has a great deal the appearance of being fabulous, and is also anonymous. I pass on to the book of Job.

The book of Job differs in character from all the books we have hitherto passed over. Treachery and murder make no part of this book; it is the meditations of a mind strongly impressed with the vicissitudes of human life, and by turns sinking under, and struggling against the pressure. It is a highly wrought composition, between willing submission and involuntary discontent; and shews man, as he sometimes is, more disposed to be resigned than he is capable of being. Patience has but a small share in the character of the person of whom the book treats; on the contrary, his grief is often impetuous; but he still endeavours to keep a guard upon it, and seems determined, in the midst of accumulating ills, to impose upon himself the hard duty of contentment.

I have spoken in a respectful manner of the book of Job in the former part of the *Age of Reason,* but without knowing at that time what I have learned since; which is, that

from all the evidence that can be collected, the book of Job
does not belong to the Bible.

I have seen the opinion of two Hebrew commentators,
Abenezra and Spinoza, upon this subject; they both say
that the book of Job carries no internal evidence of being
an Hebrew book; that the genius of the composition, and
the drama of the piece, are not Hebrew; that it has been
translated from another language into Hebrew, and that
the author of the book was a Gentile; that the character
represented under the name of Satan (which is the first and
only time this name is mentioned in the Bible)[1] does not
correspond to any Hebrew idea; and that the two convoca-
tions which the Deity is supposed to have made of those
whom the poem calls sons of God, and the familiarity which
this supposed Satan is stated to have with the Deity, are in
the same case.

It may also be observed, that the book shews itself to be
the production of a mind cultivated in science, which the
Jews, so far from being famous for, were very ignorant of.
The allusions to objects of natural philosophy are frequent
and strong, and are of a different cast to any thing in the
books known to be Hebrew. The astronomical names,
Pleïades, Orion, and Arcturus, are Greek and not Hebrew
names, and it does not appear from any thing that is to be
found in the Bible that the Jews knew any thing of astronomy, or that they studied it, they had no translation of those
names into their own language, but adopted the names as
they found them in the poem.[2]

---

[1] In a later work Paine notes that in "the Bible" (by which he always means
the Old Testament alone) the word Satan occurs also in 1 Chron. xxi. 1, and re-
marks that the action there ascribed to Satan is in 2 Sam. xxiv. 1, attributed to
Jehovah ("Essay on Dreams"). In these places, however, and in Ps. cix. 6,
Satan means "adversary," and is so translated (A. S. version) in 2 Sam. xix.
22, and 1 Kings v. 4, xi. 25. As a proper name, with the article, Satan (שָׂטָן)
appears in the Old Testament only in Job and in Zech. iii. 1, 2. But the
authenticity of the passage in Zechariah has been questioned, and it may be
that in finding the proper name of Satan in Job alone, Paine was following
some opinion met with in one of the authorities whose comments are condensed
in his paragraph.—*Editor.*

[2] Paine's Jewish critic, David Levi, fastened on this slip ("Defence of the

That the Jews did translate the literary productions of
the Gentile nations into the Hebrew language, and mix
them with their own, is not a matter of doubt; Proverbs
xxxi. 1, is an evidence of this: it is there said, *The word of
king Lemuel, the prophecy which his mother taught him.*
This verse stands as a preface to the proverbs that follow,
and which are not the proverbs of Solomon, but of Lemuel;
and this Lemuel was not one of the kings of Israel, nor of
Judah, but of some other country, and consequently a Gentile. The Jews however have adopted his proverbs; and as
they cannot give any account who the author of the book
of Job was, nor how they came by the book, and as it differs
in character from the Hebrew writings, and stands totally
unconnected with every other book and chapter in the Bible
before it and after it, it has all the circumstantial evidence
of being originally a book of the Gentiles.*

The Bible-makers, and those regulators of time, the Bible
chronologists, appear to have been at a loss where to place
and how to dispose of the book of Job; for it contains no
one historical circumstance, nor allusion to any, that might

Old Testament," 1797, p. 152). In the original the names are *Ash* (Arcturus),
Kesil' (Orion), *Kimah'* (Pleiades), though the identifications of the constellations
in the A. S. V. have been questioned.—*Editor.*

* The prayer known by the name of *Agur's Prayer*, in Proverbs xxx.,—immediately preceding the proverbs of Lemuel,—and which is the only sensible,
well-conceived, and well-expressed prayer in the Bible, has much the appearance of being a prayer taken from the Gentiles. The name of Agur occurs on no
other occasion than this ; and he is introduced, together with the prayer ascribed
to him, in the same manner, and nearly in the same words, that Lemuel and
his proverbs are introduced in the chapter that follows. The first verse says,
" The words of Agur, the son of Jakeh, even the prophecy : " here the word
prophecy is used with the same application it has in the following chapter of
Lemuel, unconnected with anything of prediction. The prayer of Agur is in
the 8th and 9th verses, " Remove far from me vanity and lies ; give me neither
riches nor poverty, but feed me with food convenient for me ; lest 1 be full and
deny thee and say, Who is the Lord ? or lest I be poor and steal, and take the
name of my God in vain." This has not any of the marks of being a Jewish
prayer, for the Jews never prayed but when they were in trouble, and never for
anything but victory, vengeance, or riches.—*Author.* [Prov. xxx.1, and xxxi.
1, the word "prophecy" in these verses is translated "oracle" or "burden"
(marg.) in the revised version.—The prayer of Agur was quoted by Paine in his
plea for the officers of Excise, 1772.—*Editor.*]

serve to determine its place in the Bible.　But it would not
have answered the purpose of these men to have informed
the world of their ignorance; and, therefore, they have
affixed it to the æra of B.C. 1520, which is during the time
the Israelites were in Egypt, and for which they have just
as much authority and no more than I should have for saying it was a thousand years before that period.　The probability however is, that it is older than any book in the Bible;
and it is the only one that can be read without indignation
or disgust.

We know nothing of what the ancient Gentile world (as
it is called) was before the time of the Jews, whose practice
has been to calumniate and blacken the character of all
other nations; and it is from the Jewish accounts that we
have learned to call them heathens.　But, as far as we know
to the contrary, they were a just and moral people, and not
addicted, like the Jews, to cruelty and revenge, but of whose
profession of faith we are unacquainted.　It appears to have
been their custom to personify both virtue and vice by
statues and images, as is done now-a-days both by statuary
and by painting; but it does not follow from this that they
worshipped them any more than we do.—I pass on to the
book of

Psalms, of which it is not necessary to make much observation.　Some of them are moral, and others are very
revengeful; and the greater part relates to certain local
circumstances of the Jewish nation at the time they were
written, with which we have nothing to do.　It is, however,
an error or an imposition to call them the Psalms of David;
they are a collection, as song-books are now-a-days, from
different song-writers, who lived at different times.　The
137th Psalm could not have been written till more than
400 years after the time of David, because it is written
in commemoration of an event, the capitivity of the Jews
in Babylon, which did not happen till that distance of time.
"*By the rivers of Babylon we sat down; yea, we wept when
we remembered Zion.　We hanged our harps upon the willows,
in the midst thereof; for there they that carried us away*

captive required of us a song, saying, sing us one of the songs of Zion." As a man would say to an American, or to a Frenchman, or to an Englishman, sing us one of your American songs, or your French songs, or your English songs. This remark, with respect to the time this psalm was written, is of no other use than to shew (among others already mentioned) the general imposition the world has been under with respect to the authors of the Bible. No regard has been paid to time, place, and circumstance; and the names of persons have been affixed to the several books which it was as impossible they should write, as that a man should walk in procession at his own funeral.

The Book of Proverbs. These, like the Psalms, are a collection, and that from authors belonging to other nations than those of the Jewish nation, as I have shewn in the observations upon the book of Job; besides which, some of the Proverbs ascribed to Solomon did not appear till two hundred and fifty years after the death of Solomon; for it is said in xxv. 1, " *These are also proverbs of Solomon which the men of Hezekiah, king of Judah, copied out.*" It was two hundred and fifty years from the time of Solomon to the time of Hezekiah. When a man is famous and his name is abroad he is made the putative father of things he never said or did ; and this, most probably, has been the case with Solomon. It appears to have been the fashion of that day to make proverbs, as it is now to make jest-books, and father them upon those who never saw them.[1]

The book of *Ecclesiastes*, or the *Preacher*, is also ascribed to Solomon, and that with much reason, if not with truth. It is written as the solitary reflections of a worn-out debauchee, such as Solomon was, who looking back on scenes he can no longer enjoy, cries out *All is Vanity !* A great deal of the metaphor and of the sentiment is obscure, most probably by translation; but enough is left to shew they were strongly pointed in the original.* From what is trans-

---

[1] A " Tom Paine's Jest Book " had appeared in London with little or nothing of Paine in it.—*Editor*.

* *Those that look out of the window shall be darkened*, is an obscure figure in translation for loss of sight.—*Author*.

mitted to us of the character of Solomon, he was witty, ostentatious, dissolute, and at last melancholy. He lived fast, and died, tired of the world, at the age of fifty-eight years.

Seven hundred wives, and three hundred concubines, are worse than none ; and, however it may carry with it the appearance of heightened enjoyment, it defeats all the felicity of affection, by leaving it no point to fix upon ; divided love is never happy. This was the case with Solomon ; and if he could not, with all his pretensions to wisdom, discover it beforehand, he merited, unpitied, the mortification he afterwards endured. In this point of view, his preaching is unnecessary, because, to know the consequences, it is only necessary to know the cause. Seven hundred wives, and three hundred concubines would have stood in place of the whole book. It was needless after this to say that all was vanity and vexation of spirit ; for it is impossible to derive happiness from the company of those whom we deprive of happiness.

To be happy in old age it is necessary that we accustom ourselves to objects that can accompany the mind all the way through life, and that we take the rest as good in their day. The mere man of pleasure is miserable in old age ; and the mere drudge in business is but little better : whereas, natural philosophy, mathematical and mechanical science, are a continual source of tranquil pleasure, and in spite of the gloomy dogmas of priests, and of superstition, the study of those things is the study of the true theology ; it teaches man to know and to admire the Creator, for the principles of science are in the creation, and are unchangeable, and of divine origin.

Those who knew Benjaman Franklin will recollect, that his mind was ever young ; his temper ever serene ; science, that never grows grey, was always his mistress. He was never without an object ; for when we cease to have an object we become like an invalid in an hospital waiting for death.

Solomon's Songs, amorous and foolish enough, but which

wrinkled fanaticism has called divine.—The compilers of the
Bible have placed these songs after the book of Ecclesiastes;
and the chronologists have affixed to them the æra of B.C.
1014, at which time Solomon, according to the same chronology, was nineteen years of age, and was then forming his
seraglio of wives and concubines. The Bible-makers and
the chronologists should have managed this matter a little
better, and either have said nothing about the time, or
chosen a time less inconsistent with the supposed divinity
of those songs; for Solomon was then in the honey-moon of
one thousand debaucheries.

It should also have occurred to them, that as he wrote,
if he did write, the book of Ecclesiastes, long after these
songs, and in which he exclaims that all is vanity and vexation of spirit, that he included those songs in that description.
This is the more probable, because he says, or somebody for
him, Ecclesiastes ii. 8, *I got me men-singers, and women-
singers* [most probably to sing those songs], *and musical
instruments of all sorts;* and behold (Ver. 11), " all was
vanity and vexation of spirit." The compilers however
have done their work but by halves; for as they have given
us the songs they should have given us the tunes, that we
might sing them.

The books called the books of the Prophets fill up all the remaining part of the Bible; they are sixteen in number, beginning with Isaiah and ending with Malachi, of which I have
given a list in the observations upon Chronicles. Of these
sixteen prophets, all of whom except the last three lived
within the time the books of Kings and Chronicles were
written, two only, Isaiah and Jeremiah, are mentioned in the
history of those books. I shall begin with those two, reserv-
ing, what I have to say on the general character of the men
called prophets to another part of the work.

Whoever will take the trouble of reading the book ascribed to Isaiah, will find it one of the most wild and dis-
orderly compositions ever put together; it has neither
beginning, middle, nor end; and, except a short historical
part, and a few sketches of history in the first two or three

chapters, is one continued incoherent, bombastical rant, full of extravagant metaphor, without application, and destitute of meaning ; a school-boy would scarcely have been excusable for writing such stuff ; it is (at least in translation) that kind of composition and false taste that is properly called prose run mad.

The historical part begins at chapter xxxvi., and is continued to the end of chapter xxxix. It relates some matters that are said to have passed during the reign of Hezekiah, king of Judah, at which time Isaiah lived. This fragment of history begins and ends abruptly ; it has not the least connection with the chapter that precedes it, nor with that which follows it, nor with any other in the book. It is probable that Isaiah wrote this fragment himself, because he was an actor in the circumstances it treats of ; but except this part there are scarcely two chapters that have any connection with each other. One is entitled, at the beginning of the first verse, the burden of Babylon ; another, the burden of Moab ; another, the burden of Damascus ; another, the burden of Egypt ; another, the burden of the Desert of the Sea ; another, the burden of the Valley of Vision : as you would say the story of the Knight of the Burning Mountain, the story of Cinderella, or the glassen slipper, the story of the Sleeping Beauty in the Wood, etc., etc.

I have already shewn, in the instance of the last two verses of 2 Chronicles, and the first three in Ezra, that the compilers of the Bible mixed and confounded the writings of different authors with each other ; which alone, were there no other cause, is sufficient to destroy the authenticity of any compilation, because it is more than presumptive evidence that the compilers are ignorant who the authors were. A very glaring instance of this occurs in the book ascribed to Isaiah : the latter part of the 44th chapter, and the beginning of the 45th, so far from having been written by Isaiah, could only have been written by some person who lived at least an hundred and fifty years after Isaiah was dead.

These chapters are a compliment to *Cyrus*, who per-

mitted the Jews to return to Jerusalem from the Babylonian captivity, to rebuild Jerusalem and the temple, as is
stated in Ezra. The last verse of the 44th chapter, and the
beginning of the 45th [Isaiah] are in the following words:
" *That saith of Cyrus, he is my shepherd, and shall per-*
form all my pleasure ; even saying to Jerusalem, thou shalt
be built ; and to the temple, thy foundations shall be laid :
thus saith the Lord to his anointed, to Cyrus, whose right
hand I have holden to subdue nations before him, and I will
loose the loins of kings to open before him the two-leaved gates,
and the gates shall not be shut ; I will go before thee," etc.

What audacity of church and priestly ignorance it is to impose this book upon the world as the writing of Isaiah, when
Isaiah, according to their own chronology, died soon after
the death of Hezekiah, which was B.C. 698 ; and the decree
of Cyrus, in favour of the Jews returning to Jerusalem, was,
according to the same chronology, B.C. 536 ; which is a
distance of time between the two of 162 years. I do not
suppose that the compilers of the Bible made these books,
but rather that they picked up some loose, anonymous
essays, and put them together under the names of such
authors as best suited their purpose. They have encouraged the imposition, which is next to inventing it ; for it
was impossible but they must have observed it.

When we see the studied craft of the scripture-makers,
in making every part of this romantic book of school-boy's
eloquence bend to the monstrous idea of a Son of God,
begotten by a ghost on the body of a virgin, there is no
imposition we are not justified in suspecting them of.
Every phrase and circumstance are marked with the bar-
barous hand of superstitious torture, and forced into meanings it was impossible they could have. The head of every
chapter, and the top of every page, are blazoned with the
names of Christ and the Church, that the unwary reader
might suck in the error before he began to read.

Behold a virgin shall conceive, and bear a son (Isa. vii. 14),
has been interpreted to mean the person called Jesus Christ,
and his mother Mary, and has been echoed through christen-

dom for more than a thousand years; and such has been the rage of this opinion, that scarcely a spot in it but has been stained with blood and marked with desolation in consequence of it. Though it is not my intention to enter into controversy on subjects of this kind, but to confine myself to shew that the Bible is spurious,—and thus, by taking away the foundation, to overthrow at once the whole structure of superstition raised thereon,—I will however stop a moment to expose the fallacious application of this passage.

Whether Isaiah was playing a trick with Ahaz, king of Judah, to whom this passage is spoken, is no business of mine; I mean only to shew the misapplication of the passage, and that it has no more reference to Christ and his mother, than it has to me and my mother. The story is simply this:

The king of Syria and the king of Israel (I have already mentioned that the Jews were split into two nations, one of which was called Judah, the capital of which was Jerusalem, and the other Israel) made war jointly against Ahaz, king of Judah, and marched their armies towards Jerusalem. Ahaz and his people became alarmed, and the account says (Is. vii. 2), *Their hearts were moved as the trees of the wood are moved with the wind.*

In this situation of things, Isaiah addresses himself to Ahaz, and assures him in the *name of the Lord* (the cant phrase of all the prophets) that these two kings should not succeed against him; and to satisfy Ahaz that this should be the case, tells him to ask a sign. This, the account says, Ahaz declined doing; giving as a reason that he would not tempt the Lord; upon which Isaiah, who is the speaker, says, ver. 14, " Therefore the Lord himself shall give you a sign; *behold a virgin shall conceive and bear a son;* " and the 16th verse says, " *And before this child shall know to refuse the evil, and choose the good, the land* which thou abhorrest or dreadest [meaning Syria and the kingdom of Israel] shall be forsaken of both her kings." Here then was the sign, and the time limited for the completion of the assurance or promise; namely, before this child shall know to refuse the evil and choose the good.

Isaiah having committed himself thus far, it became necessary to him, in order to avoid the imputation of being a false
prophet, and the consequences thereof, to take measures to
make this sign appear. It certainly was not a difficult thing,
in any time of the world, to find a girl with child, or to make
her so ; and perhaps Isaiah knew of one beforehand ; for I
do not suppose that the prophets of that day were any more
to be trusted than the priests of this : be that, however, as
it may, he says in the next chapter, ver. 2, " And I took unto
me faithful witnesses to record, Uriah the priest, and Zechariah the son of Jeberechiah, and *I went unto the prophetess,
and she conceived and bare a son.*"

Here then is the whole story, foolish as it is, of this child
and this virgin ; and it is upon the barefaced perversion of
this story that the book of Matthew, and the impudence and
sordid interest of priests in later times, have founded a
theory, which they call the gospel ; and have applied this
story to signify the person they call Jesus Christ ; begotten,
they say, by a ghost, whom they call holy, on the body of a
woman, engaged in marriage, and afterwards married, whom
they call a virgin, seven hundred years after this foolish story
was told ; a theory which, speaking for myself, I hesitate not
to believe, and to say, is as fabulous and as false as God is
true.*

But to shew the imposition and falsehood of Isaiah we
have only to attend to the sequel of this story ; which,
though it is passed over in silence in the book of Isaiah, is
related in 2 Chronicles, xxviii ; and which is, that instead of
these two kings failing in their attempt against Ahaz, king
of Judah, as Isaiah had pretended to foretel in the name of
the Lord, they *succeeded :* Ahaz was defeated and destroyed ;
an hundred and twenty thousand of his people were slaugh-
tered ; Jerusalem was plundered, and two hundred thousand
women and sons and daughters carried into captivity. Thus

---

* In Is. vii. 14, it is said that the child should be called Immanuel ; but this
name was not given to either of the children, otherwise than as a character,
which the word signifies. That of the prophetess was called Maher-shalal-
hash-baz, and that of Mary was called Jesus.—*Author.*

much for this lying prophet and imposter Isaiah, and the
book of falsehoods that bears his name. I pass on to the
book of

Jeremiah. This prophet, as he is called, lived in the time
that Nebuchadnezzar besieged Jerusalem, in the reign of
Zedekiah, the last king of Judah; and the suspicion was
strong against him that he was a traitor in the interest of
Nebuchadnezzar. Every thing relating to Jeremiah shews
him to have been a man of an equivocal character: in his
metaphor of the potter and the clay, (ch. xviii.) he guards
his prognostications in such a crafty manner as always to
leave himself a door to escape by, in case the event should
be contrary to what he had predicted. In the 7th and 8th
verses he makes the Almighty to say, " At what instant I
shall speak concerning a nation, and concerning a kingdom,
to pluck up, and to pull down, and destroy it, if that nation,
against whom I have pronounced, turn from their evil, I will
repent me of the evil that I thought to do unto them."
Here was a proviso against one side of the case: now for
the other side. Verses 9 and 10, " At what instant I shall
speak concerning a nation, and concerning a kingdom, to
build and to plant it, if it do evil in my sight, that it obey
not my voice, then I will repent me of the good wherewith
I said I would benefit them." Here is a proviso against
the other side; and, according to this plan of prophesying, a
prophet could never be wrong, however mistaken the Almighty might be. This sort of absurd subterfuge, and this
manner of speaking of the Almighty, as one would speak of a
man, is consistent with nothing but the stupidity of the Bible.

As to the authenticity of the book, it is only necessary to
read it in order to decide positively that, though some passages recorded therein may have been spoken by Jeremiah,
he is not the author of the book. The historical parts, if
they can be called by that name, are in the most confused
condition; the same events are several times repeated, and
that in a manner different, and sometimes in contradiction
to each other; and this disorder runs even to the last chapter, where the history, upon which the greater part of the

book has been employed, begins anew, and ends abruptly. The book has all the appearance of being a medley of un-connected anecdotes respecting persons and things of that time, collected together in the same rude manner as if the various and contradictory accounts that are to be found in a bundle of newspapers, respecting persons and things of the present day, were put together without date, order, or explanation. I will give two or three examples of this kind.

It appears, from the account of chapter xxxvii. that the army of Nebuchadnezzer, which is called the army of the Chaldeans, had besieged Jerusalem some time; and on their hearing that the army of Pharaoh of Egypt was marching against them, they raised the siege and retreated for a time. It may here be proper to mention, in order to understand this confused history, that Nebuchadnezzar had besieged and taken Jerusalem during the reign of Jehoakim, the predecessor of Zedekiah; and that it was Nebuchadnezzar who had make Zedekiah king, or rather vice-roy; and that this second siege, of which the book of Jeremiah treats, was in consequence of the revolt of Zedekiah against Nebuchadnezzar. This will in some measure account for the suspicion that affixes itself to Jeremiah of being a traitor, and in the interest of Nebuchadnezzar,—whom Jeremiah calls, xliii. 10, the servant of God.

Chapter xxxvii. 11–13, says, "And it came to pass, that, when the army of the Chaldeans was broken up from Jerusalem, for fear of Pharaoh's army, that Jeremiah went forth out of Jerusalem, to go (as this account states) into the land of Benjamin, to separate himself thence in the midst of the people; and when he was in the gate of Benjamin a captain of the ward was there, whose name was Irijah . . . and he took Jeremiah the prophet, saying, *Thou fallest away to the Chaldeans;* then Jeremiah said, *It is false; I fall not away to the Chaldeans.*" Jeremiah being thus stopt and accused, was, after being examined, committed to prison, on suspicion of being a traitor, where he remained, as is stated in the last verse of this chapter.

But the next chapter gives an account of the imprisonment of Jeremiah, which has no connection with *this* account, but ascribes his imprisonment to another circumstance, and for which we must go back to chapter xxi. It is there stated, ver. 1, that Zedekiah sent Pashur the son of Malchiah, and Zephaniah the son of Maaseiah the priest, to Jeremiah, to enquire of him concerning Nebuchadnezzar, whose army was then before Jerusalem ; and Jeremiah said to them, ver. 8, "Thus saith the Lord, Behold I set before you the way of life, and the way of death; he that abideth in this city shall die by the sword and by the famine, and by the pestilence ; *but he that goeth out and falleth to the Chaldeans that besiege you, he shall live, and his life shall be unto him for a prey.*"

This interview and conference breaks off abruptly at the end of the 10th verse of chapter xxi.; and such is the disorder of this book that we have to pass over sixteen chapters upon various subjects, in order to come at the continuation and event of this conference; and this brings us to the first verse of chapter xxxviii., as I have just mentioned. The chapter opens with saying, "Then Shaphatiah, the son of Mattan, Gedaliah the son of Pashur, and Jucal the son of Shelemiah, and Pashur the son of Malchiah, (here are more persons mentioned than in chapter xxi.) heard the words that Jeremiah spoke unto all the people, saying, Thus saith the Lord, He that remaineth in this city, shall die by the sword, by famine, and by the pestilence ; but he that goeth forth to the Chaldeans shall live ; for he shall have his life for a prey, and shall live " ; [which are the words of the conference;] therefore, (say they to Zedekiah,) "We beseech thee, let this man be put to death, for thus he weakeneth the hands of the men of war that remain in this city, and the hands of all the people, in speaking such words unto them ; for this man seeketh not the welfare of the people, but the hurt:" and at the 6th verse it is said, "Then they took Jeremiah, and put him into the dungeon of Malchiah."

These two accounts are different and contradictory. The one ascribes his imprisonment to his attempt to *escape out of the city ;* the other to his *preaching and prophesying in the* *city;* the one to his being seized by the guard at the gate; the other to his being accused before Zedekiah by the conferees.*

In the next chapter (Jer. xxxix.) we have another instance of the disordered state of this book; for notwithstanding the siege of the city by Nebuchadnezzar has been the subject of several of the preceding chapters, particularly xxxvii. and xxxviii., chapter xxxix. begins as if not a word had been said upon the subject, and as if the reader was still to be informed of every particular respecting it; for it begins with saying, ver. 1, "In the ninth year of Zedekiah king of Judah, in the tenth month, came Nebuchadnezzar king of Babylon, and all his army, against Jerusalem, and besieged it," etc.

* I observed two chapters in 1 Samuel (xvi. and xvii.) that contradict each other with respect to David, and the manner he became acquainted with Saul; as Jeremiah xxxvii. and xxxviii. contradict each other with respect to the cause of Jeremiah's imprisonment.

In 1 Samuel, xvi., it is said, that an evil spirit of God troubled Saul, and that his servants advised him (as a remedy,) " to seek out a man who was a cunning player upon the harp." And Saul said, ver. 17, " Provide me now a man that can play well, and bring him to me. Then answered one of his servants, and said, Behold, I have seen a son of Jesse, the Bethlehemite, that is cunning in playing, and a mighty man, and a man of war, and prudent in matters, and a comely person, and the Lord is with him ; wherefore Saul sent messengers unto Jesse, and said, Send me David, thy son. And (verse 21) David came to Saul, and stood before him, and he loved him greatly, and he became his armour-bearer ; and when the evil spirit from God was upon Saul, (verse 23) David took his harp, and played with his hand, and Saul was refreshed, and was well."

But the next chapter (xvii.) gives an account, all different to this, of the manner that Saul and David became acquainted. Here it is ascribed to David's encounter with Goliah, when David was sent by his father to carry provision to his brethren in the camp. In the 55th verse of this chapter it is said, " And when Saul saw David go forth against the Philistine (Goliah) he said to Abner, the captain of the host, Abner, whose son is this youth ? And Abner said, As thy soul liveth, O king, I cannot tell. And the king said, Enquire thou whose son the stripling is. And as David returned from the slaughter of the Philistine, Abner took him and brought him before Saul, with the head of the Philistine in his hand ; and Saul said unto him, Whose son art thou, thou young man ? And David answered, I am the son of thy servant, Jesse, the Bethlehemite." These two accounts belie each other, because each of them supposes Saul and David not to have known each other before. This book, the Bible, is too ridiculous for criticism.—*Author.*

But the instance in the last chapter (lii.) is still more glaring; for though the story has been told over and over again, this chapter still supposes the reader not to know anything of it, for it begins by saying, ver. 1, "Zedekiah was one and twenty years old when he began to reign, and he reigned eleven years in Jerusalem, and his mother's name was Hamutal, the daughter of Jeremiah of Libnah." (Ver. 4,) "And it came to pass in the ninth year of his reign, in the tenth month, that Nebuchadnezzar king of Babylon came, he and all his army, against Jerusalem, and pitched against it, and built forts against it," etc.

It is not possible that any one man, and more particularly Jeremiah, could have been the writer of this book. The errors are such as could not have been committed by any person sitting down to compose a work. Were I, or any other man, to write in such a disordered manner, no body would read what was written, and every body would suppose that the writer was in a state of insanity. The only way, therefore, to account for the disorder is, that the book is a medley of detached unauthenticated anecdotes, put together by some stupid book-maker, under the name of Jeremiah; because many of them refer to him, and to the circumstances of the times he lived in.

Of the duplicity, and of the false predictions of Jeremiah, I shall mention two instances, and then proceed to review the remainder of the Bible.

It appears from chapter xxxviii. that when Jeremiah was in prison, Zedekiah sent for him, and at this interview, which was private, Jeremiah pressed it strongly on Zedekiah to surrender himself to the enemy. "If," says he, (ver. 17,) "thou wilt assuredly go forth unto the king of Babylon's princes, then thy soul shall live," etc. Zedekiah was apprehensive that what passed at this conference should be known; and he said to Jeremiah, (ver. 25,) "If the princes [meaning those of Judah] hear that I have talked with thee, and they come unto thee, and say unto thee, Declare unto us now what thou hast said unto the king; hide it not from us, and we will not put thee to death; and also what the king said unto thee; then thou shalt say unto them, I presented my supplication before the king that he would not cause me to return to Jonathan's house, to die there. Then came all the princes unto Jeremiah, and asked him, and " he told them according to all the words the king had commanded." Thus, this man of God, as he is called, could tell a lie, or very strongly prevaricate, when he supposed it would answer his purpose; for certainly he did not go to Zedekiah to make this supplication, neither did he make it; he went because he was sent for, and he employed that opportunity to advise Zedekiah to surrender himself to Nebuchadnezzar.

In chapter xxxiv. 2–5, is a prophecy of Jeremiah to Zedekiah in these words: " Thus saith the Lord, Behold I will give this city into the hand of the king of Babylon, and he will burn it with fire; and thou shalt not escape out of his hand, but thou shalt surely be taken, and delivered into his hand; and thine eyes shall behold the eyes of the king of Babylon, and he shall speak with thee mouth to mouth, and thou shalt go to Babylon. *Yet hear the word of the Lord; O Zedekiah, king of Judah, thus saith the Lord, Thou shalt not die by the sword, but thou shalt die in peace; and with the burnings of thy fathers, the former kings that were before thee, so shall they burn odours for thee, and they will lament thee, saying, Ah, Lord! for I have pronounced the word, saith the Lord.*"

Now, instead of Zedekiah beholding the eyes of the king of Babylon, and speaking with him mouth to mouth, and dying in peace, and with the burning of odours, as at the funeral of his fathers, (as Jeremiah had declared the Lord himself had pronounced,) the reverse, according to chapter lii., 10, 11 was the case; it is there said, that the king of Babylon slew the sons of Zedekiah before his eyes: then he put out the eyes of Zedekiah, and bound him in chains, and carried him to Babylon, and put him in prison till the day of his death.

What then can we say of these prophets, but that they are impostors and liars?

As for Jeremiah, he experienced none of those evils. He
was taken into favour by Nebuchadnezzar, who gave him in
charge to the captain of the guard (xxxix, 12), "Take him
(said he) and look well to him, and do him no harm ; but do
unto him even as he shall say unto thee." Jeremiah joined
himself afterwards to Nebuchadnezzar, and went about
propnesying for him against the Egyptians, who had
marched to the relief of Jerusalem while it was besieged.
Thus much for another of the lying prophets, and the book
that bears his name.

I have been the more particular in treating of the books
ascribed to Isaiah and Jeremiah, because those two are
spoken of in the books of Kings and Chronicles, which the
others are not.   The remainder of the books ascribed to the
men called prophets I shall not trouble myself much about ;
but take them collectively into the observations I shall offer
on the character of the men stiled prophets.

In the former part of the *Age of Reason*, I have said that
the word prophet was the Bible-word for poet, and that the
flights and metaphors of Jewish poets have been foolishly
erected into what are now called prophecies.   I am sufficiently justified in this opinion, not only because the books
called the prophecies are written in poetical language, but
because there is no word in the Bible, except it be the word
prophet, that describes what we mean by a poet.   I have
also said, that the word signified a performer upon musical
instruments, of which I have given some instances ; such as
that of a company of prophets, prophesying with psalteries,
with tabrets, with pipes, with harps, etc., and that Saul
prophesied with them, 1 Sam. x., 5.   It appears from this
passage, and from other parts in the book of Samuel, that
the word prophet was confined to signify poetry and music ;
for the person who was supposed to have a visionary insight
into concealed things, was not a prophet but a *seer*,* (1 Sam.

---

* I know not what is the Hebrew word that corresponds to the word seer in
English ; but I observe it is translated into French by Le Voyant, from the verb
voir to *see*, and which means the person who *sees*, or the seer.—*Author*.

The Hebrew word for Seer, in 1 Samuel ix., transliterated, is *chozéh*, the
gazer ; it is translated in Is. xlvii. 13, " the stargazers."—*Editor*.

ix. 9;) and it was not till after the word *seer* went out of use (which most probably was when Saul banished those he called wizards) that the profession of the seer, or the art of seeing, became incorporated into the word prophet.

According to the *modern* meaning of the word prophet and prophesying, it signifies foretelling events to a great distance of time; and it became necessary to the inventors of the gospel to give it this latitude of meaning, in order to apply or to stretch what they call the prophecies of the Old Testament, to the times of the New. But according to the Old Testament, the prophesying of the seer, and afterwards of the prophet, so far as the meaning of the word "seer" was incorporated into that of prophet, had reference only to things of the time then passing, or very closely connected with it; such as the event of a battle they were going to engage in, or of a journey, or of any enterprize they were going to undertake, or of any circumstance then pending, or of any difficulty they were then in; all of which had immediate reference to themselves (as in the case already mentioned of Ahaz and Isaiah with respect to the expression, *Behold a virgin shall conceive and bear a son,*) and not to any distant future time. It was that kind of prophesying that corresponds to what we call fortune-telling; such as casting nativities, predicting riches, fortunate or unfortunate marriages, conjuring for lost goods, etc.; and it is the fraud of the Christian church, not that of the Jews, and the ignorance and the superstition of modern, not that of ancient times, that elevated those poetical, musical, conjuring, dreaming, strolling gentry, into the rank they have since had.

But, besides this general character of all the prophets, they had also a particular character. They were in parties, and they prophesied for or against, according to the party they were with; as the poetical and political writers of the present day write in defence of the party they associate with against the other.

After the Jews were divided into two nations, that of Judah and that of Israel, each party had its prophets, who

abused and accused each other of being false prophets, lying
prophets, impostors, etc.

The prophets of the party of Judah prophesied against the
prophets of the party of Israel ; and those of the party of
Israel against those of Judah. This party prophesying
shewed itself immediately on the separation under the first
two rival kings, Rehoboam and Jeroboam. The prophet that
cursed, or prophesied against the altar that Jeroboam had
built in Bethel, was of the party of Judah, where Rehoboam
was king ; and he was way-laid on his return home by a
prophet of the party of Israel, who said unto him (1 Kings
xiii.) " *Art thou the man of God that came from Judah ? and
he said, I am.*" Then the prophet of the party of Israel said
to him " I am a prophet also, as thou art, [signifying of
Judah,] and an angel spake unto me by the word of the
Lord, saying, Bring him back with thee unto thine house, that
he may eat bread and drink water ; but (says the 18th verse)
he lied unto him." The event, however, according to the
story, is, that the prophet of Judah never got back to Judah ;
for he was found dead on the road by the contrivance of the
prophet of Israel, who no doubt was called a true prophet
by his own party, and the prophet of Judah a lying prophet.

In 2 Kings, iii., a story is related of prophesying or conjuring that shews, in several particulars, the character of a
prophet. Jehoshaphat king of Judah, and Joram king of
Israel, had for a while ceased their party animosity, and
entered into an alliance ; and these two, together with
the king of Edom, engaged in a war against the king
of Moab. After uniting and marching their armies, the
story says, they were in great distress for water, upon
which Jehoshaphat said, " Is there not here a prophet of
the Lord, that we may enquire of the Lord by him ? and
one of the servants of the king of Israel said here is Elisha.
[Elisha was of the party of Judah.] And Jehoshaphat the
king of Judah said, The word of the Lord is with him."
The story then says, that these three kings went down to
Elisha ; and when Elisha [who, as I have said, was a Judah-
mite prophet] saw the King of Israel, he said unto him,

" What have I to do with thee, get thee to the prophets of
thy father and the prophets of thy mother. Nay but, said
the king of Israel, the Lord hath called these three kings together, to deliver them into the hands of the king of Moab,"
(meaning because of the distress they were in for water ;)
upon which Elisha said, " As the Lord of hosts liveth
before whom I stand, surely, were it not that I regard the
presence of Jehoshaphat, king of Judah, I would not look
towards thee nor see thee." Here is all the venom and
vulgarity of a party prophet. We are now to see the
performance, or manner of prophesying.

Ver. 15. " Bring me," (said Elisha), " a minstrel ; and it
came to pass, when the minstrel played, that the hand of
the Lord came upon him." Here is the farce of the con-
jurer. Now for the prophecy : " And Elisha said, [singing
most probably to the tune he was playing], Thus saith the
Lord, Make this valley full of ditches ; " which was just telling them what every countryman could have told them
without either fiddle or farce, that the way to get water was
to dig for it.

But as every conjuror is not famous alike for the same
thing, so neither were those prophets ; for though all of
them, at least those I have spoken of, were famous for lying,
some of them excelled in cursing. Elisha, whom I have
just mentioned, was a chief in this branch of prophesying ;
it was he that cursed the forty-two children in the name of
the Lord, whom the two she-bears came and devoured. We
are to suppose that those children were of the party of
Israel ; but as those who will curse will lie, there is just as
much credit to be given to this story of Elisha's two she-
bears as there is to that of the Dragon of Wantley, of whom
it is said :

Poor children three devoured he,
That could not with him grapple ;
And at one sup he eat them up,
As a man would eat an apple.

There was another description of men called prophets,
that amused themselves with dreams and visions ; but

whether by night or by day we know not. These, if they were not quite harmless, were but little mischievous. Of this class are

EZEKIEL and DANIEL ; and the first question upon these books, as upon all the others, is, Are they genuine? that is, were they written by Ezekiel and Daniel?

Of this there is no proof ; but so far as my own opinion goes, I am more inclined to believe they were, than that they were not. My reasons for this opinion are as follows : First, Because those books do not contain internal evidence to prove they were not written by Ezekiel and Daniel, as the books ascribed to Moses, Joshua, Samuel, etc., prove they were not written by Moses, Joshua, Samuel, etc.

Secondly, Because they were not written till after the Babylonish captivity began ; and there is good reason to believe that not any book in the bible was written before that period ; at least it is proveable, from the books themselves, as I have already shewn, that they were not written till after the commencement of the Jewish monarchy.

Thirdly, Because the manner in which the books ascribed to Ezekiel and Daniel are written, agrees with the condition these men were in at the time of writing them.

Had the numerous commentators and priests, who have foolishly employed or wasted their time in pretending to expound and unriddle those books, been carried into captivity, as Ezekiel and Daniel were, it would greatly have improved their intellects in comprehending the reason for this mode of writing, and have saved them the trouble of racking their invention, as they have done to no purpose ; for they would have found that themselves would be obliged to write whatever they had to write, respecting their own affairs, or those of their friends, or of their country, in a concealed manner, as those men have done.

These two books differ from all the rest ; for it is only these that are filled with accounts of dreams and visions : and this difference arose from the situation the writers were in as prisoners of war, or prisoners of state, in a foreign country, which obliged them to convey even the most

trifling information to each other, and all their political
projects or opinions, in obscure and metaphorical terms.
They pretend to have dreamed dreams, and seen visions,
because it was unsafe for them to speak facts or plain
language. We ought, however, to suppose, that the persons
to whom they wrote understood what they meant, and that
it was not intended anybody else should. But these busy
commentators and priests have been puzzling their wits to
find out what it was not intended they should know, and
with which they have nothing to do.

Ezekiel and Daniel were carried prisoners to Babylon,
under the first captivity, in the time of Jehoiakim, nine
years before the second captivity in the time of Zedekiah.
The Jews were then still numerous, and had considerable
force at Jerusalem; and as it is natural to suppose that
men in the situation of Ezekiel and Daniel would be medi-
tating the recovery of their country, and their own deliverance, it is reasonable to suppose that the accounts of dreams
and visions with which these books are filled, are no other
than a disguised mode of correspondence to facilitate those
objects: it served them as a cypher, or secret alphabet. If
they are not this, they are tales, reveries, and nonsense;
or at least a fanciful way of wearing off the wearisome-
ness of captivity; but the presumption is, they are the
former.

Ezekiel begins his book by speaking of a vision of
cherubims, and of a *wheel within a wheel*, which he says
he saw by the river Chebar, in the land of his captivity.
Is it not reasonable to suppose that by the cherubims he
meant the temple at Jerusalem, where they had figures of
cherubims? and by a wheel within a wheel (which as a
figure has always been understood to signify political contrivance) the project or means of recovering Jerusalem? In
the latter part of his book he supposes himself trans-
ported to Jerusalem, and into the temple; and he refers
back to the vision on the river Chebar, and says, (xliii. 3,)
that this last vision was like the vision on the river
Chebar; which indicates that those pretended dreams and

visions had for their object the recovery of Jerusalem, and nothing further.

As to the romantic interpretations and applications, wild as the dreams and visions they undertake to explain, which commentators and priests have made of those books, that of converting them into things which they call prophecies, and making them bend to times and circumstances as far remote even as the present day, it shews the fraud or the extreme folly to which credulity or priestcraft can go.

Scarcely anything can be more absurd than to suppose that men situated as Ezekiel and Daniel were, whose country was over-run, and in the possession of the enemy, all their friends and relations in captivity abroad, or in slavery at home, or massacred, or in continual danger of it ; scarcely any thing, I say, can be more absurd than to suppose that such men should find nothing to do but that of employing their time and their thoughts about what was to happen to other nations a thousand or two thousand years after they were dead ; at the same time nothing more natural than that they should meditate the recovery of Jerusalem, and their own deliverance ; and that this was the sole object of all the obscure and apparently frantic writing contained in those books.

In this sense the mode of writing used in those two books being forced by necessity, and not adopted by choice, is not irrational ; but, if we are to use the books as prophecies, they are false.   In Ezekiel xxix. 11., speaking of Egypt, it is said, " No foot of man shall pass through it, nor foot of beast pass through it ; neither shall it be inhabited for forty years."   This is what never came to pass, and consequently it is false, as all the books I have already reviewed are.—I here close this part of the subject.

In the former part of *The Age of Reason* I have spoken of Jonah, and of the story of him and the whale.—A fit story for ridicule, if it was written to be believed ; or of laughter, if it was intended to try what credulity could swallow ; for, if it could swallow Jonah and the whale it could swallow anything.

But, as is already shewn in the observations on the book of Job and of Proverbs, it is not always certain which of the books in the Bible are originally Hebrew, or only translations from the books of the Gentiles into Hebrew ; and, as the book of Jonah, so far from treating of the affairs of the Jews, says nothing upon that subject, but treats altogether of the Gentiles, it is more probable that it is a book of the Gentiles than of the Jews,[1] and that it has been written as a fable to expose the nonsense, and satyrize the vicious and malignant character, of a Bible-prophet, or a predicting priest.

Jonah is represented, first as a disobedient prophet, running away from his mission, and taking shelter aboard a vessel of the Gentiles, bound from Joppa to Tarshish ; as if he ignorantly supposed, by such a paltry contrivance, he could hide himself where God could not find him. The vessel is overtaken by a storm at sea ; and the mariners, all of whom are Gentiles, believing it to be a judgement on account of some one on board who had committed a crime, agreed to cast lots to discover the offender ; and the lot fell upon Jonah. But before this they had cast all their wares and merchandise over-board to lighten the vessel, while Jonah, like a stupid fellow, was fast asleep in the hold.

After the lot had designated Jonah to be the offender, they questioned him to know who and what he was? and he told them *he was an Hebrew ;* and the story implies that he confessed himself to be guilty. But these Gentiles, instead of sacrificing him at once without pity or mercy, as a company of Bible-prophets or priests would have done by a Gentile in the same case, and as it is related Samuel had done by Agag, and Moses by the women and children, they endeavoured to save him, though at the risk of their own lives : for the account says, " Nevertheless [that is, though Jonah was a Jew and a foreigner, and the cause of all their misfortunes, and the loss of their cargo] the men rowed

---

[1] I have read in an ancient Persian poem (Saadi, I believe, but have mislaid the reference) this phrase : "And now the whale swallowed Jonah : the sun set."—*Editor.*

hard to bring the boat to land, but they could not, for the sea wrought and was tempestuous against them." Still however they were unwilling to put the fate of the lot into execution ; and they cried, says the account, unto the Lord, saying, " We beseech thee, O Lord, let us not perish for this man's life, and lay not upon us innocent blood ; for thou, O Lord, hast done as it pleased thee." Meaning thereby, that they did not presume to judge Jonah guilty, since that he might be innocent ; but that they considered the lot that had fallen upon him as a decree of God, or as it *pleased God.* The address of this prayer shews that the Gentiles worshipped one *Supreme Being,* and that they were not idolaters as the Jews represented them to be. But the storm still continuing, and the danger encreasing, they put the fate of the lot into execution, and cast Jonah in the sea ; where, according to the story, a great fish swallowed him up whole and alive !

We have now to consider Jonah securely housed from the storm in the fish's belly. Here we are told that he prayed ; but the prayer is a made-up prayer, taken from various parts of the Psalms, without connection or con-sistency, and adapted to the distress, but not at all to the condition that Jonah was in. It is such a prayer as a Gen-tile, who might know something of the Psalms, could copy out for him. This circumstance alone, were there no other, is sufficient to indicate that the whole is a made-up story. The prayer, however, is supposed to have answered the purpose, and the story goes on, (taking-off at the same time the cant language of a Bible-prophet,) saying, " The Lord spake unto the fish, and it vomited out Jonah upon dry land."

Jonah then received a second mission to Nineveh, with which he sets out ; and we have now to consider him as a preacher. The distress he is represented to have suffered, the remembrance of his own disobedience as the cause of it, and the miraculous escape he is supposed to have had, were sufficient, one would conceive, to have impressed him with sympathy and benevolence in the execution of his mission ;

but, instead of this, he enters the city with denunciation
and malediction in his mouth, crying, "Yet forty days, and
Nineveh shall be overthrown."

We have now to consider this supposed missionary in the
last act of his mission ; and here it is that the malevolent
spirit of a Bible-prophet, or of a predicting priest, appears in
all that blackness of character that men ascribe to the being
they call the devil.

Having published his predictions, he withdrew, says the
story, to the east side of the city.—But for what ? not to
contemplate in retirement the mercy of his Creator to himself or to others, but to wait, with malignant impatience, the
destruction of Nineveh. It came to pass, however, as the
story relates, that the Ninevites reformed, and that God,
according to the Bible phrase, repented him of the evil he
had said he would do unto them, and did it not. This, saith
the first verse of the last chapter, *displeased Jonah exceedingly and he was very angry*. His obdurate heart would
rather that all Nineveh should be destroyed, and every soul,
young and old, perish in its ruins, than that his prediction
should not be fulfilled. To expose the character of a
prophet still more, a gourd is made to grow up in the night,
that promises him an agreeable shelter from the heat of the
sun, in the place to which he is retired ; and the next
morning it dies.

Here the rage of the prophet becomes excessive, and he
is ready to destroy himself. " It is better, *said he*, for me
to die than to live." This brings on a supposed expostula-
tion between the Almighty and the prophet ; in which the
former says, " Doest thou well to be angry for the gourd ?
And Jonah said, I do well to be angry even unto death.
Then said the Lord, Thou hast had pity on the gourd, for
which thou hast not laboured, neither madest it to grow,
which came up in a night, and perished in a night ; and
should not I spare Nineveh, that great city, in which are
more than threescore thousand persons, that cannot discern
between their right hand and their left ? "

Here is both the winding up of the satire, and the moral

of the fable. As a satire, it strikes against the character of all the Bible-prophets, and against all the indiscriminate judgements upon men, women and children, with which this lying book, the bible, is crowded; such as Noah's flood, the destruction of the cities of Sodom and Gomorrah, the extirpation of the Canaanites, even to suckling infants, and women with child; because the same reflection ' that there are more than threescore thousand persons that cannot discern between their right hand and their left,' meaning young children, applies to all their cases. It satirizes also the supposed partiality of the Creator for one nation more than for another.

As a moral, it preaches against the malevolent spirit of prediction; for as certainly as a man predicts ill, he becomes inclined to wish it. The pride of having his judgment right hardens his heart, till at last he beholds with satisfaction, or sees with disappointment, the accomplishment or the failure of his predictions.—This book ends with the same kind of strong and well-directed point against prophets, prophecies and indiscriminate judgements, as the chapter that Benjamin Franklin made for the Bible, about Abraham and the stranger, ends against the intolerant spirit of religious persecutions—Thus much for the book Jonah.[1]

Of the poetical parts of the Bible, that are called prophecies, I have spoken in the former part of *The Age of Reason*, and already in this, where I have said that the word *prophet* is the Bible-word for *poet*, and that the flights and metaphors of those poets, many of which have become obscure by the lapse of time and the change of circumstances, have been ridiculously erected into things called prophecies, and applied to purposes the writers never thought of. When a priest quotes any of those passages, he unriddles it agreeably to his own views, and imposes

---

[1] The story of Abraham and the Fire-worshipper, ascribed to Franklin, is from Saadi. (See my " Sacred Anthology," p. 61.) Paine has often been called a " mere scoffer," but he seems to have been among the first to treat with dignity the book of Jonah, so especially liable to the ridicule of superficial readers, and discern in it the highest conception of Deity known to the Old Testament.—*Editor.*

that explanation upon his congregation as the meaning of the writer. The *whore of Babylon* has been the common whore of all the priests, and each has accused the other of keeping the strumpet; so well do they agree in their explanations.

There now remain only a few books, which they call books of the lesser prophets; and as I have already shewn that the greater are impostors, it would be cowardice to disturb the repose of the little ones. Let them sleep, then, in the arms of their nurses, the priests, and both be forgotten together.

I have now gone through the Bible, as a man would go through a wood with an axe on his shoulder, and fell trees. Here they lie; and the priests, if they can, may replant them. They may, perhaps, stick them in the ground, but they will never make them grow.—I pass on to the books of the New Testament.

CHAPTER II.

THE NEW TESTAMENT.

THE New Testament, they tell us, is founded upon the prophecies of the Old; if so, it must follow the fate of its foundation.

As it is nothing extraordinary that a woman should be with child before she was married, and that the son she might bring forth should be executed, even unjustly, I see no reason for not believing that such a woman as Mary, and such a man as Joseph, and Jesus, existed; their mere existence is a matter of indifference, about which there is no ground either to believe or to disbelieve, and which comes under the common head of, *It may be so, and what then?* The probability however is that there were such persons, or at least such as resembled them in part of the circumstances, because almost all romantic stories have been suggested by some actual circumstance; as the adventures of Robinson Crusoe, not a word of which is true, were suggested by the case of Alexander Selkirk.

It is not then the existence or the non-existence, of the persons that I trouble myself about; it is the fable of Jesus Christ, as told in the New Testament, and the wild and visionary doctrine raised thereon, against which I contend. The story, taking it as it is told, is blasphemously obscene. It gives an account of a young woman engaged to be married, and while under this engagement, she is, to speak plain language, debauched by a ghost, under the impious pretence, (Luke i. 35,) that *"the Holy Ghost shall come upon thee, and the power of the Highest shall overshadow thee."* Notwithstanding which, Joseph afterwards marries her, cohabits with her as his wife, and in his turn rivals the ghost. This is putting the story into intelligible language, and when told in this manner, there is not a priest but must be ashamed to own it.*

Obscenity in matters of faith, however wrapped up, is always a token of fable and imposture; for it is necessary to our serious belief in God, that we do not connect it with stories that run, as this does, into ludicrous interpretations. This story is, upon the face of it, the same kind of story as that of Jupiter and Leda, or Jupiter and Europa, or any of the amorous adventures of Jupiter; and shews, as is already stated in the former part of *The Age of Reason,* that the Christian faith is built upon the heathen Mythology.

As the historical parts of the New Testament, so far as concerns Jesus Christ, are confined to a very short space of time, less than two years, and all within the same country, and nearly to the same spot, the discordance of time, place, and circumstance, which detects the fallacy of the books of the Old Testament, and proves them to be impositions, cannot be expected to be found here in the same abundance. The New Testament compared with the Old, is like a farce of one act, in which there is not room for very numerous violations of the unities. There are, however, some glaring contradictions, which, exclusive of the fallacy of the pretended prophecies, are sufficient to shew the story of Jesus Christ to be false.

I lay it down as a position which cannot be controverted, first, that the *agreement* of all the parts of a story does not prove that story to be true, because the parts may agree, and the whole may be false; secondly, that the *disagreement* of the parts of a story *proves the whole cannot be true.* The agreement does not prove truth, but the disagreement proves falsehood positively.

The history of Jesus Christ is contained in the four books ascribed to Matthew, Mark, Luke, and John.—The first chapter of Matthew begins with giving a genealogy of Jesus

---

* Mary, the supposed virgin, mother of Jesus, had several other children, sons and daughters. See Matt. xiii. 55, 56.—*Author.*

Christ; and in the third chapter of Luke there is also given
a genealogy of Jesus Christ. Did these two agree, it would
not prove the genealogy to be true, because it might nevertheless be a fabrication; but as they contradict each other
in every particular, it proves falsehood absolutely. If Matthew speaks truth, Luke speaks falsehood; and if Luke speaks
truth, Matthew speaks falsehood: and as there is no authority for believing one more than the other, there is no authority for believing either; and if they cannot be believed even
in the very first thing they say, and set out to prove, they
are not entitled to be believed in any thing they say afterwards. Truth is an uniform thing; and as to inspiration
and revelation, were we to admit it, it is impossible to suppose it can be contradictory. Either then the men called
apostles were imposters, or the books ascribed to them have
been written by other persons, and fathered upon them, as
is the case in the Old Testament.

The book of Matthew gives (i. 6), a genealogy by name
from David, up, through Joseph, the husband of Mary, to
Christ; and makes there to be *twenty-eight* generations. The
book of Luke gives also a genealogy by name from Christ,
through Joseph the husband of Mary, down to David, and
makes there to be *forty-three* generations; besides which, there
is only the two names of David and Joseph that are alike in
the two lists.—I here insert both genealogical lists, and for
the sake of perspicuity and comparison, have placed them
both in the same direction, that is, from Joseph down to
David.

Genealogy, according to Matthew.	Genealogy, according to Luke.
Christ	Christ
2 Joseph	2 Joseph
3 Jacob	3 Heli
4 Matthan	4 Matthat
5 Eleazer	5 Levi
6 Eliud	6 Melchi
7 Achim	7 Janna
8 Sadoc	8 Joseph
9 Azor	9 Mattathias
10 Eliakim	10 Amos

Genealogy, according to Matthew.	Genealogy, according to Luke.
11 Abiud	11 Naum
12 Zorobabel	12 Esli
13 Salathiel	13 Nagge
14 Jechonias	14 Maath
15 Josias	15 Mattathias
16 Amon	16 Semei
17 Manasses	17 Joseph
18 Ezekias	18 Juda
19 Achaz	19 Joanna
20 Joatham	20 Rhesa
21 Ozias	21 Zorobabel
22 Joram	22 Salathiel
23 Josaphat	23 Neri
24 Asa	24 Melchi
25 Abia	25 Addi
26 Roboam	26 Cosam
27 Solomon	27 Elmodam
28 David *	28 Er
	29 Jose
	30 Eliezer
	31 Jorim
	32 Matthat
	33 Levi
	34 Simeon
	35 Juda
	36 Joseph
	37 Jonan
	38 Eliakim
	39 Melea
	40 Menan
	41 Mattatha
	42 Nathan
	43 David

* From the birth of David to the birth of Christ is upwards of 1080 years; and as the life-time of Christ is not included, there are but 27 full generations. To find therefore the average age of each person mentioned in the list, at the time his first son was born, it is only necessary to divide 1080 by 27, which gives 40 years for each person. As the life-time of man was then but of the same extent it is now, it is an absurdity to suppose, that 27 following generations should all be old bachelors, before they married; and the more so, when we are told that Solomon, the next in succession to David, had a house full of wives and mistresses before he was twenty-one years of age. So far from this genealogy being a solemn truth, it is not even a reasonable lie. The list of Luke gives about twenty-six years for the average age, and this is too much.—*Author.*

Now, if these men, Matthew and Luke, set out with a falsehood between them (as these two accounts shew they do) in the very commencement of their history of Jesus Christ, and of who, and of what he was, what authority (as I have before asked) is there left for believing the strange things they tell us afterwards? If they cannot be believed in their account of his natural genealogy, how are we to believe them when they tell us he was the son of God, begotten by a ghost ; and that an angel announced this in secret to his mother? If they lied in one genealogy, why are we to believe them in the other? If his natural gene- alogy be manufactured, which it certainly is, why are we not to suppose that his celestial genealogy is manufactured also, and that the whole is fabulous? Can any man of serious reflection hazard his future happiness upon the belief of a story naturally impossible, repugnant to every idea of decency, and related by persons already detected of false- hood? Is it not more safe that we stop ourselves at the plain, pure, and unmixed belief of one God, which is deism, than that we commit ourselves on an ocean of improbable, irrational, indecent, and contradictory tales?

The first question, however, upon the books of the New Testament, as upon those of the Old, is, Are they genuine? were they written by the persons to whom they are ascribed? For it is upon this ground only that the strange things related therein have been credited. Upon this point, there is no *direct proof for or against ;* and all that this state of a case proves is *doubtfulness ;* and doubtfulness is the opposite of belief. The state, therefore, that the books are in, proves against themselves as far as this kind of proof can go.

But, exclusive of this, the presumption is that the books called the Evangelists, and ascribed to Matthew, Mark, Luke, and John, were not written by Matthew, Mark, Luke, and John ; and that they are impositions. The dis- ordered state of the history in these four books, the silence of one book upon matters related in the other, and the dis- agreement that is to be found among them, implies that they are the productions of some unconnected individuals, many years after the things they pretend to relate, each of whom made his own legend; and not the writings of men living intimately together, as the men called apostles are supposed to have done: in fine, that they have been manufactured, as the books of the Old Testament have been, by other persons than those whose names they bear.

The story of the angel announcing what the church calls the *immaculate conception,* is not so much as mentioned in the books ascribed to Mark, and John; and is differently related in Matthew and Luke. The former says the angel, appeared to Joseph; the latter says, it was to Mary; but either Joseph or Mary was the worst evidence that could have been thought of; for it was others that should have testified *for them,* and not they for themselves. Were any girl that is now with child to say, and even to swear it, that she was gotten with child by a ghost, and that an angel told her so, would she be believed? Certainly she would not. Why then are we to believe the same thing of another girl whom we never saw, told by nobody knows who, nor when, nor where? How strange and inconsistent is it, that the same circumstance that would weaken the belief even of a probable story, should be given as a motive for believing this one, that has upon the face of it every token of absolute impossibility and imposture.

The story of Herod destroying all the children under two years old, belongs altogether to the book of Matthew; not one of the rest mentions anything about it. Had such a circumstance been true, the universality of it must have made it known to all the writers, and the thing would have been too striking to have been omitted by any. This writer tell us, that Jesus escaped this slaughter, because Joseph and Mary were warned by an angel to flee with him into Egypt; but he forgot to make provision for John [the Baptist], who was then under two years of age. John, however, who staid behind, fared as well as Jesus, who fled; and therefore the story circumstantially belies itself.

Not any two of these writers agree in reciting, *exactly in the same words,* the written inscription, short as it is, which

they tell us was put over Christ when he was crucified; and
besides this, Mark says, He was crucified at the third hour,
(nine in the morning;) and John says it was the sixth hour,
(twelve at noon.*)

The inscription is thus stated in those books:

Matthew—This is Jesus the king of the Jews.
Mark ——The king of the Jews.
Luke ——This is the king of the Jews.
John ——Jesus of Nazareth the king of the Jews.

We may infer from these circumstances, trivial as they
are, that those writers, whoever they were, and in whatever
time they lived, were not present at the scene. The only
one of the men called apostles who appears to have been
near to the spot was Peter, and when he was accused of
being one of Jesus's followers, it is said, (Matthew xxvi. 74,)
" *Then Peter began to curse and to swear, saying, I know not
the man:* " yet we are now called to believe the same Peter,
convicted, by their own account, of perjury. For what
reason, or on what authority, should we do this?

The accounts that are given of the circumstances, that
they tell us attended the crucifixion, are differently related
in those four books.

The book ascribed to Matthew says *there was darkness over
all the land from the sixth hour unto the ninth hour—that the
veil of the temple was rent in twain from the top to the bottom
—that there was an earthquake—that the rocks rent—that the
graves opened, that the bodies of many of the saints that slept
arose and came out of their graves after the resurrection, and
went into the holy city and appeared unto many.* Such is the
account which this dashing writer of the book of Matthew
gives, but in which he is not supported by the writers of the
other books.

The writer of the book ascribed to Mark, in detailing the

---

* According to John, (xix. 14) the sentence was not passed till about the
sixth hour (noon,) and consequently the execution could not be till the after-
noon; but Mark (xv. 25) says expressly that he was crucified at the third hour,
(nine in the morning,)—*Author.*

circumstances of the crucifixion, makes no mention of any earthquake, nor of the rocks rending, nor of the graves open-ing, nor of the dead men walking out. The writer of the book of Luke is silent also upon the same points. And as to the writer of the book of John, though he details all the circumstances of the crucifixion down to the burial of Christ, he says nothing about either the darkness—the veil of the temple—the earthquake—the rocks—the graves—nor the dead men.

Now if it had been true that these things had happened, and if the writers of these books had lived at the time they did happen, and had been the persons they are said to be —namely, the four men called apostles, Matthew, Mark, Luke, and John,—it was not possible for them, as true historians, even without the aid of inspiration, not to have recorded them. The things, supposing them to have been facts, were of too much notoriety not to have been known, and of too much importance not to have been told. All these supposed apostles must have been witnesses of the earthquake, if there had been any, for it was not possible for them to have been absent from it: the opening of the graves and resurrection of the dead men, and their walking about the city, is of still greater importance than the earth-quake. An earthquake is always possible, and natural, and proves nothing; but this opening of the graves is super-natural, and directly in point to their doctrine, their cause, and their apostleship. Had it been true, it would have filled up whole chapters of those books, and been the chosen theme and general chorus of all the writers; but instead of this, little and trivial things, and mere prattling conversation of *he said this* and *she said that* are often tediously detailed, while this most important of all, had it been true, is passed off in a slovenly manner by a single dash of the pen, and that by one writer only, and not so much as hinted at by the rest.

It is an easy thing to tell a lie, but it is difficult to support the lie after it is told. The writer of the book of Matthew should have told us who the saints were that came to life

again, and went into the city, and what became of them
afterwards, and who it was that saw them ; for he is not
hardy enough to say that he saw them himself ;—whether
they came out naked, and all in natural buff, he-saints and
she-saints, or whether they came full dressed, and where
they got their dresses ; whether they went to their former
habitations, and reclaimed their wives, their husbands, and
their property, and how they were received ; whether they
entered ejectments for the recovery of their possessions, or
brought actions of *crim. con.* against the rival interlopers ;
whether they remained on earth, and followed their former
occupation of preaching or working ; or whether they died
again, or went back to their graves alive, and buried themselves.

Strange indeed, that an army of saints should return to
life, and nobody know who they were, nor who it was that
saw them, and that not a word more should be said upon the
subject, nor these saints have any thing to tell us ! Had it
been the prophets who (as we are told) had formerly prophesied of these things, *they* must have had a great deal to say.
They could have told us everything, and we should have had
posthumous prophecies, with notes and commentaries upon
the first, a little better at least than we have now. Had it
been Moses, and Aaron, and Joshua, and Samuel, and David,
not an unconverted Jew had remained in all Jerusalem.
Had it been John the Baptist; and the saints of the times
then present, everybody would have known them, and they
would have out-preached and out-famed all the other apostles.
But, instead of this, these saints are made to pop up, like
Jonah's gourd in the night, for no purpose at all but to wither
in the morning.—Thus much for this part of the story.

The tale of the resurrection follows that of the crucifixion ;
and in this as well as in that, the writers, whoever they were,
disagree so much as to make it evident that none of them
were there.

The book of Matthew states, that when Christ was put in
the sepulchre the Jews applied to Pilate for a watch or a
guard to be placed over the sepulchre, to prevent the body

being stolen by the disciples ; and that in consequence of this request the sepulchre *was made sure, sealing the stone* that covered the mouth, and setting a watch. But the other books say nothing about this application, nor about the sealing, nor the guard, nor the watch ; and according to their accounts, there were none. Matthew, however, follows up this part of the story of the guard or the watch with a second part, that I shall notice in the conclusion, as it serves to detect the fallacy of those books.

The book of Matthew continues its account, and says, (xxviii. 1,) that at the end of the Sabbath, as it began to *dawn*, towards the first day of the week, came *Mary Magdalene* and the *other Mary*, to see the sepulchre. Mark says it was sun-rising, and John says it was dark. Luke says it was Mary Magdalene and Joanna, and *Mary the mother* of James, and *other women*, that came to the sepulchre ; and John states that Mary Magdalene came alone. So well do they agree about their first evidence! They all, however, appear to have known most about Mary Magdalene ; she was a woman of large acquaintance, and it was not an ill conjecture that she might be upon the stroll.[1]

The book of Matthew goes on to say (ver. 2): "And behold there was a great earthquake, for the angel of the Lord descended from heaven, and came and rolled back the stone from the door, and *sat upon it.*" But the other books say nothing about any earthquake, nor about the angel rolling back the stone, and *sitting upon it ;* and, according to their account, there was no angel *sitting there.* Mark says the angel[2] was *within the sepulchre, sitting* on the right side. Luke says there were two, and they were both standing up ; and John says they were both sitting down, one at the head and the other at the feet.

Matthew says, that the angel that was sitting upon the

---

[1] The Bishop of Llandaff, in his famous " Apology," censured Paine severely for this insinuation against Mary Magdalene, but the censure really falls on our English version, which, by a chapter-heading (Luke vii.), has unwarrantably identified her as the sinful woman who anointed Jesus, and irrevocably branded her.—*Editor.*

[2] Mark says " a young man," and Luke " two men."—*Editor.*

stone on the outside of the sepulchre told the two Marys that Christ was risen, and that the women went *away* quickly. Mark says, that the women, upon seeing the stone rolled away, and wondering at it, went *into* the sepulchre, and that it was the angel that was *sitting* within on the right side, that told them so. Luke says, it was the two angels that were standing up; and John says, it was Jesus Christ himself that told it to Mary Magdalene; and that she did not go into the sepulchre, but only stooped down and looked in.

Now, if the writers of these four books had gone into a court of justice to prove an *alibi*, (for it is of the nature of an alibi that is here attempted to be proved, namely, the absence of a dead body by supernatural means,) and had they given their evidence in the same contradictory manner as it is here given, they would have been in danger of having their ears cropt for perjury, and would have justly deserved it. Yet this is the evidence, and these are the books, that have been imposed upon the world as being given by divine inspiration, and as the unchangeable word of God.

The writer of the book of Matthew, after giving this account, relates a story that is not to be found in any of the other books, and which is the same I have just before alluded to. "Now," says he, [that is, after the conversation the women had had with the angel sitting upon the stone,] "behold some of the watch [meaning the watch that he had said had been placed over the sepulchre] came into the city, and shewed unto the chief priests all the things that were done; and when they were assembled with the elders and had taken counsel, they gave large money unto the soldiers, saying, Say ye, that his disciples came by night, and stole him away while we *slept;* and if this come to the governor's ears, we will persuade him, and secure you. So they took the money, and did as they were taught; and this saying [that his disciples stole him away] is commonly reported among the Jews *until this day*."

The expression, *until this day*, is an evidence that the book ascribed to Matthew was not written by Matthew, and that it has been manufactured long after the times and things of which it pretends to treat; for the expression implies a great length of intervening time. It would be inconsistent in us to speak in this manner of any thing happening in our own time. To give, therefore, intelligible meaning to the expression, we must suppose a lapse of some generations at least, for this manner of speaking carries the mind back to ancient time.

The absurdity also of the story is worth noticing; for it shews the writer of the book of Matthew to have been an exceeding weak and foolish man. He tells a story that contradicts itself in point of possibility; for though the guard, if there were any, might be made to say that the body was taken away while they were *asleep*, and to give that as a reason for their not having prevented it, that same sleep must also have prevented their knowing how, and by whom, it was done; and yet they are made to say that it was the disciples who did it. Were a man to tender his evidence of something that he should say was done, and of the manner of doing it, and of the person who did it, while he was asleep, and could know nothing of the matter, such evidence could not be received: it will do well enough for Testament evidence, but not for any thing where truth is concerned.

I come now to that part of the evidence in those books, that respects the pretended appearance of Christ after this pretended resurrection.

The writer of the book of Matthew relates, that the angel that was sitting on the stone at the mouth of the sepulchre, said to the two Marys (xxviii. 7), " *Behold Christ is gone before you into Galilee, there ye shall see him ; lo, I have told you.*" And the same writer at the next two verses (8, 9,) makes Christ himself to speak to the same purpose to these women immediately after the angel had told it to them, and that they ran quickly to tell it to the disciples; and it is said (ver. 16), " *Then the eleven disciples went away into Galilee,* into a mountain where Jesus had appointed them; and, when they saw him, they worshipped him."

But the writer of the book of John tells us a story very

different to this; for he says (xx. 19) " Then the same day
at evening, being the first day of the week, [that is, the same
day that Christ is said to have risen,] when the doors were
shut, where the disciples were assembled, for fear of the
Jews, came Jesus and stood in the midst of them."

According to Matthew the eleven were marching to
Galilee, to meet Jesus in a mountain, by his own appointment, at the very time when, according to John, they were
assembled in another place, and that not by appointment,
but in secret, for fear of the Jews.

The writer of the book of Luke xxiv. 13, 33–36, contradicts that of Matthew more pointedly than John does; for
he says expressly, that the meeting was in Jerusalem the
evening of the same day that he (Christ) rose, and that the
eleven were *there*.

Now, it is not possible, unless we admit these supposed
disciples the right of wilful lying, that the writers of these
books could be any of the eleven persons called disciples;
for if, according to Matthew, the eleven went into Galilee
to meet Jesus in a mountain by his own appointment, on the
same day that he is said to have risen, Luke and John must
have been two of that eleven; yet the writer of Luke says
expressly, and John implies as much, that the meeting was
that same day, in a house in Jerusalem; and, on the other
hand, if, according to Luke and John, the *eleven* were assembled in a house in Jerusalem, Matthew must have been
one of that eleven; yet Matthew says the meeting was in a
mountain in Galilee, and consequently the evidence given in
those books destroy each other.

The writer of the book of Mark says nothing about any
meeting in Galilee; but he says (xvi. 12) that Christ, after
his resurrection, appeared in *another form* to two of them, as
they walked into the country, and that these two told it to
the residue, who would not believe them.[1] Luke also tells
a story, in which he keeps Christ employed the whole of the
day of this pretended resurrection, until the evening, and

---

[1] This belongs to the late addition to Mark, which originally ended with
xvi. 8.—*Editor*.

which totally invalidates the account of going to the mountain in Galilee. He says, that two of them, without saying
which two, went that *same day* to a village called Emmaus,
three score furlongs (seven miles and a half) from Jerusalem,
and that Christ in disguise went with them, and staid with
them unto the evening, and supped with them, and then
vanished out of their sight, and re-appeared that same evening, at the meeting of the eleven in Jerusalem.

This is the contradictory manner in which the evidence of
this pretended re-appearance of Christ is stated : the only
point in which the writers agree, is the skulking privacy of
that re-appearance ; for whether it was in the recess of a
mountain in Galilee, or in a shut-up house in Jerusalem, it
was still skulking. To what cause then are we to assign
this skulking? On the one hand, it is directly repugnant to
the supposed or pretended end, that of convincing the world
that Christ was risen ; and, on the other hand, to have
asserted the publicity of it would have exposed the writers
of those books to public detection ; and, therefore, they have
been under the necessity of making it a private affair.

As to the account of Christ being seen by more than five
hundred at once, it is Paul only who says it, and not the
five hundred who say it for themselves. It is, therefore, the
testimony of but one man, and that too of a man, who did
not, according to the same account, believe a word of the
matter himself at the time it is said to have happened. His
evidence, supposing him to have been the writer of Corinthians xv., where this account is given, is like that of a man
who comes into a court of justice to swear that what he had
sworn before was false. A man may often see reason, and
he has too always the right of changing his opinion ; but
this liberty does not extend to matters of fact.

I now come to the last scene, that of the ascension into
heaven.—Here all fear of the Jews, and of every thing else,
must necessarily have been out of the question : it was that
which, if true, was to seal the whole ; and upon which the
reality of the future mission of the disciples was to rest for
proof. Words, whether declarations or promises, that

passed in private, either in the recess of a mountain in Galilee, or in a shut-up house in Jerusalem, even supposing them to have been spoken, could not be evidence in public; it was therefore necessary that this last scene should preclude the possibility of denial and dispute; and that it should be, as I have stated in the former part of *The Age of Reason,* as public and as visible as the sun at noon-day; at least it ought to have been as public as the crucifixion is reported to have been.—But to come to the point.

In the first place, the writer of the book of Matthew does not say a syllable about it; neither does the writer of the book of John.   This being the case, is it possible to suppose that those writers, who affect to be even minute in other matters, would have been silent upon this, had it been true? The writer of the book of Mark passes it off in a careless, slovenly manner, with a single dash of the pen, as if he was tired of romancing, or ashamed of the story.   So also does the writer of Luke.   And even between these two, there is not an apparent agreement, as to the place where this final parting is said to have been.[1]

The book of Mark says that Christ appeared to the eleven as they sat at meat, alluding to the meeting of the eleven at Jerusalem: he then states the conversation that he says passed at that meeting; and immediately after says (as a school-boy would finish a dull story,) " *So then,* after the Lord had spoken unto them, he was received up into heaven, and sat on the right hand of God."   But the writer of Luke says, that the ascension was from Bethany; that *he* (Christ) *led them out as far as Bethany, and was parted from them there, and was carried up into heaven.*   So also was Mahomet: and, as to Moses, the *apostle* Jude says, ver. 9, *That Michael and the devil disputed about his body.*   While we believe such fables as these, or either of them, we believe unworthily of the Almighty.

I have now gone through the examination of the four

---

[1] The last nine verses of Mark being ungenuine, the story of the ascension rests exclusively on the words in Luke xxiv. 51, " was carried up into heaven," —words omitted by several ancient authorities.—*Editor.*

books ascribed to Matthew, Mark, Luke and John; and when it is considered that the whole space of time, from the crucifixion to what is called the ascension, is but a few days, apparently not more than three or four, and that all the circumstances are reported to have happened nearly about the same spot, Jerusalem, it is, I believe, impossible to find in any story upon record so many and such glaring absurdities, contradictions, and falsehoods, as are in those books. They are more numerous and striking than I had any expectation of finding, when I began this examination, and far more so than I had any idea of when I wrote the former part of *The Age of Reason*. I had then neither Bible nor Testament to refer to, nor could I procure any. My own situation, even as to existence, was becoming every day more precarious; and as I was willing to leave something behind me upon the subject, I was obliged to be quick and concise. The quotations I then made were from memory only, but they are correct; and the opinions I have advanced in that work are the effect of the most clear and long-established conviction, —that the Bible and the Testament are impositions upon the world;—that the fall of man, the account of Jesus Christ being the Son of God, and of his dying to appease the wrath of God, and of salvation by that strange means, are all fabulous inventions, dishonourable to the wisdom and power of the Almighty;—that the only true religion is deism, by which I then meant and now mean the belief of one God, and an imitation of his moral character, or the practice of what are called moral virtues;—and that it was upon this only (so far as religion is concerned) that I rested all my hopes of happiness hereafter. So say I now—and so help me God.

But to return to the subject.—Though it is impossible, at this distance of time, to ascertain as a fact who were the writers of those four books (and this alone is sufficient to hold them in doubt, and where we doubt we do not believe) it is not difficult to ascertain negatively that they were not written by the persons to whom they are ascribed. The contradictions in those books demonstrate two things:

First, that the writers cannot have been eye-witnesses and ear-witnesses of the matters they relate, or they would have related them without those contradictions ; and, consequently that the books have not been written by the persons called apostles, who are supposed to have been witnesses of this kind.

Secondly, that the writers, whoever they were, have not acted in concerted imposition, but each writer separately and individually for himself, and without the knowledge of the other.

The same evidence that applies to prove the one, applies equally to prove both cases; that is, that the books were not written by the men called apostles, and also that they are not a concerted imposition. As to inspiration, it is altogether out of the question ; we may as well attempt to unite truth and falsehood, as inspiration and contradiction.

If four men are eye-witnesses and ear-witnesses to a scene, they will without any concert between them, agree as to time and place, when and where that scene happened. Their individual knowledge of the *thing*, each one knowing it for himself, renders concert totally unnecessary ; the one will not say it was in a mountain in the country, and the other at a house in town ; the one will not say it was at sunrise, and the other that it was dark. For in whatever place it was, and whatever time it was, they know it equally alike.

And on the other hand, if four men concert a story, they will make their separate relations of that story agree and corroborate with each other to support the whole. *That* concert supplies the want of fact in the one case, as the knowledge of the fact supersedes, in the other case, the necessity of a concert. The same contradictions, therefore, that prove there has been no concert, prove also that the reporters had no knowledge of the fact, (or rather of that which they relate as a fact,) and detect also the falsehood of their reports. Those books, therefore, have neither been written by the men called apostles, nor by imposters in concert.—How then have they been written?

I am not one of those who are fond of believing there is

much of that which is called wilful lying, or lying originally, except in the case of men setting up to be prophets, as in the Old Testament; for prophesying is lying professionally. In almost all other cases it is not difficult to discover the progress by which even simple supposition, with the aid of credulity, will in time grow into a lie, and at last be told as a fact; and whenever we can find a charitable reason for a thing of this kind, we ought not to indulge a severe one.

The story of Jesus Christ appearing after he was dead is the story of an apparition, such as timid imaginations can always create in vision, and credulity believe. Stories of this kind had been told of the assassination of Julius Cæsar not many years before, and they generally have their origin in violent deaths, or in execution of innocent persons. In cases of this kind, compassion lends its aid, and benevolently stretches the story. It goes on a little and a little farther, till it becomes a *most certain truth*. Once start a ghost, and credulity fills up the history of its life, and assigns the cause of its appearance; one tells it one way, another another way, till there are as many stories about the ghost, and about the proprietor of the ghost, as there are about Jesus Christ in these four books.

The story of the appearance of Jesus Christ is told with that strange mixture of the natural and impossible, that distinguishes legendary tale from fact. He is represented as suddenly coming in and going out when the doors are shut, and of vanishing out of sight, and appearing again, as one would conceive of an unsubstantial vision; then again he is hungry, sits down to meat, and eats his supper. But as those who tell stories of this kind never provide for all the cases, so it is here: they have told us, that when he arose he left his grave-clothes behind him; but they have forgotten to provide other clothes for him to appear in afterwards, or to tell us what he did with them when he ascended; whether he stripped all off, or went up clothes and all. In the case of Elijah, they have been careful enough to make him throw down his mantle; how it happened not to be burnt in the chariot of fire, *they* also have not told us ; but as imagination supplies all deficiencies of this kind, we may suppose if we please that it was made of salamander's wool.

Those who are not much acquainted with ecclesiastical history, may suppose that the book called the New Testament has existed ever since the time of Jesus Christ, as they suppose that the books ascribed to Moses have existed ever since the time of Moses. But the fact is historically otherwise ; there was no such book as the New Testament till more than three hundred years after the time that Christ is said to have lived.

At what time the books ascribed to Matthew, Mark, Luke and John, began to appear, is altogether a matter of uncertainty. There is not the least shadow of evidence of who the persons were that wrote them, nor at what time they were written ; and they might as well have been called by the names of any of the other supposed apostles as by the names they are now called. The originals are not in the possession of any Christian Church existing, any more than the two tables of stone written on, they pretend, by the finger of God, upon Mount Sinai, and given to Moses, are in the possession of the Jews. And even if they were, there is no possibility of proving the hand-writing in either case. At the time those four books were written there was no printing, and consequently there could be no publication otherwise than by written copies, which any man might make or alter at pleasure, and call them originals. Can we suppose it is consistent with the wisdom of the Almighty to commit himself and his will to man upon such precarious means as these ; or that it is consistent we should pin our faith upon such uncertainties? We cannot make nor alter, nor even imitate, so much as one blade of grass that he has made, and yet we can make or alter *words of God* as easily as words of man.*

---

* The former part of the *Age of Reason* has not been published two years, and there is already an expression in it that is not mine. The expression is : *The book of Luke was carried by a majority of one voice only.* It may be true,

About three hundred and fifty years after the time that Christ is said to have lived, several writings of the kind I am speaking of were scattered in the hands of divers individuals; and as the church had begun to form itself into an hierarchy, or church government, with temporal powers, it set itself about collecting them into a code, as we now see them, called *The New Testament.* They decided by vote, as I have before said in the former part of the *Age of Reason,* which of those writings, out of the collection they had made, should be the *word of God,* and which should not. The Rabbins of the Jews had decided, by vote, upon the books of the Bible before.

As the object of the church, as is the case in all national establishments of churches, was power and revenue, and terror the means it used, it is consistent to suppose that the most miraculous and wonderful of the writings they had collected stood the best chance of being voted. And as to the authenticity of the books, the *vote stands in the place of it;* for it can be traced no higher.

Disputes, however, ran high among the people then calling themselves Christians, not only as to points of doctrine, but as to the authenticity of the books. In the contest between the person called St. Augustine, and Fauste, about the year 400, the latter says, " The books called the Evan-

---

but it is not I that have said it. Some person who might know of that circumstance, has added it in a note at the bottom of the page of some of the editions, printed either in England or in America ; and the printers, after that, have erected it into the body of the work, and made me the author of it. If this has happened within such a short space of time, notwithstanding the aid of printing, which prevents the alteration of copies individually, what may not have happened in a much greater length of time, when there was no printing, and when any man who could write could make a written copy and call it an original by Matthew, Mark, Luke, or John?—*Author.*

The spurious addition to Paine's work alluded to in his footnote drew on him a severe criticism from Dr. Priestley (" Letters to a Philosophical Unbeliever," p. 75), yet it seems to have been Priestley himself who, in his quotation, first incorporated into Paine's text the footnote added by the editor of the American edition (1794). The American added: "Vide Moshiem's (*sic*) Ecc. History," which Priestley omits. In a modern American edition I notice four verbal alterations introduced into the above footnote.—*Editor.*

gelists have been composed long after the times of the apostles, by some obscure men, who, fearing that the world would not give credit to their relation of matters of which they could not be informed, have published them under the names of the apostles; and which are so full of sottishness and discordant relations, that there is neither agreement nor connection between them."

And in another place, addressing himself to the advocates of those books, as being the word of God, he says, " It is thus that your predecessors have inserted in the scriptures of our Lord many things which, though they carry his name, agree not with his doctrine. This is not surprising, *since that we have often proved* that these things have not been written by himself, nor by his apostles, but that for the greatest part they are founded upon *tales*, upon *vague reports*, and put together by I know not what half Jews, with but little agreement between them; and which they have nevertheless published under the name of the apostles of our Lord, and have thus attributed to them their own *errors and their lies.**

The reader will see by those extracts that the authenticity of the books of the New Testament was denied, and the books treated as tales, forgeries, and lies, at the time they were voted to be the word of God. But the interest of the church, with the assistance of the faggot, bore down the opposition, and at last suppressed all investigation. Miracles followed upon miracles, if we will believe them, and men were taught to say they believed whether they believed or not. But (by way of throwing in a thought) the French Revolution has excommunicated the church from the power of working miracles; she has not been able, with the assistance of all her saints, to work *one* miracle since the revolution began; and as she never stood in greater need than now, we

---

* I have taken these two extracts from Boulanger's Life of Paul, written in French; Boulanger has quoted them from the writings of Augustine against Fauste, to which he refers.—*Author.*

This Bishop Faustus is usually styled " The Manichæan," Augustine having entitled his book, *Contra Faustum Manichæum Libri xxxiii.*, in which nearly the whole of Faustus' very able work is quoted.—*Editor.*

may, without the aid of divination, conclude that all her former miracles are tricks and lies.*

When we consider the lapse of more than three hundred years intervening between the time that Christ is said to have lived and the time the New Testament was formed into a book, we must see, even without the assistance of historical evidence, the exceeding uncertainty there is of its authenticity. The authenticity of the book of Homer, so far as regards the authorship, is much better established than that of the New Testament, though Homer is a thousand years the most ancient. It was only an exceeding good poet that could have written the book of Homer, and, therefore, few men only could have attempted it; and a man capable of doing it would not have thrown away his own fame by giving it to another. In like manner, there were but few that could have composed Euclid's Elements, because none but an exceeding good geometrician could have been the author of that work.

---

* Boulanger in his life of Paul, has collected from the ecclesiastical histories, and the writings of the fathers as they are called, several matters which shew the opinions that prevailed among the different sects of Christians, at the time the Testament, as we now see it, was voted to be the word of God. The following extracts are from the second chapter of that work:

The Marcionists (a Christian sect) asserted that the evangelists were filled with falsities. The Manichæans, who formed a very numerous sect at the commencement of Christianity, *rejected as false all the New Testament*, and shewed other writings quite different that they gave for authentic. The Cerinthians, like the Marcionists, admitted not the Acts of the Apostles. The Encratites and the Sevenians adopted neither the Acts, nor the Epistles of Paul. Chrysostom, in a homily which he made upon the Acts of the Apostles, says that in his time, about the year 400, many people knew nothing either of the author or of the book. St. Irene, who lived before that time, reports that the Valentinians, like several other sects of the Christians, accused the scriptures of being filled with imperfections, errors, and contradictions. The Ebionites, or Nazarenes, who were the first Christians, rejected all the Epistles of Paul, and regarded him as an impostor. They report, among other things, that he was originally a Pagan; that he came to Jerusalem, where he lived some time; and that having a mind to marry the daughter of the high priest, he had himself been circumcised; but that not being able to obtain her, he quarrelled with the Jews and wrote against circumcision, and against the observation of the Sabbath, and against all the legal ordinances.—*Author*. [Much abridged from the *Exam. Crit. de la Vie de St. Paul*, by N. A. Boulanger, 1770.—*Editor*.]

But with respect to the books of the New Testament, particularly such parts as tell us of the resurrection and ascension
of Christ, any person who could tell a story of an apparition,
or of a *man's walking*, could have made such books ; for the
story is most wretchedly told.   The chance, therefore, of
forgery in the Testament is millions to one greater than in
the case of Homer or Euclid.   Of the numerous priests or
parsons of the present day, bishops and all, every one of
them can make a sermon, or translate a scrap of Latin,
especially if it has been translated a thousand times before ;
but is there any amongst them that can write poetry like
Homer, or science like Euclid ?   The sum total of a parson's
learning, with very few exceptions, is a, b, ab, and hic, hæc,
hoc ; and their knowledge of science is, three times one is
three ; and this is more than sufficient to have enabled them,
had they lived at the time, to have written all the books of
the New Testament.

As the opportunities of forgery were greater, so also was
the inducement.   A man could gain no advantage by
writing under the name of Homer or Euclid ; if he could
write equal to them, it would be better that he wrote under
his own name ; if inferior, he could not succeed.   Pride
would prevent the former, and impossibility the latter.   But
with respect to such books as compose the New Testament,
all the inducements were on the side of forgery.   The best
imagined history that could have been made, at the distance
of two or three hundred years after the time, could not have
passed for an original under the name of the real writer ; the
only chance of success lay in forgery ; for the church wanted
pretence for its new doctrine, and truth and talents were out
of the question.

But as it is not uncommon (as before observed) to relate
stories of persons *walking* after they are dead, and of ghosts
and apparitions of such as have fallen by some violent or
extraordinary means ; and as the people of that day were in
the habit of believing such things, and of the appearance of
angels, and also of devils, and of their getting into people's
insides, and skaking them like a fit of an ague, and of their

being cast out again as if by an emetic—(Mary Magdalene,
the book of Mark tells us had brought up, or been brought
to bed of seven devils;) it was nothing extraordinary that
some story of this kind should get abroad of the person
called Jesus Christ, and become afterwards the foundation
of the four books ascribed to Matthew, Mark, Luke, and
John. Each writer told a tale as he heard it, or thereabouts,
and gave to his book the name of the saint or the apostle
whom tradition had given as the eye-witness. It is only
upon this ground that the contradictions in those books can
be accounted for; and if this be not the case, they are downright impositions, lies, and forgeries, without even the apology of credulity.

That they have been written by a sort of half Jews, as the
foregoing quotations mention, is discernible enough. The
frequent references made to that chief assassin and impostor
Moses, and to the men called prophets, establishes this
point; and, on the other hand, the church has complimented
the fraud, by admitting the Bible and the Testament to
reply to each other. Between the Christian-Jew and the
Christian-Gentile, the thing called a prophecy, and the thing
prophesied of, the type and the thing typified, the sign and
the thing signified, have been industriously rummaged up,
and fitted together like old locks and pick-lock keys. The
story foolishly enough told of Eve and the serpent, and
naturally enough as to the enmity between men and ser-
pents (for the serpent always bites about the *heel*, because it
cannot reach higher, and the man always knocks the serpent
about the *head*, as the most effectual way to prevent its
biting;*) this foolish story, I say, has been made into a
prophecy, a type, and a promise to begin with; and the
lying imposition of Isaiah to Ahaz, *That a virgin shall conceive and bear a son*, as a sign that Ahaz should conquer,
when the event was that he was defeated (as already noticed
in the observations on the book of Isaiah), has been per-
verted, and made to serve as a winder up.

* " It shall bruise thy *head*, and thou shalt bruise his *heel*."   Gen. iii. 15.—
Author.

Jonah and the whale are also made into a sign and type. Jonah is Jesus, and the whale is the grave; for it is said, (and they have made Christ to say it of himself, Matt. xii. 40), "For as Jonah was *three days* and *three nights* in the whale's belly, so shall the Son of man be *three days* and *three nights* in the heart of the earth." But it happens, aukwardly enough, that Christ, according to their own account, was but one day and two nights in the grave; about 36 hours instead of 72; that is, the Friday night, the Saturday, and the Saturday night; for they say he was up on the Sunday morning by sunrise, or before. But as this fits quite as well as the *bite* and the *kick* in Genesis, or the *virgin* and her *son* in Isaiah, it will pass in the lump of *orthodox* things.—Thus much for the historical part of the Testament and its evidences.

Epistles of Paul.—The epistles ascribed to Paul, being fourteen in number, almost fill up the remaining part of the Testament. Whether those epistles were written by the person to whom they are ascribed is a matter of no great importance, since that the writer, whoever he was, attempts to prove his doctrine by argument. He does not pretend to have been witness to any of the scenes told of the resurrection and the ascension; and he declares that he had not believed them.

The story of his being struck to the ground as he was journeying to Damascus, has nothing in it miraculous or extraordinary; he escaped with life, and that is more than many others have done, who have been struck with lightning; and that he should lose his sight for three days, and be unable to eat or drink during that time, is nothing more than is common in such conditions. His companions that were with him appear not to have suffered in the same manner, for they were well enough to lead him the remainder of the journey; neither did they pretend to have seen any vision.

The character of the person called Paul, according to the accounts given of him, has in it a great deal of violence and fanaticism; he had persecuted with as much heat as he preached afterwards; the stroke he had received had changed his thinking, without altering his constitution; and either as a Jew or a Christian he was the same zealot. Such men are never good moral evidences of any doctrine they preach. They are always in extremes, as well of action as of belief.

The doctrine he sets out to prove by argument, is the resurrection of the same body: and he advances this as an evidence of immortality. But so much will men differ in their manner of thinking, and in the conclusions they draw from the same premises, that this doctrine of the resurrection of the same body, so far from being an evidence of immortality, appears to me to be an evidence against it; for if I have already died in this body, and am raised again in the same body in which I have died, it is presumptive evidence that I shall die again. That resurrection no more secures me against the repetition of dying, than an ague-fit, when past, secures me against another. To believe therefore in immortality, I must have a more elevated idea than is contained in the gloomy doctrine of the resurrection.

Besides, as a matter of choice, as well as of hope, I had rather have a better body and a more convenient form than the present. Every animal in the creation excels us in something. The winged insects, without mentioning doves or eagles, can pass over more space with greater ease in a few minutes than man can in an hour. The glide of the smallest fish, in proportion to its bulk, exceeds us in motion almost beyond comparison, and without weariness. Even the sluggish snail can ascend from the bottom of a dungeon, where man, by the want of that ability, would perish; and a spider can launch itself from the top, as a playful amusement. The personal powers of man are so limited, and his heavy frame so little constructed to extensive enjoyment, that there is nothing to induce us to wish the opinion of Paul to be true. It is too little for the magnitude of the scene, too mean for the sublimity of the subject.

But all other arguments apart, the *consciousness of existence* is the only conceivable idea we can have of another life, and the continuance of that consciousness is immortality. The consciousness of existence, or the knowing that we exist, is not necessarily confined to the same form, nor to the same matter, even in this life.

We have not in all cases the same form, nor in any case the same matter, that composed our bodies twenty or thirty years ago; and yet we are conscious of being the same persons. Even legs and arms, which make up almost half the human frame, are not necessary to the consciousness of existence. These may be lost or taken away, and the full consciousness of existence remain; and were their place supplied by wings, or other appendages, we cannot conceive that it could alter our consciousness of existence. In short, we know not how much, or rather how little, of our composition it is, and how exquisitely fine that little is, that creates in us this consciousness of existence; and all beyond that is like the pulp of a peach, distinct and separate from the vegetative speck in the kernel.

Who can say by what exceeding fine action of fine matter it is that a thought is produced in what we call the mind? and yet that thought when produced, as I now produce the thought I am writing, is capable of becoming immortal, and is the only production of man that has that capacity.

Statues of brass and marble will perish; and statues made in imitation of them are not the same statues, nor the same workmanship, any more than the copy of a picture is the same picture. But print and reprint a thought a thousand times over, and that with materials of any kind, carve it in wood, or engrave it on stone, the thought is eternally and identically the same thought in every case. It has a capacity of unimpaired existence, unaffected by change of matter, and is essentially distinct, and of a nature different from every thing else that we know of, or can conceive. If then the thing produced has in itself a capacity of being immortal, it is more than a token that the power that produced it, which is the self-same thing as consciousness of existence, can be immortal also; and that as independently of the matter it was first connected with, as the thought is of the printing or writing it first appeared in. The one idea is not more difficult to believe than the other; and we can see that one is true.

That the consciousness of existence is not dependent on the same form or the same matter, is demonstrated to our senses in the works of the creation, as far as our senses are capable of receiving that demonstration. A very numerous part of the animal creation preaches to us, far better than Paul, the belief of a life hereafter. Their little life resembles an earth and a heaven, a present and a future state; and comprises, if it may be so expressed, immortality in miniature.

The most beautiful parts of the creation to our eye are the winged insects, and they are not so originally. They acquire that form and that inimitable brilliancy by progressive changes. The slow and creeping caterpillar worm of to day, passes in a few days to a torpid figure, and a state resembling death; and in the next change comes forth in all the miniature magnificence of life, a splendid butterfly. No resemblance of the former creature remains; every thing is changed; all his powers are new, and life is to him another thing. We cannot conceive that the consciousness of existence is not the same in this state of the animal as before; why then must I believe that the resurrection of the same body is necessary to continue to me the consciousness of existence hereafter?

In the former part of *The Age of Reason*, I have called the creation the true and only real word of God; and this instance, or this text, in the book of creation, not only shews to us that this thing may be so, but that it is so; and that the belief of a future state is *a rational belief*, founded upon facts visible in the creation: for it is not more difficult to believe that we shall exist hereafter in a better state and form than at present, than that a worm should become a butterfly, and quit the dunghill for the atmosphere, if we did not know it as a fact.

As to the doubtful jargon ascribed to Paul in 1 Corinthians xv., which makes part of the burial service of some Christian

sectaries, it is as destitute of meaning as the tolling of a bell
at the funeral; it explains nothing to the understanding, it
illustrates nothing to the imagination, but leaves the reader
to find any meaning if he can. "All flesh," says he, "is not
the same flesh. There is one flesh of men, another of beasts,
another of fishes, and another of birds." And what then?
nothing. A cook could have said as much. "There are
also," says he, "bodies celestial and bodies terrestrial; the
glory of the celestial is *one* and the glory of the terrestrial is
the *other.*" And what then? nothing. And what is the
difference? nothing that he has told. "There is," says he,
"one glory of the sun, and another glory of the moon, and
another glory of the stars." And what then? nothing; except that he says that *one star differeth from another star in
glory*, instead of distance; and he might as well have told
us that the moon did not shine so bright as the sun. All
this is nothing better than the jargon of a conjuror, who
picks up phrases he does not understand to confound the
credulous people who come to have their fortune told.
Priests and conjurors are of the same trade.

Sometimes Paul affects to be a naturalist, and to prove
his system of resurrection from the principles of vegetation.
"*Thou fool,*" says he, "*that which thou sowest is not quickened
except it die.*" To which one might reply in his own language, and say, Thou fool, Paul, that which thou sowest is
not quickened except it die *not;* for the grain that dies in
the ground never does, nor can vegetate. It is only the
living grains that produce the next crop. But the metaphor, in any point of view, is no simile. It is succession,
and [not] resurrection.

The progress of an animal from one state of being to another, as from a worm to a butterfly, applies to the case;
but this of a. grain does not, and shews Paul to have been
what he says of others, *a fool.*

Whether the fourteen epistles ascribed to Paul were written by him or not, is a matter of indifference; they are
either argumentative or dogmatical; and as the argument is
defective, and the dogmatical part is merely presumptive, it

signifies not who wrote them. And the same may be said
for the remaining parts of the Testament. It is not upon
the Epistles, but upon what is called the Gospel, contained
in the four books ascribed to Matthew, Mark, Luke, and
John, and upon the pretended prophecies, that the theory
of the church, calling itself the Christian Church, is founded.
The Epistles are dependant upon those, and must follow
their fate; for if the story of Jesus Christ be fabulous, all
reasoning founded upon it, as a supposed truth, must fall
with it.

We know from history, that one of the principal leaders
of this church, Athanasius, lived at the time the New Testament was formed; * and we know also, from the absurd jargon he has left us under the name of a creed, the character
of the men who formed the New Testament; and we know
also from the same history that the authenticity of the books
of which it is composed was denied at the time. It was
upon the vote of such as Athanasius that the Testament
was decreed to be the word of God; and nothing can present to us a more strange idea than that of decreeing the
word of God by vote. Those who rest their faith upon
such authority put man in the place of God, and have no
true foundation for future happiness. Credulity, however,
is not a crime, but it becomes criminal by resisting conviction. It is strangling in the womb of the conscience the
efforts it makes to ascertain truth. We should never force
belief upon ourselves in any thing.

I here close the subject on the Old Testament and the
New. The evidence I have produced to prove them forgeries, is extracted from the books themselves, and acts,
like a two-edge sword, either way. If the evidence be denied, the authenticity of the Scriptures is denied with it, for
it is Scripture evidence: and if the evidence be admitted,
the authenticity of the books is disproved. The contradictory impossibilities, contained in the Old Testament and the
New, put them in the case of a man who swears *for* and

* Athanasius died, according to the Church chronology, in the year 371.—
Author.

against. Either evidence convicts him of perjury, and equally destroys reputation.

Should the Bible and the Testament hereafter fall, it is not that I have done it. I have done no more than extracted the evidence from the confused mass of matters with which it is mixed, and arranged that evidence in a point of light to be clearly seen and easily comprehended; and, having done this, I leave the reader to judge for himself, as I have judged for myself.

CHAPTER III.

CONCLUSION.

In the former part of *The Age of Reason* I have spoken of the three frauds, *mystery*, *miracle*, and *prophecy;* and as I have seen nothing in any of the answers to that work that in the least affects what I have there said upon those subjects, I shall not encumber this Second Part with additions that are not necessary.

I have spoken also in the same work upon what is called *revelation*, and have shewn the absurd misapplication of that term to the books of the Old Testament and the New; for certainly revelation is out of the question in reciting any thing of which man has been the actor or the witness. That which man has done or seen, needs no revelation to tell him he has done it, or seen it—for he knows it already—nor to enable him to tell it or to write it. It is ignorance, or imposition, to apply the term revelation in such cases; yet the Bible and Testament are classed under this fraudulent description of being all *revelation*.

Revelation then, so far as the term has relation between God and man, can only be applied to something which God reveals of his will to man; but though the power of the Almighty to make such a communication is necessarily admitted, because to that power all things are possible, yet, the thing so revealed (if any thing ever was revealed, and which, by the bye, it is impossible to prove) is revelation to the person *only to whom it is made.* His account of it to another is not revelation; and whoever puts faith in that account, puts it in the man from whom the account comes; and that man may have been deceived, or may have dreamed

it ; or he may be an impostor and may lie. There is no possible criterion whereby to judge of the truth of what he tells ;
for even the morality of it would be no proof of revelation.
In all such cases, the proper answer should be, " When it is
revealed to me, I will believe it to be revelation ; but it is
not and cannot be incumbent upon me to believe it to be
revelation before; neither is it proper that I should take the
word of man as the word of God, and put man in the place
of God." This is the manner in which I have spoken of
revelation in the former part of *The Age of Reason ;* and
which, whilst it reverentially admits revelation as a possible
thing, because, as before said, to the Almighty all things are
possible, it prevents the imposition of one man upon another,
and precludes the wicked use of pretended revelation.

But though, speaking for myself, I thus admit the possibility of revelation, I totally disbelieve that the Almighty
ever did communicate any thing to man, by any mode of
speech, in any language, or by any kind of vision, or appearance, or by any means which our senses are capable of receiving, otherwise than by the universal display of himself
in the works of the creation, and by that repugnance we feel
in ourselves to bad actions, and disposition to good ones.[1]

The most detestable wickedness, the most horrid cruelties,
and the greatest miseries, that have afflicted the human race,
have had their origin in this thing called revelation, or revealed religion. It has been the most dishonourable belief
against the character of the divinity, the most destructive
to morality, and the peace and happiness of man, that ever

[1] A fair parallel of the then unknown aphorism of Kant : " Two things fill the
soul with wonder and reverence, increasing evermore as I meditate more closely
upon them : the starry heavens above me and the moral law within me." (*Kritik
der praktischen Vernunft*, 1788). Kant's religious utterances at the beginning
of the French Revolution brought on him a royal mandate of silence, because he
had worked out from " the moral law within" a principle of human equality precisely similar to that which Paine had derived from his Quaker doctrine of the
" inner light " of every man. About the same time Paine's writings were suppressed in England. Paine did not understand German, but Kant, though
always independent in the formation of his opinions, was evidently well acquainted with the literature of the Revolution, in America, England, and
France.—*Editor*.

was propagated since man began to exist. It is better, far better, that we admitted, if it were possible, a thousand devils to roam at large, and to preach publicly the doctrine of devils, if there were any such, than that we permitted one such impostor and monster as Moses, Joshua, Samuel, and the Bible prophets, to come with the pretended word of God in his mouth, and have credit among us.

Whence arose all the horrid assassinations of whole nations of men, women, and infants, with which the Bible is filled ; and the bloody persecutions, and tortures unto death and religious wars, that since that time have laid Europe in blood and ashes ; whence arose they, but from this impious thing called revealed religion, and this monstrous belief that God has spoken to man ? The lies of the Bible have been the cause of the one, and the lies of the Testament [of] the other.

Some Christians pretend that Christianity was not estab-lished by the sword ; but of what period of time do they speak ? It was impossible that twelve men could begin with the sword : they had not the power ; but no sooner were the professors of Christianity sufficiently powerful to employ the sword than they did so, and the stake and faggot too ; and Mahomet could not do it sooner. By the same spirit that Peter cut off the ear of the high priest's servant (if the story be true) he would cut off his head, and the head of his master, had he been able. Besides this, Christianity grounds itself originally upon the [Hebrew] Bible, and the Bible was established altogether by the sword, and that in the worst use of it—not to terrify, but to extirpate. The Jews made no converts : they butchered all. The Bible is the sire of the [New] Testament, and both are called the *word of God.* The Christians read both books ; the minis-ters preach from both books ; and this thing called Christi-anity is made up of both. It is then false to say that Christianity was not established by the sword.

The only sect that has not persecuted are the Quakers ; and the only reason that can be given for it is, that they are rather Deists than Christians. They do not believe much about Jesus Christ, and they call the scriptures a dead letter.¹ Had they called them by a worse name, they had been nearer the truth.

It is incumbent on every man who reverences the character of the Creator, and who wishes to lessen the catalogue of artificial miseries, and remove the cause that has sown persecutions thick among mankind, to expel all ideas of a revealed religion as a dangerous heresy, and an impious fraud. What is it that we have learned from this pretended thing called revealed religion? Nothing that is useful to man, and every thing that is dishonourable to his Maker. What is it the Bible teaches us?—rapine, cruelty, and murder. What is it the Testament teaches us?—to believe that the Almighty committed debauchery with a woman engaged to be married; and the belief of this debauchery is called faith.

As to the fragments of morality that are irregularly and thinly scattered in those books, they make no part of this pretended thing, revealed religion. They are the natural dictates of conscience, and the bonds by which society is held together, and without which it cannot exist ; and are nearly the same in all religions, and in all societies. The Testament teaches nothing new upon this subject, and where it attempts to exceed, it becomes mean and ridiculous. The doctrine of not retaliating injuries is much better expressed in Proverbs, which is a collection as well from the Gentiles as the Jews, than it is in the Testament. It is there said, (xxv. 21) "*If thine enemy be hungry, give him bread to eat ; and if he be thirsty, give him water to drink :* " * but when it is

---

¹ This is an interesting and correct testimony as to the beliefs of the earlier Quakers, one of whom was Paine's father.—*Editor.*

* According to what is called Christ's sermon on the mount, in the book of Matthew, where, among some other [and] good things, a great deal of this feigned morality is introduced, it is there expressly said, that the doctrine of forbearance, or of not retaliating injuries, *was not any part of the doctrine of the Jews ;* but as this doctrine is found in " Proverbs," it must, according to that statement, have been copied from the Gentiles, from whom Christ had learned it. Those men whom Jewish and Christian idolators have abusively called heathen, had much better and clearer ideas of justice and morality than are to be found in the Old Testament, so far as it is Jewish, or in the New. The answer of Solon on the question, " Which is the most perfect popular govern-

said, as in the Testament, "*If a man smite thee on the right cheek, turn to him the other also,*" it is assassinating the dignity of forbearance, and sinking man into a spaniel.

Loving of enemies is another dogma of feigned morality, and has besides no meaning. It is incumbent on man, as a moralist, that he does not revenge an injury; and it is equally as good in a political sense, for there is no end to retaliation; each retaliates on the other, and calls it justice: but to love in proportion to the injury, if it could be done, would be to offer a premium for a crime. Besides, the word *enemies* is too vague and general to be used in a moral maxim, which ought always to be clear and defined, like a proverb. If a man be the enemy of another from mistake and prejudice, as in the case of religious opinions, and sometimes in politics, that man is different to an enemy at heart with a criminal intention; and it is incumbent upon us, and it contributes also to our own tranquillity, that we put the best construction upon a thing that it will bear. But even this erroneous motive in him makes no motive for love on the other part; and to say that we can love voluntarily, and without a motive, is morally and physically impossible.

Morality is injured by prescribing to it duties that, in the first place, are impossible to be performed, and if they could be would be productive of evil; or, as before said, be premiums for crime. The maxim *of doing as we would be done unto* does not include this strange doctrine of loving enemies; for no man expects to be loved himself for his crime or for his enmity.

Those who preach this doctrine of loving their enemies, are in general the greatest persecutors, and they act consistently by so doing; for the doctrine is hypocritical, and it is natural that hypocrisy should act the reverse of what it preaches. For my own part, I disown the doctrine, and consider it as a feigned or fabulous morality; yet the man

ment," has never been exceeded by any man since his time, as containing a maxim of political morality. "That," says he, "where the least injury done to the meanest individual, is considered as an insult on the whole constitution." Solon lived about 500 years before Christ.—*Author.*

does not exist that can say I have persecuted him, or any man, or any set of men, either in the American Revolution, or in the French Revolution; or that I have, in any case, returned evil for evil. But it is not incumbent on man to reward a bad action with a good one, or to return good for evil; and wherever it is done, it is a voluntary act, and not a duty. It is also absurd to suppose that such doctrine can make any part of a revealed religion. We imitate the moral character of the Creator by forbearing with each other, for he forbears with all; but this doctrine would imply that he loved man, not in proportion as he was good, but as he was bad.

If we consider the nature of our condition here, we must see there is no occasion for such a thing as *revealed religion*. What is it we want to know? Does not the creation, the universe we behold, preach to us the existence of an Almighty power, that governs and regulates the whole? And is not the evidence that this creation holds out to our senses infinitely stronger than any thing we can read in a book, that any imposter might make and call the word of God? As for morality, the knowledge of it exists in every man's conscience.

Here we are. The existence of an Almighty power is sufficiently demonstrated to us, though we cannot conceive, as it is impossible we should, the nature and manner of its existence. We cannot conceive how we came here ourselves, and yet we know for a fact that we are here. We must know also, that the power that called us into being, can if he please, and when he pleases, call us to account for the manner in which we have lived here; and therefore, without seeking any other motive for the belief, it is rational to believe that he will, for we know beforehand that he can. The probability or even possibility of the thing is all that we ought to know; for if we knew it as a fact, we should be the mere slaves of terror; our belief would have no merit, and our best actions no virtue.

Deism then teaches us, without the possibility of being deceived, all that is necessary or proper to be known. The creation is the Bible of the deist. He there reads, in the hand-writing of the Creator himself, the certainty of his existence, and the immutability of his power; and all other Bibles and Testaments are to him forgeries. The probability that we may be called to account hereafter, will, to reflecting minds, have the influence of belief; for it is not our belief or disbelief that can make or unmake the fact. As this is the state we are in, and which it is proper we should be in, as free agents, it is the fool only, and not the philosopher, nor even the prudent man, that will live as if there were no God.

But the belief of a God is so weakened by being mixed with the strange fable of the Christian creed, and with the wild adventures related in the Bible, and the obscurity and obscene nonsense of the Testament, that the mind of man is bewildered as in a fog. Viewing all these things in a confused mass, he confounds fact with fable; and as he cannot believe all, he feels a disposition to reject all. But the belief of a God is a belief distinct from all other things, and ought not to be confounded with any. The notion of a Trinity of Gods has enfeebled the belief of *one* God. A multiplication of beliefs acts as a division of belief; and in proportion as anything is divided, it is weakened.

Religion, by such means, becomes a thing of form instead of fact; of notion instead of principle: morality is banished to make room for an imaginary thing called faith, and this faith has its origin in a supposed debauchery; a man is preached instead of a God; an execution is an object for gratitude; the preachers daub themselves with the blood, like a troop of assassins, and pretend to admire the brilliancy it gives them; they preach a humdrum sermon on the merits of the execution; then praise Jesus Christ for being executed, and condemn the Jews for doing it.

A man, by hearing all this nonsense lumped and preached together, confounds the God of the Creation with the imagined God of the Christians, and lives as if there were none.

Of all the systems of religion that ever were invented,

there is none more derogatory to the Almighty, more unedi-
fying to man, more repugnant to reason, and more contradictory in itself, than this thing called Christianity.   Too
absurd for belief, too impossible to convince, and too inconsistent for practice, it renders the heart torpid, or produces
only atheists and fanatics.   As an engine of power, it serves
the purpose of despotism ; and as a means of wealth, the
avarice of priests ; but so far as respects the good of man in
general, it leads to nothing here or hereafter.

The only religion that has not been invented, and that
has in it every evidence of divine originality, is pure and
simple deism.   It must have been the first and will probably be the last that man believes.   But pure and simple
deism does not answer the purpose of despotic governments.   They cannot lay hold of religion as an engine but
by mixing it with human inventions, and making their own
authority a part ; neither does it answer the avarice of
priests, but by incorporating themselves and their functions
with it, and becoming, like the government, a party in the
system.   It is this that forms the otherwise mysterious connection of church and state ; the church human, and the
state tyrannic.

Were a man impressed as fully and strongly as he ought
to be with the belief of a God, his moral life would be
regulated by the force of belief ; he would stand in awe of
God, and of himself, and would not do the thing that could
not be concealed from either.   To give this belief the full
opportunity of force, it is necessary that it acts alone.   This
is deism.

But when, according to the Christian Trinitarian scheme,
one part of God is represented by a dying man, and another
part, called the Holy Ghost, by a flying pigeon, it is impossible that belief can attach itself to such wild conceits.*

* The book called the book of Matthew, says, (iii. 16,) that *the Holy Ghost
descended in the shape of a dove.*   It might as well have said a goose ; the
creatures are equally harmless, and the one is as much a nonsensical lie as the
other.   Acts, ii. 2, 3, says, that it descended in a mighty *rushing wind*, in the
shape of *cloven tongues :* perhaps it was cloven feet.   Such absurd stuff is fit
only for tales of witches and wizards.—*Author.*

It has been the scheme of the Christian church, and of all the other invented systems of religion, to hold man in ignorance of the Creator, as it is of government to hold him in ignorance of his rights. The systems of the one are as false as those of the other, and are calculated for mutual support. The study of theology as it stands in Christian churches, is the study of nothing; it is founded on nothing; it rests on no principles; it proceeds by no authorities; it has no data; it can demonstrate nothing; and admits of no conclusion. Not any thing can be studied as a science without our being in possession of the principles upon which it is founded; and as this is not the case with Christian theology, it is therefore the study of nothing.

Instead then of studying theology, as is now done, out of the Bible and Testament, the meanings of which books are always controverted, and the authenticity of which is disproved, it is necessary that we refer to the Bible of the creation. The principles we discover there are eternal, and of divine origin: they are the foundation of all the science that exists in the world, and must be the foundation of theology.

We can know God only through his works. We cannot have a conception of any one attribute, but by following some principle that leads to it. We have only a confused idea of his power, if we have not the means of comprehending something of its immensity. We can have no idea of his wisdom, but by knowing the order and manner in which it acts. The principles of science lead to this knowledge; for the Creator of man is the Creator of science, and it is through that medium that man can see God, as it were, face to face.

Could a man be placed in a situation, and endowed with power of vision to behold at one view, and to contemplate deliberately, the structure of the universe, to mark the movements of the several planets, the cause of their varying appearances, the unerring order in which they revolve, even to the remotest comet, their connection and dependence on each other, and to know the system of laws estab-

lished by the Creator, that governs and regulates the whole;
he would then conceive, far beyond what any church theology
can teach him, the power, the wisdom, the vastness, the
munificence of the Creator. He would then see that all the
knowledge man has of science, and that all the mechanical
arts by which he renders his situation comfortable here, are
derived from that source: his mind, exalted by the scene,
and convinced by the fact, would increase in gratitude as it
increased in knowledge: his religion or his worship would
become united with his improvement as a man : any employ-
ment he followed that had connection with the principles of
the creation,—as everything of agriculture, of science, and
of the mechanical arts, has,—would teach him more of God,
and of the gratitude he owes to him, than any theological
Christian sermon he now hears. Great objects inspire great
thoughts; great munificence excites great gratitude; but the
grovelling tales and doctrines of the Bible and the Testament are fit only to excite contempt.

Though man cannot arrive, at least in this life, at the
actual scene I have described, he can demonstrate it, because he has knowledge of the principles upon which the
creation is constructed. We know that the greatest works
can be represented in model, and that the universe can be
represented by the same means. The same principles by
which we measure an inch or an acre of ground will measure
to millions in extent. A circle of an inch diameter has the
same geometrical properties as a circle that would circum-
scribe the universe. The same properties of a triangle that
will demonstrate upon paper the course of a ship, will do it
on the ocean; and, when applied to what are called the
heavenly bodies, will ascertain to a minute the time of an
eclipse, though those bodies are millions of miles distant
from us. This knowledge is of divine origin; and it is from
the Bible of the creation that man has learned it, and not
from the stupid Bible of the church, that teaches man
nothing.*

* The Bible-makers have undertaken to give us, in the first chapter of
Genesis, an account of the creation; and in doing this they have demonstrated

All the knowledge man has of science and of machinery, by the aid of which his existence is rendered comfortable upon earth, and without which he would be scarcely distinguishable in appearance and condition from a common animal, comes from the great machine and structure of the universe. The constant and unwearied observations of our ancestors upon the movements and revolutions of the heavenly bodies, in what are supposed to have been the early ages of the world, have brought this knowledge upon earth. It is not Moses and the prophets, nor Jesus Christ, nor his apostles, that have done it. The Almighty is the great mechanic of the creation, the first philosopher, and original teacher of all science. Let us then learn to reverence our master, and not forget the labours of our ancestors.

Had we, at this day, no knowledge of machinery, and were it possible that man could have a view, as I have before described, of the structure and machinery of the universe, he would soon conceive the idea of constructing some at least of the mechanical works we now have ; and the idea so conceived would progressively advance in practice. Or could a model of the universe, such as is called an orrery, be presented before him and put in motion, his mind would arrive at the same idea. Such an object and such a subject would, whilst it improved him in knowledge

nothing but their ignorance. They make there to have been three days and three nights, evenings and mornings, before there was any sun ; when it is the presence or absence of the sun that is the cause of day and night—and what is called his rising and setting, that of morning and evening. Besides, it is a puerile and pitiful idea, to suppose the Almighty to say, " Let there be light." It is the imperative manner of speaking that a conjuror uses when he says to his cups and balls, Presto, be gone—and most probably has been taken from it, as Moses and his rod is a conjuror and his wand. Longinus calls this expression the sublime ; and by the same rule the conjuror is sublime too ; for the manner of speaking is expressively and grammatically the same. When authors and critics talk of the sublime, they see not how nearly it borders on the ridiculous. The sublime of the critics, like some parts of Edmund Burke's sublime and beautiful, is like a windmill just visible in a fog, which imagination might distort into a flying mountain, or an archangel, or a flock of wild geese.—*Author.*

useful to himself as a man and a member of society, as well
as entertaining, afford far better matter for impressing him
with a knowledge of, and a belief in the Creator, and of the
reverence and gratitude that man owes to him, than the
stupid texts of the Bible and the Testament, from which,
be the talents of the preacher what they may, only stupid
sermons can be preached. If man must preach, let him
preach something that is edifying, and from the texts that
are known to be true.

The Bible of the creation is inexhaustible in texts. Every
part of science, whether connected with the geometry of the
universe, with the systems of animal and vegetable life, or
with the properties of inanimate matter, is a text as well for
devotion as for philosophy—for gratitude, as for human improvement. It will perhaps be said, that if such a revolution
in the system of religion takes place, every preacher ought to
be a philosopher. *Most certainly*, and every house of devotion a school of science.

It has been by wandering from the immutable laws of
science, and the light of reason, and setting up an invented thing called "revealed religion," that so many wild
and blasphemous conceits have been formed of the Almighty. The Jews have made him the assassin of the
human species, to make room for the religion of the Jews.
The Christians have made him the murderer of himself,
and the founder of a new religion to supersede and expel
the Jewish religion. And to find pretence and admission
for these things, they must have supposed his power or his
wisdom imperfect, or his will changeable; and the change-
ableness of the will is the imperfection of the judgement.
The philosopher knows that the laws of the Creator have
never changed, with respect either to the principles of
science, or the properties of matter. Why then is it to be
supposed they have changed with respect to man?

I here close the subject. I have shewn in all the foregoing parts of this work that the Bible and Testament are
impositions and forgeries; and I leave the evidence I have

produced in proof of it to be refuted, if any one can do it; and I leave the ideas that are suggested in the conclusion of the work to rest on the mind of the reader; certain as I am that when opinions are free, either in matters of government or religion, truth will finally and powerfully prevail.

END OF "THE AGE OF REASON."

III.

LETTERS CONCERNING "THE AGE OF REASON."

I.

AN ANSWER TO A FRIEND.

PARIS, May 12, 1797.

IN your letter of the 20th of March, you give me several quotations from the Bible, which you call the *word of God*, to shew me that my opinions on religion are wrong, and I could give you as many, from the same book to shew that yours are not right; consequently, then, the Bible decides nothing, because it decides any way, and every way, one chooses to make it.

But by what authority do you call the Bible the *word of God?* for this is the first point to be settled. It is not your calling it so that makes it so, any more than the Mahometans calling the Koran the *word of God* makes the Koran to be so. The Popish Councils of Nice and Laodicea, about 350 years after the time the person called Jesus Christ is said to have lived, voted the books that now compose what is called the New Testament to be the *word of God*. This was done by *yeas* and *nays*, as we now vote a law. The pharisees of the second Temple, after the Jews returned from captivity in Babylon, did the same by the books that now compose the Old Testament, and this is all the authority there is, which to me is no authority at all. I am as capable of judging for myself as they were, and I think more so, because, as they made a living by their religion, they had a self-interest in the vote they gave.

You may have an opinion that a man is inspired, but you

cannot prove it, nor can you have any proof of it yourself,
because you cannot see into his mind in order to know how
he comes by his thoughts; and the same is the case with the
word *revelation.* There can be no evidence of such a thing,
for you can no more prove revelation than you can prove
what another man dreams of, neither can he prove it himself.

It is often said in the Bible that God spake unto Moses,
but how do you know that God spake unto Moses? Because, you will say, the Bible says so. The Koran says, that
God spake unto Mahomet, do you believe that too? No.
Why not? Because, you will say, you do not believe it;
and so because you *do*, and because you *don't* is all the reason
you can give for believing or disbelieving except that you
will say that Mahomet was an impostor. And how do you
know Moses was not an impostor? For my own part, I believe that all are impostors who pretend to hold verbal communication with the Deity. It is the way by which the
world has been imposed upon; but if you think otherwise
you have the same right to your opinion that I have to
mine, and must answer for it in the same manner. But all
this does not settle the point, whether the Bible be the *word
of God*, or not. It is therefore necessary to go a step further. The case then is :—

You form your opinion of God from the account given of
him in the Bible; and I form my opinion of the Bible from
the wisdom and goodness of God manifested in the structure
of the universe, and in all works of Creation. The result in
these two cases will be, that you, by taking the Bible for
your standard, will have a bad opinion of God; and I, by
taking God for my standard, shall have a bad opinion of the
Bible.

The Bible represents God to be a changeable, passionate,
vindictive Being; making a world and then drowning it,
afterwards repenting of what he had done, and promising
not to do so again. Setting one nation to cut the throats of
another, and stopping the course of the sun till the butchery
should be done. But the works of God in the Creation
preach to us another doctrine. In that vast volume we see

nothing to give us the idea of a changeable, passionate, vindictive God ; everything we there behold impresses us with a contrary idea,—that of unchangeableness and of eternal order, harmony, and goodness. The sun and the seasons return at their appointed time, and every thing in the Creation proclaims that God is unchangeable. Now, which am I to believe, a book that any impostor might make and call the *word of God*, or the Creation itself which none but an Almighty Power could make? For the Bible says one thing, and the Creation says the contrary. The Bible represents God with all the passions of a mortal, and the Creation proclaims him with all the attributes of a God.

It is from the Bible that man has learned cruelty, rapine, and murder; for the belief of a cruel God makes a cruel man. That bloodthirsty man, called the prophet Samuel, makes God to say, (1 Sam. xv. 3,) " Now go and smite Amaleck, and utterly destroy all that they have, and *spare them not, but slay both man and woman, infant and suckling, ox and sheep, camel and ass.*"

That Samuel or some other impostor might say this, is what, at this distance of time, can neither be proved nor disproved, but in my opinion it is blasphemy to say, or to believe, that God said it. All our ideas of the justice and goodness of God revolt at the impious cruelty of the Bible. It is not a God, just and good, but a devil, under the name of God, that the Bible describes.

What makes this pretended order to destroy the Amalekites appear the worse, is the reason given for it. The Amalekites, four hundred years before, according to the account in Exodus xvii. (but which has the appearance of fable from the magical account it gives of Moses holding up his hands,) had opposed the Israelites coming into their country, and this the Amalekites had a right to do, because the Israelites were the invaders, as the Spaniards were the invaders of Mexico ; and this opposition by the Amalekites, *at that time*, is given as a reason, that the men, women, infants and sucklings, sheep and oxen, camels and asses, that were born four hundred years afterwards, should be put to death ; and to complete the horror, Samuel hewed Agag, the chief of the Amalekites, in pieces, as you would hew a stick of wood. I will bestow a few observations on this case.

In the first place, nobody knows who the author, or writer, of the book of Samuel was, and, therefore, the fact itself has no other proof than anonymous or hearsay evidence, which is no evidence at all. In the second place, this anonymous book says, that this slaughter was done by *the express command of God :* but all our ideas of the justice and goodness of God give the lie to the book, and as I never will believe any book that ascribes cruelty and injustice to God, I therefore reject the Bible as unworthy of credit.

As I have now given you my reasons for believing that the Bible is not the word of God, that it is a falsehood, I have a right to ask you your reasons for believing the contrary ; but I know you can give me none, except that *you were educated to believe the Bible ;* and as the Turks give the same reason for believing the Koran, it is evident that education makes all the difference, and that reason and truth have nothing to do in the case. You believe in the Bible from the accident of birth, and the Turks believe in the Koran from the same accident, and each calls the other *infidel.* But leaving the prejudice of education out of the case, the unprejudiced truth is, that all are infidels who believe falsely of God, whether they draw their creed from the Bible, or from the Koran, from the Old Testament, or from the New.

When you have examined the Bible with the attention that I have done, (for I do not think you know much about it,) and permit yourself to have just ideas of God, you will most probably believe as I do. But I wish you to know that this answer to your letter is not written for the purpose of changing your opinion. It is written to satisfy you, and some other friends whom I esteem, that my disbelief of the Bible is founded on a pure and religious belief in God ; for in my opinion the Bible is a gross libel against the justice and goodness of God, in almost every part of it.

THOMAS PAINE.

II.

CORRESPONDENCE WITH THE HON. SAMUEL ADAMS.[1]

[*To the Editor of the " National Intelligencer," Federal City.*]

TOWARDS the latter end of last December I received a letter from a venerable patriot, Samuel Adams, dated Boston, Nov. 30. It came by a private hand, which I suppose was the cause of the delay. I wrote Mr. Adams an answer, dated Jan. 1st, and that I might be certain of his receiving it, and also that I might know of that reception, I desired a

[1] The Hon. Samuel Adams (1722–1803) was from the Stamp Act agitation of 1764 to the Declaration of Independence in 1776 the pre-eminent revolutionary leader in Massachusetts, and General Gage was given orders to send him over to London, where a newspaper predicted that his head would appear on Temple Bar. He was sent by Massachusetts, with his cousin, John Adams, afterwards President, to the first Continental Congress (1774), where he was suspected, with justice, of being favorable to separation from England. When Paine published his famous appeal for American Independence (January 10, 1776), Samuel Adams was the first member of the Congress at his side, and a cordial lifelong relation existed between the two. It is to my mind certain that these two men were the real pioneers of American Independence, and they were both inspired therein by their widely different religious sentiments. Samuel Adams was the son of a deacon of the Old South Church, Boston, who sent his son to Harvard College with the hope that he would graduate into a minister. The son had no taste for theology, but he made up for it by retaining through all his career as a lawyer and public man a rigid Puritanism, of which the first article was hatred of the British system of royalty and prelacy. While Adams's desire for American independency was largely an inheritance from New England Puritans, Paine beheld in it a means of establishing a Republic based on the principles of Quakerism,—the divine Light in every man by virtue of which all were equal. Samuel Adams died October 2, 1803. The correspondence here given was printed in the *National Intelligencer*, Washington City, February 2, 1803, as one of a series of Ten Letters addressed to " The Citizens of the United States " on his return after his fifteen eventful years in Europe. These Letters were printed in a pamphlet in London, 1804, by his friend Thomas Clio Rickman, whose task, however, was achieved under sad intimidation. Rickman's preface opens with the words: " The following little work would not have been published, had there been anything in it the least offending against the government or individuals." Under this deadly fear the much prosecuted Rickman mutilated Paine's letter to Adams a good deal. I have been fortunate in being able to print the letter from Paine's own manuscript, which was recently discovered among the papers of George Bancroft, the historian, when they passed into the possession of the Lenox Library, New York, to whose excellent librarian I owe thanks for this and other favors.—*Editor.*

friend of mine at Washington to put it under cover to some friend of his at Boston, and desire him to present it to Mr. Adams. The letter was accordingly put under cover while I was present, and given to one of the clerks of the post office to seal and put in the mail. The clerk put it in his pocket book, and either forgot to put it into the mail, or supposed he had done so among other letters. The post-master general, on learning this mistake, informed me of it last Saturday, and as the cover was then out of date, the letter was put under a new cover, with the same request, and forwarded by the post. I felt concern at this accident, lest Mr. Adams should conclude I was unmindful of his attention to me ; and therefore, lest any further accident should prevent or delay his receiving it, as well as to relieve myself from that concern, I give the letter an opportunity of reaching him by the newspapers. I am the more induced to do this, because some manuscript copies have been taken of both letters, and therefore there is a possibility of imperfect copies getting into print ; and besides this, if some of the Federal[ist] printers (for I hope they are not all base alike) could get hold of a copy, they would make no scruple of altering it, and publishing it as mine. I therefore send you the original letter of Mr. Adams, and my own copy of the answer.

THOMAS PAINE.

FEDERAL CITY.

BOSTON, Nov. 30, 1802.

SIR :

I have frequently with pleasure reflected on your services to my native and your adopted country. Your *Common Sense* and your *Crisis* unquestionably awakened the public mind, and led the people loudly to call for a Declaration of our national Independence. I therefore esteemed you as a warm friend to the liberty and lasting welfare of the human race. But when I heard that you had turned your mind to a defence of infidelity, I felt myself much astonished and more grieved that you had attempted a measure so injurious to the feelings and so repugnant to the true interest of so great a part of the citizens of the United States. The people of New England, if you will allow me to use a scripture phrase, are fast returning to their first love. Will you excite among them the spirit of angry controversy, at a time when they are hastening to unity and peace? I am told that some of our newspapers have announced your intention to publish an additional pamphlet upon the principles of your *Age of Reason.* Do you think that your pen, or the pen of any other man, can unchristianize the mass of our citizens, or have you hopes of converting a few of them to assist you in so bad a cause? We ought to think ourselves happy in the enjoyment of opinion without the danger of persecution by civil or ecclesiastical law.

Our friend, the President of the United States,[1] has been calumniated for his liberal sentiments, by men who have attributed that liberality to a latent design to promote the cause of infidelity. This and all other slanders have been made without a shadow of proof. Neither religion nor liberty can long subsist in the tumult of altercation, and amidst the noise and violence of faction.

 Felix qui cautus.
 Adieu.
SAMUEL ADAMS.

Mr. THOMAS PAINE.

MY DEAR AND VENERABLE FRIEND SAMUEL ADAMS:

 I received with great pleasure your friendly and affectionate letter of November 30, and I thank you also for the frankness of it. Between men in pursuit of truth, and whose object is the Happiness of Man both here and hereafter, there ought to be no reserve. Even Error has a claim to indulgence, if not to respect, when it is believed to be truth.

 I am obliged to you for your affectionate remembrance of what you stile my services in awakening the public mind to a declaration of Independance, and supporting it after it was declared. I also, like you, have often looked back on those

----

[1] Thomas Jefferson.

times, and have thought that if independance had not been
declared at the time it was, the public mind could not have
been brought up to it afterwards. It will immediately occur
to you, who were so intimately acquainted with the situation
of things at that time, that I allude to the black times of
seventy-six ; for though I know, and you my friend also
know, they were no other than the natural consequence of
the military blunders of that campaign, the country might
have viewed them as proceeding from a natural inability to
support its Cause against the enemy, and have sunk under
the despondency of that misconceived Idea. This was the
impression against which it was necessary the Country should
be strongly animated.

I come now to the second part of your letter, on which I
shall be as frank with you as you are with me.

"But, (say you) when I *heard* you had turned your mind
to a defence of *Infidelity* I felt myself much astonished &c."
—What, my good friend, do you call believing in God
infidelity? for that is the great point maintained in *The Age
of Reason* against all divided beliefs and *allegorical* divini-
ties.[1] The bishop of Landaff (Doctor Watson) not only ac-
knowledges this, but pays me some compliments upon it (in
his answer to the second part of that work). " *There is* (says
he) *a philosophical sublimity in some of your Ideas when speaking of the Creator of the Universe.*"

What then (my much esteemed friend for I do not respect
you the less because we differ, and that perhaps not much,
in religious sentiments), what, I ask, is this thing called
infidelity? If we go back to your ancestors and mine three
or four hundred years ago, for we must have had fathers and
grandfathers or we should not be here, we shall find them
praying to Saints and Virgins, and believing in purgatory
and transubstantiation; and therefore all of us are infidels
according to our forefathers' belief. If we go back to times
more ancient we shall again be infidels according to the
belief of some other forefathers.

[1] The ten concluding words of this sentence were omitted from Rickman's
edition, the close being " in the work alluded to."—*Editor.*

The case my friend is, that the World has been over-run with fable and creeds of human invention, with sectaries of whole Nations against all other Nations, and sectaries of those sectaries in each of them against each other. Every sectary, except the quakers, has been a persecutor. Those who fled from persecution persecuted in their turn, and it is this confusion of creeds that has filled the World with persecution and deluged it with blood. Even the depredation on your commerce by the barbary powers sprang from the Cruisades of the church against those powers. It was a war of creed against creed, each boasting of God for its author, and reviling each other with the name of Infidel. If I do not believe as you believe, it proves that you do not believe as I believe, and this is all that it proves.

There is however one point of Union wherein all religions meet, and that is in the first article of every Man's Creed, and of every Nation's Creed, that has any Creed at all : *I believe in God.* Those who rest here, and there are millions who do, cannot be wrong as far as their Creed goes. Those who chuse to go further *may be wrong*, for it is impossible that all can be right, since there is so much contradiction among them. The first therefore are, in my opinion, on the safest side.

I presume you are so far acquainted with ecclesiastical history as to know, and the bishop who has answered me has been obliged to acknowledge the fact, that the books that compose the New Testament were voted by *Yeas* and *Nays* to be the Word of God, as you now vote a law, by the popish Councils of Nice and Laodocia about 1450 years ago. With respect to the fact there is no dispute, neither do I mention it for the sake of controversy. This Vote may appear authority enough to some, and not authority enough to others. It is proper however that everybody should know the fact.[1]

---

[1] This paragraph was omitted by Rickman with a footnote saying : " A paragraph of eleven lines is here omitted, it being a principle with the Editor to offend neither the government nor individuals. Its insertion is also unnecessary, as the curious reader will find it answered in a way well worth his notice by the

With respect to *The Age of Reason*, which you so much condemn, and that I believe without having read it, for you say only that you *heard* of it, I will inform you of a Circumstance, because you cannot know it by other means.

I have said in the first page of the First Part of that work that it had long been my intention to publish my thoughts upon Religion, but that I had reserved it to a later time of life. I have now to inform you why I wrote it and published it at the time I did.

In the first place, I saw my life in continual danger. My friends were falling as fast as the guilleotine could cut their heads off, and as I every day expected the same fate, I resolved to begin my Work. I appeared to myself to be on my death-bed, for death was on every side of me, and I had no time to lose. This accounts for my writing it at the time I did ; and so nicely did the time and the intention meet, that I had not finished the first part of that Work more than six hours before I was arrested and taken to prison. Joel Barlow was with me and knows the fact.

In the second place, the people of france were running headlong into Atheism, and I had the work translated and published in their own language to stop them in that carreer, and fix them to the first article (as I have before said) of every man's Creed who has any Creed at all, *I believe in God.* I endangered my own life, in the first place, by opposing in the Convention the execution of the king, and by labouring to shew they were trying the Monarchy and not the Man, and that the crimes imputed to him were the crimes of the monarchical [1] system ; and I endangered it a second time by opposing Atheism ; and yet *some* of your priests, for I do not believe that all are perverse, cry out, in the war-whoop of monarchical priestcraft, What an Infidel, what a wicked Man, is Thomas Paine ! They might as well add, for he believes in God and is against shedding blood.

---

bishop of Llandaff. See his apology for the Bible, from page 300 to 307." The title " Age of Reason " is also suppressed in the next paragraph, and elsewhere. —*Editor.*

[1] This word is omitted by Rickman.—*Editor.*

But all this *war-whoop* of the pulpit [1] has some concealed object. Religion is not the Cause, but is the stalking horse. They put it forward to conceal themselves behind it. It is not a secret that there has been a party composed of the leaders of the federalists, for I do not include all federalists with their leaders, who have been working by various means for several years past to overturn the federal Constitution established on the representative system, and place Government in the new World on the corrupt system of the old.[2] To accomplish this, a large standing army was necessary, and as a pretence for such an army the danger of a foreign invasion must be bellowed forth from the pulpit, from the press, and by their public orators.

I am not of a disposition inclined to suspicion. It is in its nature a mean and cowardly passion, and upon the whole, even admitting error into the case, it is better, I am sure it is more generous, to be wrong on the side of confidence than on the side of suspicion.[3] But I know as a fact that the english Government distributes annually fifteen hundred pounds sterling among the presbyterian ministers in England and one thousand among those of Ireland ;[4] and when I hear of the strange discourses of some of your ministers and professors of Colleges, I cannot, as the quakers say, find freedom in my mind to acquit them. Their anti-revolutionary doctrines invite suspicion even against one's will, and in spite of one's charity to believe well of them.

As you have given me one scripture phrase I will give you another for those ministers. It is said in Exodus xxii. 28, " *Thou shalt not revile the Gods nor curse the ruler of thy people.*" But those ministers, such I mean as Dr. Emmons,[5]

---

[1] The words " of the pulpit " omitted by Rickman.—*Editor.*

[2] The preceding fourteen words omitted by Rickman.—*Editor.*

[3] The words "it is better " and " on the side of Confidence than " are dropped out of the sentence in Rickman's edition.—*Editor.*

[4] See vol. iii. p. 85, of my edition of *Paine's Writings,* where the amounts are stated as £1700 to the dissenting Ministers in England, and £800 to those of Ireland.—The preceding 29 words, and the remainder of this paragraph, are omitted by Rickman.—*Editor*

[5] Nathaniel Emmons, D.D. (1745–1840), fifty-four years minister of the

curse ruler and people both, for the majority are, politically, the people, and it is those who have chosen the ruler whom they curse. As to the first part of the verse, that of *not reviling the Gods*, it makes no part of my scripture. I have but one God.[1]

Since I began this letter, for I write it by piece-meals as I have leisure, I have seen the four letters that passed between you and John Adams. In your first letter you say, " Let divines and Philosophers, statesmen and patriots, unite their endeavours to *renovate the age* by inculcating in the minds of youth *the fear and love of the Deity and universal philanthropy.*" Why, my dear friend, this is exactly *my* religion, and is the whole of it. That you may have an Idea that *The Age of Reason* (for I believe you have not read it) inculcates this reverential fear and love of the Deity I will give you a paragraph from it.

" Do we want to contemplate his power ? We see it in the immensity of the Creation. Do we want to contemplate his wisdom : We see it in the unchangeable order by which the incomprehensible Whole is governed. Do we want to contemplate his munificence ? We see it in the abundance with which he fills the Earth. Do we want to contemplate his mercy ? We see it in his not withholding that abundance even from the unthankful."

As I am fully with you in your first part, that respecting the Deity, so am I in your second, that of *universal philanthropy ;* by which I do not mean merely the sentimental benevolence of wishing well, but the practical benevolence of doing good. We cannot serve the Deity in the manner we serve those who cannot do without that service. He needs no service from us. We can add nothing to eternity. But it is in our power to render a service *acceptable* to him, and that is not by praying, but by endeavouring to make

Franklin, Mass., Congregational Church. He was a vehement Federalist, and assailant of President Jefferson.—*Editor*.

[1] This and the preceding sentence are omitted by Rickman.—*Editor*.

his creatures happy.   A man does not serve God when he prays, for it is himself he is trying to serve; and as to hiring or paying men to pray, as if the Deity needed instruction, it is, in my opinion, an abomination.   One good schoolmaster is of more use and of more value than a load of such persons as Dr. Emmons and some others.[1]

You, my dear and much respected friend, are now far in the vale of years; I have yet, I believe, some years in store, for I have a good state of health and a happy mind, and I take care of both, by nourishing the first with temperance and the latter with abundance.   This, I believe, you will allow to be the true philosophy of life.   You will see by my third letter to the Citizens of the United States that I have been exposed to, and preserved through, many dangers; but instead of buffetting the Deity with prayers as if I distrusted him, or must dictate to him,[2] I reposed myself on his protection; and you, my friend, will find, even in your last moments, more consolation in the silence of resignation than in the murmuring wish of a prayer.

In every thing which you say in your second letter to John Adams, respecting our Rights as Men and Citizens in this World, I am perfectly with you.   On other points we have to answer to our Creator and not to each other.   The key of heaven is not in the keeping of any sect, nor ought the road to it be obstructed by any.   Our relation to each other in this World is as Men, and the Man who is a friend to Man and to his rights, let his religious opinions be what they may, is a good citizen, to whom I can give, as I ought to do, and as every other ought, the right hand of fellowship, and to none with more hearty good will, my dear friend, than to you.

THOMAS PAINE.

FEDERAL CITY, January 1, 1803.

[1] This and the preceding sentence omitted by Rickman.—*Editor.*
[2] This and the seventeen preceding words omitted by Rickman.—*Editor.*

STICKLEY CRAFTSMAN FURNITURE CATALOGS, Gustav Stickley and L. & J. G. Stickley. Beautiful, functional furniture in two authentic catalogs from 1910. 594 illustrations, including 277 photos, show settles, rockers, armchairs, reclining chairs, bookcases, desks, tables. 183pp. 6½ x 9¼. 0-486-23838-5

AMERICAN LOCOMOTIVES IN HISTORIC PHOTOGRAPHS: 1858 to 1949, Ron Ziel (ed.). A rare collection of 126 meticulously detailed official photographs, called "builder portraits," of American locomotives that majestically chronicle the rise of steam locomotive power in America. Introduction. Detailed captions. xi+ 129pp. 9 x 12. 0-486-27393-8

AMERICA'S LIGHTHOUSES: An Illustrated History, Francis Ross Holland, Jr. Delightfully written, profusely illustrated fact-filled survey of over 200 American lighthouses since 1716. History, anecdotes, technological advances, more. 240pp. 8 x 10¾. 0-486-25576-X

TOWARDS A NEW ARCHITECTURE, Le Corbusier. Pioneering manifesto by founder of "International School." Technical and aesthetic theories, views of industry, economics, relation of form to function, "mass-production split" and much more. Profusely illustrated. 320pp. 6⅛ x 9¼. (Available in U.S. only.) 0-486-25023-7

HOW THE OTHER HALF LIVES, Jacob Riis. Famous journalistic record, exposing poverty and degradation of New York slums around 1900, by major social reformer. 100 striking and influential photographs. 233pp. 10 x 7⅞. 0-486-22012-5

FRUIT KEY AND TWIG KEY TO TREES AND SHRUBS, William M. Harlow. One of the handiest and most widely used identification aids. Fruit key covers 120 deciduous and evergreen species; twig key 160 deciduous species. Easily used. Over 300 photographs. 126pp. 5⅜ x 8½. 0-486-20511-8

COMMON BIRD SONGS, Dr. Donald J. Borror. Songs of 60 most common U.S. birds: robins, sparrows, cardinals, bluejays, finches, more—arranged in order of increasing complexity. Up to 9 variations of songs of each species.
Cassette and manual 0-486-99911-4

ORCHIDS AS HOUSE PLANTS, Rebecca Tyson Northen. Grow cattleyas and many other kinds of orchids–in a window, in a case, or under artificial light. 63 illustrations. 148pp. 5⅜ x 8½. 0-486-23261-1

MONSTER MAZES, Dave Phillips. Masterful mazes at four levels of difficulty. Avoid deadly perils and evil creatures to find magical treasures. Solutions for all 32 exciting illustrated puzzles. 48pp. 8¼ x 11. 0-486-26005-4

MOZART'S DON GIOVANNI (DOVER OPERA LIBRETTO SERIES), Wolfgang Amadeus Mozart. Introduced and translated by Ellen H. Bleiler. Standard Italian libretto, with complete English translation. Convenient and thoroughly portable–an ideal companion for reading along with a recording or the performance itself. Introduction. List of characters. Plot summary. 121pp. 5¼ x 8½. 0-486-24944-1

FRANK LLOYD WRIGHT'S DANA HOUSE, Donald Hoffmann. Pictorial essay of residential masterpiece with over 160 interior and exterior photos, plans, elevations, sketches and studies. 128pp. 9¼ x 10¾. 0-486-29120-0

THE CLARINET AND CLARINET PLAYING, David Pino. Lively, comprehensive work features suggestions about technique, musicianship, and musical interpretation, as well as guidelines for teaching, making your own reeds, and preparing for public performance. Includes an intriguing look at clarinet history. "A godsend," *The Clarinet,* Journal of the International Clarinet Society. Appendixes. 7 illus. 320pp. 5⅜ x 8½. 0-486-40270-3

HOLLYWOOD GLAMOR PORTRAITS, John Kobal (ed.). 145 photos from 1926-49. Harlow, Gable, Bogart, Bacall; 94 stars in all. Full background on photographers, technical aspects. 160pp. 8⅜ x 11¼. 0-486-23352-9

THE RAVEN AND OTHER FAVORITE POEMS, Edgar Allan Poe. Over 40 of the author's most memorable poems: "The Bells," "Ulalume," "Israfel," "To Helen," "The Conqueror Worm," "Eldorado," "Annabel Lee," many more. Alphabetic lists of titles and first lines. 64pp. 5³⁄₁₆ x 8¼. 0-486-26685-0

PERSONAL MEMOIRS OF U. S. GRANT, Ulysses Simpson Grant. Intelligent, deeply moving firsthand account of Civil War campaigns, considered by many the finest military memoirs ever written. Includes letters, historic photographs, maps and more. 528pp. 6⅛ x 9¼. 0-486-28587-1

ANCIENT EGYPTIAN MATERIALS AND INDUSTRIES, A. Lucas and J. Harris. Fascinating, comprehensive, thoroughly documented text describes this ancient civilization's vast resources and the processes that incorporated them in daily life, including the use of animal products, building materials, cosmetics, perfumes and incense, fibers, glazed ware, glass and its manufacture, materials used in the mummification process, and much more. 544pp. 6⅛ x 9¼. (Available in U.S. only.) 0-486-40446-3

RUSSIAN STORIES/RUSSKIE RASSKAZY: A Dual-Language Book, edited by Gleb Struve. Twelve tales by such masters as Chekhov, Tolstoy, Dostoevsky, Pushkin, others. Excellent word-for-word English translations on facing pages, plus teaching and study aids, Russian/English vocabulary, biographical/critical introductions, more. 416pp. 5⅜ x 8½. 0-486-26244-8

PHILADELPHIA THEN AND NOW: 60 Sites Photographed in the Past and Present, Kenneth Finkel and Susan Oyama. Rare photographs of City Hall, Logan Square, Independence Hall, Betsy Ross House, other landmarks juxtaposed with contemporary views. Captures changing face of historic city. Introduction. Captions. 128pp. 8¼ x 11. 0-486-25790-8

NORTH AMERICAN INDIAN LIFE: Customs and Traditions of 23 Tribes, Elsie Clews Parsons (ed.). 27 fictionalized essays by noted anthropologists examine religion, customs, government, additional facets of life among the Winnebago, Crow, Zuni, Eskimo, other tribes. 480pp. 6⅛ x 9¼. 0-486-27377-6

TECHNICAL MANUAL AND DICTIONARY OF CLASSICAL BALLET, Gail Grant. Defines, explains, comments on steps, movements, poses and concepts. 15-page pictorial section. Basic book for student, viewer. 127pp. 5⅜ x 8½. 0-486-21843-0

THE MALE AND FEMALE FIGURE IN MOTION: 60 Classic Photographic Sequences, Eadweard Muybridge. 60 true-action photographs of men and women walking, running, climbing, bending, turning, etc., reproduced from rare 19th-century masterpiece. vi + 121pp. 9 x 12. 0-486-24745-7

FRENCH STORIES/CONTES FRANÇAIS: A Dual-Language Book, Wallace Fowlie. Ten stories by French masters, Voltaire to Camus: "Micromegas" by Voltaire; "The Atheist's Mass" by Balzac; "Minuet" by de Maupassant; "The Guest" by Camus, six more. Excellent English translations on facing pages. Also French-English vocabulary list, exercises, more. 352pp. 5⅜ x 8½.   0-486-26443-2

CHICAGO AT THE TURN OF THE CENTURY IN PHOTOGRAPHS: 122 Historic Views from the Collections of the Chicago Historical Society, Larry A. Viskochil. Rare large-format prints offer detailed views of City Hall, State Street, the Loop, Hull House, Union Station, many other landmarks, circa 1904-1913. Introduction. Captions. Maps. 144pp. 9⅜ x 12¼.   0-486-24656-6

OLD BROOKLYN IN EARLY PHOTOGRAPHS, 1865-1929, William Lee Younger. Luna Park, Gravesend race track, construction of Grand Army Plaza, moving of Hotel Brighton, etc. 157 previously unpublished photographs. 165pp. 8⅞ x 11¾.   0-486-23587-4

THE MYTHS OF THE NORTH AMERICAN INDIANS, Lewis Spence. Rich anthology of the myths and legends of the Algonquins, Iroquois, Pawnees and Sioux, prefaced by an extensive historical and ethnological commentary. 36 illustrations. 480pp. 5⅜ x 8½.   0-486-25967-6

AN ENCYCLOPEDIA OF BATTLES: Accounts of Over 1,560 Battles from 1479 B.C. to the Present, David Eggenberger. Essential details of every major battle in recorded history from the first battle of Megiddo in 1479 B.C. to Grenada in 1984. List of Battle Maps. New Appendix covering the years 1967-1984. Index. 99 illustrations. 544pp. 6½ x 9¼.   0-486-24913-1

SAILING ALONE AROUND THE WORLD, Captain Joshua Slocum. First man to sail around the world, alone, in small boat. One of great feats of seamanship told in delightful manner. 67 illustrations. 294pp. 5⅜ x 8½.   0-486-20326-3

ANARCHISM AND OTHER ESSAYS, Emma Goldman. Powerful, penetrating, prophetic essays on direct action, role of minorities, prison reform, puritan hypocrisy, violence, etc. 271pp. 5⅜ x 8½.   0-486-22484-8

MYTHS OF THE HINDUS AND BUDDHISTS, Ananda K. Coomaraswamy and Sister Nivedita. Great stories of the epics; deeds of Krishna, Shiva, taken from puranas, Vedas, folk tales; etc. 32 illustrations. 400pp. 5⅜ x 8½.   0-486-21759-0

MY BONDAGE AND MY FREEDOM, Frederick Douglass. Born a slave, Douglass became outspoken force in antislavery movement. The best of Douglass' autobiographies. Graphic description of slave life. 464pp. 5⅜ x 8½.   0-486-22457-0

FOLLOWING THE EQUATOR: A Journey Around the World, Mark Twain. Fascinating humorous account of 1897 voyage to Hawaii, Australia, India, New Zealand, etc. Ironic, bemused reports on peoples, customs, climate, flora and fauna, politics, much more. 197 illustrations. 720pp. 5⅜ x 8½.   0-486-26113-1

THE PEOPLE CALLED SHAKERS, Edward D. Andrews. Definitive study of Shakers: origins, beliefs, practices, dances, social organization, furniture and crafts, etc. 33 illustrations. 351pp. 5⅜ x 8½.   0-486-21081-2

THE MYTHS OF GREECE AND ROME, H. A. Guerber. A classic of mythology, generously illustrated, long prized for its simple, graphic, accurate retelling of the principal myths of Greece and Rome, and for its commentary on their origins and significance. With 64 illustrations by Michelangelo, Raphael, Titian, Rubens, Canova, Bernini and others. 480pp. 5⅜ x 8½.   0-486-27584-1

DRIED FLOWERS: How to Prepare Them, Sarah Whitlock and Martha Rankin. Complete instructions on how to use silica gel, meal and borax, perlite aggregate, sand and borax, glycerine and water to create attractive permanent flower arrangements. 12 illustrations. 32pp. 5⅜ x 8½. 0-486-21802-3

EASY-TO-MAKE BIRD FEEDERS FOR WOODWORKERS, Scott D. Campbell. Detailed, simple-to-use guide for designing, constructing, caring for and using feeders. Text, illustrations for 12 classic and contemporary designs. 96pp. 5⅜ x 8½. 0-486-25847-5

THE COMPLETE BOOK OF BIRDHOUSE CONSTRUCTION FOR WOOD-WORKERS, Scott D. Campbell. Detailed instructions, illustrations, tables. Also data on bird habitat and instinct patterns. Bibliography. 3 tables. 63 illustrations in 15 figures. 48pp. 5¼ x 8½. 0-486-24407-5

SCOTTISH WONDER TALES FROM MYTH AND LEGEND, Donald A. Mackenzie. 16 lively tales tell of giants rumbling down mountainsides, of a magic wand that turns stone pillars into warriors, of gods and goddesses, evil hags, powerful forces and more. 240pp. 5⅜ x 8½. 0-486-29677-6

THE HISTORY OF UNDERCLOTHES, C. Willett Cunnington and Phyllis Cunnington. Fascinating, well-documented survey covering six centuries of English undergarments, enhanced with over 100 illustrations: 12th-century laced-up bodice, footed long drawers (1795), 19th-century bustles, l9th-century corsets for men, Victorian "bust improvers," much more. 272pp. 5⅜ x 8¼. 0-486-27124-2

ARTS AND CRAFTS FURNITURE: The Complete Brooks Catalog of 1912, Brooks Manufacturing Co. Photos and detailed descriptions of more than 150 now very collectible furniture designs from the Arts and Crafts movement depict davenports, settees, buffets, desks, tables, chairs, bedsteads, dressers and more, all built of solid, quarter-sawed oak. Invaluable for students and enthusiasts of antiques, Americana and the decorative arts. 80pp. 6½ x 9¼. 0-486-27471-3

WILBUR AND ORVILLE: A Biography of the Wright Brothers, Fred Howard. Definitive, crisply written study tells the full story of the brothers' lives and work. A vividly written biography, unparalleled in scope and color, that also captures the spirit of an extraordinary era. 560pp. 6⅛ x 9¼. 0-486-40297-5

THE ARTS OF THE SAILOR: Knotting, Splicing and Ropework, Hervey Garrett Smith. Indispensable shipboard reference covers tools, basic knots and useful hitches; handsewing and canvas work, more. Over 100 illustrations. Delightful reading for sea lovers. 256pp. 5⅜ x 8½. 0-486-26440-8

FRANK LLOYD WRIGHT'S FALLINGWATER: The House and Its History, Second, Revised Edition, Donald Hoffmann. A total revision–both in text and illustrations–of the standard document on Fallingwater, the boldest, most personal architectural statement of Wright's mature years, updated with valuable new material from the recently opened Frank Lloyd Wright Archives. "Fascinating"–*The New York Times.* 116 illustrations. 128pp. 9¼ x 10¾. 0-486-27430-6

PHOTOGRAPHIC SKETCHBOOK OF THE CIVIL WAR, Alexander Gardner. 100 photos taken on field during the Civil War. Famous shots of Manassas Harper's Ferry, Lincoln, Richmond, slave pens, etc. 244pp. 10⅝ x 8¼. 0-486-22731-6

FIVE ACRES AND INDEPENDENCE, Maurice G. Kains. Great back-to-the-land classic explains basics of self-sufficient farming. The one book to get. 95 illustrations. 397pp. 5⅜ x 8½. 0-486-20974-1